"Perhaps the most important book published in the UK so far this year."

—George Monbiot, *The Guardian*

"*Treasure Islands* has prised the lid off an important and terrifying can of worms."

—*Literary Review*

"Shaxson shows us that the global financial machine is broken and that very few of us have noticed."

—*New Statesman*

"In this riveting, well-written exposé, Shaxson goes deep into the largely unexamined realm of offshore money. In the process, he reveals that this shadow world is no mere sideshow, but is troublingly central to modern finance, with the US and the UK as leaders. The resulting abuses are widespread, ranging from tax revenue stripping from African nations to individuals and corporations escaping enforcement and accountability. A must read for anyone who wants to understand the hidden reasons why financial services firms have become so powerful and impossible to reform."

—Yves Smith, creator of Naked Capitalism
and author of *ECONned*

"*Treasure Islands* shines the light on some very dark places. It reads like a thriller. The shocking thing is it's all true."

—Richard Murphy, co-author of *Tax Havens: How Globalization Really Works*

"At last, a readable—indeed gripping—book which explains the nuts and bolts of tax havens. More importantly, it lays bare the mechanism that financial capital has been using to stay in charge: capturing government policymaking around the world, shaking off such irritants as democracy and the rule of law, and making sure that suckers like you and me pay for its operators' opulent lifestyles."

—Misha Glenny, author of *McMafia: A Journey through the Global Criminal Underworld*

"Trade and investments can play a profoundly productive role on the world economy. But so much of the capital flows that we see are associated with money laundering, tax evasion, and the wholesale larsony [*sic*] of assets often of very poor countries. These thefts are greatly facilitated by special tax and accounting rules or designed to "attract capital" and embodying obscure and opaque mechanisms. Shaxson does an outstanding and socially valuable job in penetrating the impenetrable and finds a deeply shocking world."

—Nicholas Stern, former Chief Economist
for The World Bank

TREASURE ISLANDS

Uncovering the Damage of Offshore Banking and Tax Havens

NICHOLAS SHAXSON

palgrave
macmillan

TREASURE ISLANDS
Copyright © Nicholas Shaxson, 2011.
All rights reserved.

First published in 2011 by PALGRAVE MACMILLAN® in the United States–a division
of St. Martin's Press LLC, 175 Fifth Avenue, New York, NY 10010.

Where this book is distributed in the UK, Europe and the rest of the world, this is by
Palgrave Macmillan, a division of Macmillan Publishers Limited, registered in England,
company number 785998, of Houndmills, Basingstoke, Hampshire RG21 6XS.

Palgrave Macmillan is the global academic imprint of the above companies and has
companies and representatives throughout the world.

Palgrave® and Macmillan® are registered trademarks in the United States, the United
Kingdom, Europe and other countries.

ISBN 978-0-230-10501-0

Library of Congress Cataloging-in-Publication
Shaxson, Nicholas.
    Treasure islands : uncovering the damage of offshore banking and tax havens /
Nicholas Shaxson.
        p.   cm.
    Includes index.
    ISBN 978-0-230-10501-0
    1. Tax evasion—United States.   2. Tax havens.   3. Banks and banking, Foreign.
I. Title.
HV6344.U6S53   2011
364.1'338—dc22

                                                                                2010035424

A catalogue record of the book is available from the British Library.

Design by Letra Libre, Inc.

First edition: April 2011

10 9 8 7 6 5 4 3 2 1

Printed in the United States of America.

CONTENTS

ACKNOWLEDGMENTS

THIS BOOK COULD NOT HAVE BEEN WRITTEN without the help of a great many people around the world. First I must thank John Christensen, who has worked tirelessly with me on this book, and who deserves much of the credit. (Any mistakes, though, are mine.) Alongside him stand several leaders in this field, each of whom has provided remarkable help and insights, and each of whom has contributed in a range of ways. This group, in alphabetical order, includes Jack Blum, Ray Baker, Richard Murphy, Ronen Palan, Sol Picciotto and David Spencer. Special mention must also go to Paul Sagar and Ken Silverstein for their terrific contributions on the history of the British spiderweb and on Delaware, respectively.

A number of others deserve great thanks too, for their time and their help in specific areas. They are Jason Beattie, Rich Benson, Richard Brooks, Michèle, Elliot and Nicolas Christensen, Andrew Dittmer, Sven Giegold, Maurice Glasman, Bruno Gurtner, Mark Hampton, Jim Henry, Dev Kar, Pat Lucas and her merry team, Mike McIntyre and his brother Bob, Andreas Missbach, Matti Kohonen, Markus Meinzer, Prem Sikka, Father William Taylor, and Geoff Tily.

I couldn't have got this far without Karolina Sutton at Curtis Brown, and I would also like to give special thanks to the staff at Palgrave Macmillan, at Random House, and to Dan Hind. Second last, but by no means least, a particular thank you to the Joseph Rowntree Charitable Trust, and the Tax Justice Network, which made all this possible. And finally, I would like to offer my thanks, appreciation and respect to all those in the tax havens who have spoken out against the consensus, sometimes at great personal risk.

PROLOGUE
An Offshore Awakening

ONE NIGHT IN SEPTEMBER 1997 I RETURNED home to my flat in North London to find that a man with a French accent had left a message on my answering machine. Mr. Autogue, as he called himself, had heard from an editor at the *Financial Times* (whom I was writing for) that I was to visit the oil-rich country of Gabon on Africa's western coastline, and he said he wanted to help me during my visit. He left a number in Paris. Curious as hell, I rang back the next morning.

This was supposed to be a routine journalist's trip to a small African country: I wasn't expecting to find too much to write about in this sparsely populated former French colony, but the fact that English-speaking journalists almost never ventured there meant I would have the place all to myself. When I arrived, I discovered to my surprise and alarm that Mr. Autogue had flown out to the capital of Libreville with an assistant on first-class Air France tickets and they had booked themselves into the city's most expensive hotel for a week—and their sole project, he cheerfully admitted, was to help me.

I had spent years watching, living in, and writing about the curve of oil-soaked African Atlantic coastline that ranges from Nigeria, in North Africa, through Gabon and down to Angola, farther south. Today this region supplies almost a sixth of U.S. oil imports[1] and about the same share of China's; and beneath a veneer of great wealth in each place lies terrible poverty, inequality, and conflict.

Journalists are supposed to start on the trail of a great story somewhere dramatic and dangerous. I found my story here unexpectedly, in a series of polite if unsettling meetings in Libreville. Lunch with the finance minister? No problem: Monsieur Autogue arranged it with a phone call. I drank a cocktail in a hotel lobby with the powerful half-Chinese foreign minister Jean Ping, who later became president of the U.N. General Assembly; the estimable Mr. Ping gave me as much of his time as I needed for my interview and asked graciously about my family. Later, the oil minister clasped me by the shoulder and jokingly offered me an oil field—then withdrew his hand, saying, "No: these things are only for *les grands*—the people who matter."

Never more than five hundred yards from foul African poverty on the streets of Libreville, I spent a week wandering about in a bubble. Mr. Autogue's attempts to keep my diary full made me determined to find out what it was that he might be wanting to hide. My new best friend had opened for me a zone of air-conditioned splendor: I was ushered to the front of queues to meet with powerful people, who were always delighted to see me. This parallel, charmed world, underpinned by the unspoken threat of force against anyone inside or outside the bubble who would disrupt it, is easy to miss in the affluent and easy West. In Africa the jolt was enough to begin to shake me from my sleep.

I had stumbled into what later became more widely known through a scandal in Paris as the so-called Elf affair.

The scandal began in 1994 when U.S.-based Fairchild Corp. opened a commercial dispute with a French industrialist, triggering a stock exchange inquiry. Unlike in more adversarial Anglo-Saxon legal systems, where the prosecution jousts with the defense to produce a resolution, the investigating magistrate in France is more like an impartial detective inserted between the two sides. He or she is supposed to investigate the matter until the end, when the truth is uncovered. In this case Eva Joly, the Norwegian-born investigating magistrate, found that every time she investigated something new leads would emerge. Her probes just kept going deeper. She began receiving death threats: A miniature coffin was sent to her in the post, and on a raid of one business she found a Smith & Wesson revolver, fully loaded and pointed at the entrance. But she persisted: Other magistrates became involved, and as the extraordinary revelations began to accumulate, they began to discern the outlines of a gigantic system of corruption that connected the French state-owned oil company Elf Aquitaine with the French political, commercial, and intelligence establishments, via Gabon's deeply corrupt ruler Omar Bongo.

Bongo's story is a miniature tale of what happened when France formally relinquished its colonies. As countries in Africa and elsewhere gained independence, the old beneficiaries of the French empire set up new ways to stay in control behind the scenes. Gabon became independent in 1960, just as it was starting to emerge as a promising new African oil frontier, and France paid it particular attention. France needed to install the right president: an authentic African leader who would be charismatic, strong, cunning, and, when it mattered, utterly pro-French. In Omar Bongo they found the perfect candidate: He was from a tiny minority ethnic group and had no natural domestic support base, so he would have to rely on France to protect him. In 1967, aged just 32, Bongo became the world's youngest president, and for good measure France placed several hundred paratroopers in a barracks in Libreville, connected to one of his palaces by underground tunnels. This intimidating deterrent against coup plots proved so effective that by the time Bongo died in 2009, he was the world's longest-serving leader.

In exchange for France's backing Bongo gave two things. First, he gave French companies almost exclusive access to his country's minerals, on highly preferential terms that were deeply unfair to the people of Gabon. The country became known as French companies' *chasse gardée*—their private hunting ground. But the second thing Bongo provided was more interesting. He allowed his country, through its oil industry, to become the African linchpin of the gigantic, secret Elf system—a vast, spooky web of global corruption secretly connecting the oil industries of former French African colonies with mainstream politics in metropolitan France, via Switzerland, Luxembourg, and other tax havens. Parts of Gabon's oil industry, Joly discovered as she dug deeper and deeper in Paris, had been serving as a giant slush fund: a pot of secret money outside the reach of French judicial authorities in which hundreds of millions of dollars were made available for the use of French elites. An African oil cargo would be sold, and the proceeds would split up into a range of bewildering accounts in tax havens, where they could be used to supply bribes and baubles for whatever the unaccountable elites who controlled the system deemed fit.

Out of this pot, money flowed secretly to finance French political parties, the intelligence services, and other well-connected parts of French high society. Elf's secret money greased the wheels of French political and commercial diplomacy around the globe: France's biggest corporations were allowed to use this West African oil pot as a source of easy bribe money to support their bids for giant contracts ranging from Venezuela to Germany to Jersey to Taiwan—and the out-of-sight Gabon connection meant that the money trails did not lead to them. (One man told me how he once carried a suitcase of cash provided by Omar Bongo to pay off a top rebel separatist in the Angolan oil enclave of Cabinda, where Elf had a lucrative contract.)

President Bongo, for his part, was one of the smartest political operators of his generation and tapped into French Freemasonry networks and African secret societies to become one of the most important power brokers in France itself. He was the key to French leaders' ability to bind *les grands*—opinion-formers and politicians from across Africa and beyond—into France's postcolonial foreign policy. This immensely powerful, corrupt subterranean system helped France punch above its weight in global economic and political affairs and remain significantly in control after independence, behind the scenes. A local journalist summed the relationship up for me most effectively. "The French went out of the front door," he said, "and came back in through a side window."

The system emerged gradually, but by the 1970s it was already serving as a major secret financing mechanism for the main French right-wing party, the Rally for the Republic (RPR).[2] When a Socialist, François Mitterrand, became French president in 1981, he sought to break into this right-wing Franco-African offshore cash machine and installed his man Loïk le Floch-Prigent at the head of Elf to do the job. But the latter was wise enough not to cut out his rivals in the RPR. "Le Floch knew that if he cut the financing networks to the RPR and the secret services, it would be war," explained the French authors Valerie Lecasble and Airy Routier in an authoritative book on the affair.[3] "It was explained that, instead, the leaders of the RPR—Jacques Chirac and Charles Pasqua—did not mind the Socialists taking part of the cake, if it were enlarged." So the Elf system grew. It became more baroque, complex, and layered, and it began to branch out into international corruption so grand that Mitterrand's man le Floch-Prigent was moved to describe France's intelligence services, which dipped freely into the slush, as "a great brothel, where nobody knows any more who is doing what."[4]

The system was a kind of open secret: A few well-connected French insiders knew all about it, and a fair number of educated outsiders in France knew something important was afoot but didn't know the details and largely ignored it. Yet almost nobody could see the whole thing in overview. Everything was connected through tax havens. The paper trails, as the magistrates were discovering during my Libreville trip, were typically sliced among Gabon, Switzerland, Liechtenstein, Jersey, and beyond. Joly admitted that even though she probed deeply she only ever saw fragments of the whole picture. "Endless leads were lost in the shifting sands of the tax havens. The personal accounts of monarchs, elected presidents-for-life, and dictators were being protected from the curiosity of the magistrates."[5]

My trip to Gabon in late 1997 came at an exquisitely sensitive time. On November 7 of that year, less than a week after I left Libreville, Christine Deviers-Joncour, a former lingerie model, was sent to jail in the southern suburbs of Paris, still protecting the secrets of her lover Roland Dumas, the French foreign minister. She was jailed for suspected fraud after magistrates found that Elf had paid her over $6 million to help "persuade" Dumas, a haughty prince of the Paris political clans, to do certain things—notably to reverse his public opposition to the sale of Thomson missile boats to Taiwan. On an Elf credit card she had bought him gifts, including a pair of handmade ankle boots from a Paris shop so exclusive that its owner offered to wash customers' shoes once a year in champagne. Nobody thanked her for her discretion, and five and a half months in jail gave her time to reflect on her treatment. "A flower, a single flower, even sent to me anonymously [in jail] would have been enough," she later explained.[6] "I would have known it came from Roland." The following year she cast aside the code of silence and published a book, *The Whore of the Republic*, which became a best seller in France.

So when I visited Gabon at that especially tricky moment, the Elf networks must have wondered why this English journalist was nosing around in Libreville. Was I really a journalist? No wonder Mr. Autogue took such an interest in me. Recently, I tried to find him, to ask him about our week together. His old phone numbers no longer work, several Africa experts in Paris hadn't heard of him, Internet searches turned up no trace of him or the company he claimed to represent, and the only person with that name in the French phone book has, a surprised-sounding wife in a rural Dordogne village informed me, never been to Gabon.

The Elf system, when I visited, was dying. The magistrates' investigations were in full swing, and they finally secured 31 convictions in November 2004 after eight years' work. Elf Aquitaine has since been privatized and is now part of the Total group, which has an utterly different character from the old Elf. Still, Elf was not the only creature in the corrupt Franco-African system—myriad smaller pots of offshore money existed too. And though Elf is long gone, it seems that the system is not really dead. When President Nicolas Sarkozy of France came to power in 2007 the first person he called was not the president of Germany or the United States or the European

Commission but Omar Bongo. The French troops remain in place in Gabon today, connected by underground tunnels to the presidential palace. In January 2008 the French aid minister, Jean-Marie Bockel, complained that a "rupture" with a corrupt past that French leaders had promised "is taking its time to arrive." He was summarily sacked.[7] If the Elf system is dead, then French elites seem to have replaced it with something else.

––––––––––––

Gabon is on no list of tax havens anywhere. But the Elf system that it hosted was part of, and a metaphor for, the offshore world. To understand this, it is necessary to explain some fundamental truths about what a tax haven or offshore jurisdiction is.

Tax havens provide escape routes from rules and laws elsewhere. These two words, "escape" and "elsewhere," will crop up repeatedly in this book. The zero tax rates offered in the Cayman Islands, for example, are not designed for Caymanians but are set up to attract the business of North and South Americans, Europeans, Asians, Middle Easterners, and Africans alike.

In truth, the term *tax haven* is a bit of a misnomer because these places offer an escape not just from taxes but from many other rules and regulations too. If a person or entity wants to do something but is forbidden by law from doing it at home, it escapes to somewhere else to do it. (To be more precise, it isn't usually the entity but its money that escapes.) The common feature of tax havens is that they offer secrecy. Once the escape has been effected, the escapee is very hard to find. The users of tax havens might be escaping any number of different laws or regulations: taxes, criminal laws, insider trading rules, inheritance rules, environmental laws, or financial regulation. If there is a law to stop or regulate it, there will probably be places that offer escape routes from that law. A simple example of an offshore escape is when a U.S. citizen, say, parks $10 million of drug money in a bank account in Panama. It will be exceedingly difficult for the U.S. authorities to find that money, let alone tax it.

The Elf system allowed bribes to be paid and other nefarious acts to be committed *elsewhere*—without the paper trails touching French soil. Offshore. The system did not exactly exist anywhere: It flourished in the gaps *between* jurisdictions. Elsewhere became nowhere.

The Elf affair illustrates another fundamental offshore truth. The escape routes from the rules and laws of society are provided almost exclusively for the benefit of wealthy and powerful insiders—leaving the rest of us to pick up the bill. The Elf system, a gargantuan octopus of corruption, affected ordinary people in both Africa and France in the most profound, if mostly invisible, ways. Ordinary African citizens saw their nations' oil money being siphoned off to the rich world through unfair oil contracts and general corruption, while French protection made Gabon's leaders invulnerable and hence unaccountable to their citizens—at the same time that the Elf system made France's elites unaccountable to that nation's citizens too.

These very same principles apply to the offshore system more generally. Because of tax havens, we have ended up with one set of rules for the rich and powerful and another set of rules and laws for the rest of us—and this applies to citizens of rich and poor countries alike. Just like the Elf system, offshore is a project of elites against their, and our, societies. It is not so much about crime or taxes, important though they are. This is a story about how political power is distributed in the world today.

It is essential to understand from the outset that the offshore system is ultimately not about celebrity tax exiles and mobsters—though they are regular users of the system. It is about banks and financial services industries. This book will show that the offshore system is the secret underpinning for the political and financial power of Wall Street today. It is the fortified refuge of Big Finance.

The offshore system is also about a more generalized subversion of democracy by our increasingly unaccountable elites. "Taxes are for the little people," the New York millionaire Leona Helmsley once famously said. She was right, though in the end she wasn't big enough to escape prison herself. The media baron Rupert Murdoch is different. His News Corporation, which owns Fox News, MySpace, and any number of other media outlets around the globe, is a master of offshore gymnastics, using all legal means available. When *The Economist* magazine investigated in 1999, it reckoned that News Corporation paid a tax rate of just 6 percent—compared with 31 percent for its competitor Disney.[8] Neil Chenoweth, an Australian reporter, probed News Corporation's accounts and found that its profits, declared in Australian dollars, were A$364,364,000 in 1987, A$464,464,000 in 1988, A$496,496,000 in 1989, and A$282,282,000 in 1990.[9] The obvious pattern in these numbers cannot be a coincidence. As John Lanchester wrote in the *London Review of Books:* "That little grace note in the sums is accountant-speak for 'Fuck you.' Faced with this level of financial wizardry, all the ordinary taxpayer can do is cry 'Bravo l'artiste!'"

Much of what happens offshore is technically legal. A lot of it is plainly illegal and often criminal. And there is a vast gray area in between. All of it is profoundly dangerous, corrosive to democracy, and morally indefensible. Eva Joly explains what the Elf affair taught her about the distribution of power in the world. "I realized I was no longer confronted with a marginal thing but with a system," she said. "I do not see this as a terrible, multifaceted criminality which is besieging our [onshore] fortresses. I see a respectable, established system of power that has accepted grand corruption as a natural part of its daily business."[10]

From this strange Franco-African tale emerges one more important point, which will be a recurring theme of this book. In decades and centuries past, colonial systems helped rich countries preserve and boost their elites' wealth and privileges at home. When the European powers left their colonies after the Second World War, they replaced formal controls over their ex-colonies with different arrangements to retain a measure of control behind the scenes. The Elf system was the main way that France achieved this. Britain did it with the modern offshore system, its financial replacement for empire. Citizens of the United States are paying the price.

"It has taken me a long time to understand," explains Joly, "that the expansion in the use of these jurisdictions [tax havens] has a link to decolonization. It is a modern form of colonialism."[11]

———————————

Long before my first visit to Libreville I had noticed how money was pouring out of Africa, often into tax havens, but the secrecy surrounding this financial trade made it impossible to trace the connections. Financial institutions, and occasionally their accountants and lawyers, would surface in particular stories, then slip back into an offshore murk of commercial confidentiality and professional discretion. Every time a scandal broke, these intermediaries' crucial roles escaped serious scrutiny. Africa's problems, the story went, had something to do with its nations' rulers, or its cultures and societies, or the oil companies. It was their fault.

The providers of offshore secrecy were clearly a central part of all these dramas—but the racket was very hard to penetrate, and nobody seemed very interested in trying. It was only in 2005 that the threads properly started to come together for me. I was sitting with David Spencer, a New York attorney previously with Citicorp, talking about transparency in the public finances of West African oil-producing nations. Spencer was getting agitated about matters that were not at all on my agenda: accounting rules, U.S. tax exemptions on interest income, and transfer pricing. I was wondering when he was going to start talking about West African corruption when I finally began to make a serious connection. The United States, by offering tax incentives and secrecy to lure money from overseas, had been turning *itself* into a tax haven.

Tides of financial capital flow around the world in response to small changes in these kinds of tax and secrecy incentives. The U.S. government needs foreign funds to flow in, and it attracts them by offering tax-free treatment and secrecy. This is offshore business, Spencer explained, and it had become *central* to the U.S. government's global strategies for financing its deficits. Not only did almost nobody understand this, he continued, but almost nobody *wanted* to know. Once, when he gave a speech at a major United Nations event outlining some of these basic principles, a top U.S. negotiator collared him afterward and told him that his shedding light on this subject made him "a traitor to your country." The negotiator was wrong: Spencer was being disloyal only to offshore interests on Wall Street.

In the Harvard Club with Spencer I began to see how the terrible human cost of poverty and inequality in Africa, Latin America, and other parts of the world connected with the apparently impersonal world of accounting and financial regulations and tax law. Africa's supposedly natural or inevitable disasters all had one thing in common: the movement of money out of poor countries and into parts of Europe and the United States, assisted and encouraged by the tax havens and a pinstripe army of respectable bankers, lawyers, and accountants. Nobody wanted to look beyond poor countries at the system that made this movement possible. The U.S. government and many others have allowed tax havens to proliferate because the elites who use them are the world's most powerful lobbyists.

Martin Woods, a Wachovia bank employee who became a whistle-blower after seeing billions of suspect dollars flowing from currency houses in Mexico in the midst of a drug war, illustrates the problem clearly. "If you don't see the correlation between the money laundering by banks and the twenty-two thousand people killed in Mexico," he said, "you're missing the point."[12] The world has, it seems, been determined to miss the point.

The offshore system hadn't been just an exotic sideshow in the stories I was covering, as I had thought. Offshore *was* the story. It binds together Libreville, Paris, and

Jersey; Luanda, Geneva, and Moscow; Moscow, Cyprus, and London; Wall Street, Mexico City, and the Cayman Islands; Washington, the Bahamas, and Riyadh. Offshore connects the criminal underworld with financial elites and binds them together with multinational corporations and the diplomatic and intelligence establishments. Offshore drives conflict, shapes our perceptions, creates financial instability, and delivers staggering rewards to *les grands,* the people who matter. Offshore is how the world of power now works. This is what I want to show you. The offshore system is the greatest fault line in our globalized world.

An impression has been created in sections of the world's media, since a series of stirring denunciations of tax havens by world leaders in 2008 and 2009, that the offshore system has been dismantled or at least suitably tamed. As we shall see, exactly the opposite has happened. The offshore system is in robust health—and growing fast. The crackdown has turned out to be a whitewash.

1

WELCOME TO NOWHERE
An Introduction to Offshore

THE OFFSHORE WORLD IS ALL AROUND US. Over half of world trade passes, at least on paper, through tax havens.[1] Over half of all bank assets, and a third of foreign direct investment by multinational corporations, are routed offshore.[2] Some 85 percent of international banking and bond issuance takes place in the so-called Euromarkets, a stateless offshore zone that we shall soon explore.[3] Nearly every multinational corporation uses tax havens, and their largest users—by far—are on Wall Street.[4]

Tax havens don't just offer an escape from tax. They also provide wealthy and powerful elites with secrecy and all manner of ways to shrug off the laws and duties that come along with living in and obtaining benefits from society—taxes, prudent financial regulation, criminal laws, inheritance rules, and many others. Offering these escape routes is the tax havens' core line of business. It is what they *do*.

Before getting into the real story of offshore, this chapter will lay some basic groundwork for understanding tax havens, offering a few essential principles, some brief history, and a short overview of where the tax havens are located.

Nobody agrees exactly what a tax haven is, but I will offer a loose description here: It is a place that seeks to attract money by offering politically stable facilities to help people or entities get around the rules, laws, and regulations of jurisdictions elsewhere.[5] This definition is quite broad, compared to some others, and I have chosen it for two main reasons. First, I aim to challenge a common idea that it is perfectly OK for one jurisdiction to exercise its sovereign right to get rich by undermining the sovereign laws and rules of other places. Second, I am offering a lens through which to view the history of the modern world. This definition will help me show how the offshore system is not just a colorful appendage at the fringes of the global economy but rather lies at its very center.

I should also make a short point here about some confusion in the language. When I say "offshore," I obviously am not referring to offshore oil drilling. I am also not talking about "offshoring," which is what happens when a company moves a manufacturing plant or, say, a call center from the United States to India or China, perhaps to save on labor costs. When I say "offshore," I am talking about the artificial movement or use of *money* across borders, and about the jurisdictions, commonly known as tax havens, that host and facilitate this activity. Once the money has escaped offshore, it is reclassified in an accountant's ledger and it assumes a different identity—and that means, very often, that the forces of law and order will never find it.

A number of features help us spot tax havens. Here are some important ones.

First, as my colleagues have found through painstaking research, all tax havens offer secrecy, in various forms. The term *secrecy jurisdiction* emerged in the United States in the late 1990s, and in this book I will use it interchangeably with *tax haven*. I will call the whole global structure of these places, and the private infrastructure that services them, the offshore system.

Another common marker for tax havens is very low or zero taxes, of course. People and corporations use them to escape tax, legally or illegally. Secrecy jurisdictions also have very large financial services industries in comparison to the size of the local economy. These places also routinely "ring-fence" their own economies from the facilities they offer to protect themselves from their own offshore tricks. So they might, for example, offer a zero tax rate to nonresidents who park their money there but tax local residents fully. This ring-fencing is a tacit admission that what they do is harmful.

Various other telltale signs exist. Tax havens usually deny what they are and strenuously assert that they are clean. Search for "We are not a tax haven" on the Internet or "We are a transparent, well regulated, and cooperative jurisdiction," and see what comes up. Each has its own way of addressing the critics: In the Cayman Islands, for example, accusations of lax regulation after scandals are routinely dismissed as media stereotypes that do not correspond to objective reality.[6]

But there is one feature of a secrecy jurisdiction that stands out above all: that local politics is captured by financial interests from elsewhere (sometimes these financial interests are criminal interests). This is why I include "politically stable" in my definition: Meaningful opposition to the offshore business model will have been neutered in a serious tax haven, so that such irritants as local politics cannot interrupt the business of making money. And here lies one of the great offshore paradoxes: These zones of ultra-freedom for financial interests are so often repressive places, viciously intolerant of criticism. The offshore world is steeped in a pervasive inverted morality: Turning a blind eye to crime and corruption has become good business practice: a way of attracting money; while alerting forces of law and order to wrongdoing has become the punishable offense. Here in the tax havens, rugged individualism has morphed into a disregard, even a contempt, for democracy and for societies at large.

One of the first things to understand about offshore business is that it is, at heart, about artificially manipulating paper trails of money across borders. To get an idea of how artificial it can be, consider the banana.

A bunch of bananas typically takes two routes into your home: a real route and an artificial offshore paper trail. On the first route a Honduran worker, say, is employed by Big Banana, a U.S. multinational I've just invented, to pick the bananas, which are then packaged and shipped to Britain, sold to a supermarket, and sold on to a customer.

The second route—the accountants' paper trail—is different. When a banana is picked in Honduras and shipped to Britain and sold, where are the final profits generated? In Honduras? In the British supermarket? In the multinational's U.S. head office? And how do you work this out? How much do the corporation's management expertise, or the brand name, or the insurance, or the accounting business, contribute to profits and costs? Which country ought to tax each component of the final profit? Nobody can say for sure, so the accountants can, up to a point, decide for themselves.

Here, in simple form, is what they might do. They advise Big Banana to run its purchasing network from, say, the Cayman Islands, and put a financial services subsidiary in Luxembourg. The Big Banana brand might be parked in Ireland; its shipping subsidiary in the Isle of Man; it might locate certain parts of its "management expertise" in Jersey, and its insurance arm in Bermuda. All are tax havens.

Next, each part of this multinational charges the other parts for the services they provide. So Big Banana's Luxembourg finance subsidiary might lend money to Big Banana Honduras, then charge that Latin American subsidiary $10 million per year in interest payments for that loan. The Honduran subsidiary will deduct this $10 million from its local profits, cutting or wiping out its local profits (and consequently its tax bill) there. The Luxembourg finance subsidiary, however, will record this $10 million as income—but because Luxembourg is a tax haven, it pays no taxes on this. With a wave of an accountant's wand, a hefty tax bill has disappeared. Who is to say that the $10 million charged by Big Banana Luxembourg is the real going rate—or just an accountant's invention? Quite often it is hard to tell, although sometimes these prices are adjusted so aggressively that they lose all sense of reality: A kilo of toilet paper from China has been sold for $4,121.81, a liter of apple juice has been sold out of Israel at $2,052, and a ballpoint pen has been recorded leaving Trinidad valued at $8,500.

Though most examples are far less blatant than this, the cumulative total of these shenanigans is vast. About two-thirds of global cross-border world trade happens inside multinational corporations. And it is poor countries in particular, with their underpaid tax officials, that always lose out to multinationals' aggressive, highly paid accountants.

What Big Banana has done here is *transfer pricing* (or *mispricing*), a common offshore trick that U.S. Senator Carl Levin calls "the corporate equivalent of the secret offshore accounts of individual tax dodgers." The general idea is that by adjusting its internal prices a multinational can shift profits offshore, where they pay little or no tax, and shift the costs onshore, where they are deducted against tax. In the banana example, tax revenue has been drained out of a poor country and into a tax haven and funneled through to the wealthy owners of a multinational corporation. In October 2010 a Bloomberg reporter explained how Google Inc. cut its taxes by $3.1 billion in the previous three years through transfer pricing games known by names such as the "Double Irish" and "Dutch Sandwich," ending up with an overseas tax rate of 2.4 percent.[7] The problem is getting worse. Microsoft's tax bill has been falling sharply, for similar reasons. Cisco is at it.[8] They are all at it. Transfer pricing alone cost the United States an estimated $60 billion a year[9]—and that is just one form of the offshore tax game.

Worldly readers may still shrug and tell themselves that this is just part of the ugly flipside of living in a rich nation. If they do, in their reluctantly cynical way, they are suckers—for they are victims, too. The tax bill is cut not only in Honduras but in Britain and America too. The annual report of a real banana company listed in New York notes: "The company currently does not generate U.S. federal taxable income. The company's taxable earnings are substantially from foreign operations being taxed in jurisdictions at a net effective rate lower than the U.S. statutory rate."[10] (Rough translation: We don't currently pay U.S. taxes because we use tax havens.)

This may be quite legal—but when it happens, small businesses and ordinary folk must step in to pay the taxes that multinationals have escaped. "Small businesses are the lifeblood of local economies," said Frank Knapp, member of a new group formed in 2010 called Business and Investors Against Tax Haven Abuse. "We pay our fair share of taxes, shop locally, support our schools, and actually generate most of the new jobs. So why do we have to subsidize multinationals that use offshore tax havens to avoid paying taxes?"

Multinationals, it has to be said, find it hard to cut their taxes to zero because governments take countermeasures. But it is a battle the governments are losing. The U.S. Government Accountability Office reported in 2008 that two-thirds of American and foreign companies doing business in the United States avoided income tax obligations to the federal government in the years 1998–2005, despite corporate sales totaling $2.5 *trillion*.[11] Not only this, but the corporate transfer pricing abuses that I have just described are just one of several forms of tax abuse. Subsequent studies suggest the problem is getting worse.[12]

Transfer mispricing is one of the most important reasons that multinationals *are* multinationals and why they usually grow faster than smaller competitors. Anyone worried about the power of global multinationals should pay attention to tax havens.

It is not just your bananas, of course. Much of the food you eat will most likely have taken a similarly twisted route into your home. The water in your tap may have traveled on a similarly ghostly paper pathway en route to your bathtub. Your television, its component parts, and many of the programs it shows also likely took offshore routes into your living room. The offshore world envelops us.

All these offshore games make markets profoundly inefficient. Wealth has been transferred from poor taxpayers to rich shareholders—but nobody has produced a better or cheaper banana here. These are untargeted government subsidies for multinationals, courtesy of the tax havens, and they don't make multinationals more productive. When corporate managers focus on tax dodging they take their eyes off what they do best—making better goods and delivering them more cheaply to market. Add to that the time and billions wasted paying expensive accountants and lawyers to conjure up these schemes. And then there is the secrecy. A fundamental building block of modern economic theory is transparency: Markets work best when two sides to a contract have access to equal information. *Treasure Islands* explores a system that works directly and aggressively against transparency. Offshore secrecy shifts control over information and the power that flows from it toward the insiders, helping them take the cream and use the system to shift the costs and risks onto the rest of society.

David Ricardo's theory of comparative advantage elegantly describes principles that lead different jurisdictions to specialize in certain things: fine wines from France, cheap manufactures from China, and computers from the United States. But when we find that the British Virgin Islands, with fewer than twenty-five thousand inhabitants, hosts over eight hundred thousand companies, or that more than 40 percent of foreign direct investment into India comes from Mauritius, Ricardo's theory loses its traction. Companies and capital migrate not to where they are most productive but to where they can get the best tax break. There is nothing "efficient" about any of this.

————————

The world contains about 60 secrecy jurisdictions, or tax havens, which can be divided roughly into four groups: a set of continental European havens, a British zone of influence centered on the City of London and loosely shaped around parts of Britain's former empire, a zone of influence focused on the United States, and a fourth category holding unclassified oddities like Somalia and Uruguay.

The European havens got going properly from the First World War, as governments raised taxes to pay for their war costs. Switzerland's famous secrecy law, making violation of banking secrecy a criminal offense for the first time, was enacted in 1934 in response to a French tax evasion scandal, though Geneva bankers had sheltered the secret money of European elites since at least the eighteenth century.[13] Picturesque, little-known Luxembourg, specializing since 1929 in certain kinds of off-shore corporations,[14] is among the world's biggest tax havens today: Well over $2.5 trillion is parked offshore in Luxembourg.[15] In March 2010 South Korean intelligence officials indicated that North Korea's "Dear Leader" Kim Jong-Il had stashed some $4 billion in Europe—profit from the sale of nuclear technology and drugs, insurance fraud, counterfeiting, and projects using forced labor; Luxembourg, they said, is a favored destination for the money.[16]

The Netherlands is another major European tax haven. In 2006, while the Irish musician Bono browbeat Western taxpayers to boost aid to Africa, his band, U2, shifted its financial empire to the Netherlands to cut its own tax bills. Austria and Belgium are also important European havens of banking secrecy, though Belgium softened its laws in 2009. A couple of other small European micro-state havens are worth noting, including Monaco and Andorra, with occasional cameo roles from odd places like the Portuguese Islands of Madeira, which was central to a major Nigerian bribery scandal involving the U.S. oil service company Halliburton[17] that resulted in the second largest fine ever paid in a prosecution under the Foreign Corrupt Practices Act.

The second offshore group, accounting for about half the world's secrecy jurisdictions, is the biggest. This is a layered hub-and-spoke array of tax havens, centered on the City of London, which mostly emerged from the ashes of the British empire.[18] As I will show, it is no coincidence that the City of London, once the capital of the greatest empire the world has known, is the center of the most important part of the global offshore system.

The City's offshore network has three main layers. Its inner ring consists of Britain's three Crown Dependencies: the nearby islands of Jersey, Guernsey, and the Isle of Man. The authoritative U.S. publication Tax Analysts estimated conservatively in 2007 that just these three havens hosted about $1 trillion of potentially tax-evading assets.[19] At a reasonable annual rate of return of 7 percent and a top income tax rate of 40 percent, the tax evaded on those could be almost $30 billion per year—and income tax evasion is just one of several forms of offshore tax and financial losses. Other losses, which I will explain below, are far bigger.

The next, intermediate ring involves Britain's 14 overseas territories, the last surviving outposts of Britain's formal empire. With just a quarter of a million inhabitants between them, they include some of the world's top secrecy jurisdictions: the Cayman Islands, Bermuda, the British Virgin Islands, Turks and Caicos, and Gibraltar.[20] Like the Crown Dependencies, these places are partly independent from Britain—though Britain controls events behind the scenes. In the Caymans, for instance, Her Majesty the British Queen appoints His Excellency the Governor, the most powerful person on the island. He (never a she, so far) presides over a cabinet of local Caymanians who are elected locally but who have almost no power over the stuff that matters— the money. The governor handles defense, internal security, and foreign relations; he appoints the police commissioner, the complaints commissioner, the auditor general, the attorney general, the judiciary, and other top officials. The final appeal court is the Privy Council in London. MI6, Britain's Secret Intelligence Service, is highly active here[21] (as are the CIA and several other intelligence services).

The Cayman Islands is the world's fifth largest financial center, hosting eighty thousand registered companies, over three-quarters of the world's hedge funds, and $1.9 trillion on deposit—four times as much as in all the banks in New York City. And it has, at the time of writing, one cinema.

To indicate how murky things are here, the Cayman Islands reported in 2008 that institutions based there had $2.2 trillion in borrowings but had only lent out a third of that amount—even though these figures should match each other, more or less. The UK and Caymans authorities have not explained this $1.5 trillion discrepancy.[22]

The third, outer ring is a more diverse array of havens like Hong Kong and the Bahamas, which are outside Britain's direct control but nevertheless have strong historical links to the empire and deep current links to the City of London. One authoritative account estimates that this three-layered British grouping accounts for well over a third of all international bank assets worldwide. Adding the City of London itself brings the total up to nearly a half.[23]

This network of offshore satellites does several things for the City of London. First, it gives it a global reach: These havens scattered around the world attract and catch mobile international capital flowing to and from nearby jurisdictions, just as a spider's web catches passing insects. Money attracted to these jurisdictions, and much of the business of managing that money, is funneled through to London. A lot of U.S. business is attracted to the Cayman Islands, and this gives the City of London the chance to get a slice of the action. Second, the spiderweb[24] lets the City get involved in business that might be forbidden in Britain, giving the financiers in London sufficient distance from wrongdoing to allow plausible deniability. By the time the money gets to London, often via several intermediary jurisdictions, it has been washed clean. The old City of London adage "Jersey or Jail" means that if you want to do a certain type of business but don't want to get caught, you just step out into the Jersey part of the spiderweb and do it there. Sometimes, business too dirty for the Crown Dependencies is farmed out further into the spiderweb. John Christensen, formerly a Jersey financial sector professional, remembers the Overseas Territory of Gibraltar being one particular favorite. "We in Jersey regarded Gibraltar as totally subprime," he said. "This was where you put the real monkey business." Later, a Caymanian character who introduced himself to me only as "The Devil" will help illustrate just how dirty this business can be.

Britain's understated, ambiguous, but ultimately controlling role in these nodes of the spiderweb is the bedrock that reassures flighty global capital and underpins their offshore sectors. The gesture toward local representation keeps Caymanians happy and gives Britain the chance to say "it is not our business to interfere" when something unpleasant breaks the surface, or when other countries complain of abuses being perpetrated out of there. Periodically, the charade of the overseas territories is exposed: In August 2009 Britain imposed direct rule in the Turks and Caicos Islands after corruption there spun too far out of control.[25] Britain plays down these episodes, as far as is possible, to distract attention away from its real control.

The outer reaches of the British spiderweb consist of a more complex and varied set of places that are independent from Britain, but with a history of involvement with the British empire or zones of close influence, and with enduring and powerful links with the City of London. The biggest are Hong Kong, Singapore, the Bahamas, Dubai, and Ireland,[26] though many others exist, like Vanuatu in the South Pacific, whose small offshore center was created by the British government in 1971, nine years before independence. New ones continue to emerge: In February 2006, for example, Ghana said it would set up offshore legislation with help from Britain's Barclays Bank. The thought of a new African secrecy jurisdiction in the midst of a swath of legendarily corrupt African oil-producing nations—and just as Ghana takes its own first steps as a big oil producer—is almost too horrible to contemplate. Botswana, right next to South Africa, is setting up its offshore center too.

One might ask why the United States has more or less tolerated the presence of British-run places parked off its eastern and southern coastline, eroding its tax base and undermining its laws and financial regulations. The answer isn't straightforward. U.S. officials have periodically tried to crack down on offshore tax abuse, at least since 1961, when President Kennedy asked Congress for legislation to drive these tax havens "out of existence,"[27] but have been thwarted each time by powerful interests on Wall Street. A U.S. Government Accountability Office (GAO) report from December 2008 provides a clue as to their power, showing that Citigroup had 427 tax haven subsidiaries, of which 290 were in the British spiderweb. The next biggest user was Morgan Stanley with 273 offshore subsidiaries (of which 220 were in the British zone), then News Corporation with 152, of which 140 were in the British zone.[28]

In these numbers lies another important point to understand from the outset. People have traditionally seen tax havens as marginal players used by mafiosi, drug smugglers, spies, petty criminals, and celebrity tax-dodgers. Plenty of these can be found offshore, it is true.[29] But I need to stress again: The big users of the secrecy jurisdictions are the banks and other financial institutions.

I am struck by similarities between Britain's postcolonial offshore network and what I encountered in oil-rich Gabon, the epicenter of France's own very strange, quasi-offshore postcolonial system. Gabon fits no conventional definition of a tax haven, but it is, like the havens in the British spiderweb, a relic (or even a rebirth) of a colonial empire that is being used by elites to do things—often unpleasant ones—that would not be allowed at home. The Elf system, with its subterranean bargains with African rulers and French politicians, was a way for France to retain a great degree of control over its former colonies after independence. Britain's spiderweb is different—most of its former colonies in Africa, India, and elsewhere really are independent. But what Britain has done instead is to retain a large degree of control of the vast flows of wealth in and out of these places, under the table. Illicit capital flight from Africa, for example, flows mostly into the modern British spiderweb, to be managed in London. In both the French and the British systems, powerful interest groups in the old colonial powers have built secret financial relationships with the local elites, creating global alliances with each other against the ordinary citizens of these poor countries—and against their *own* citizens too.

––––––––––

The United States anchors the third big offshore pole. Before the great global offshore explosion began in the 1960s and the 1970s, the U.S. government was generally hostile to offshore business, and its leaders fought against the British spiderweb and the European havens. But as the 1970s wore on financial interests became increasingly influential in U.S. policymaking, and the country, facing large Vietnam War–era deficits and increasingly adopting an "if you can't beat 'em, join 'em" attitude toward tax havens, began consciously adopting its own offshore characteristics—particularly special tax incentives and secrecy structures available to foreigners—in efforts to attract financial capital into the United States to fill the deficits.

So there are two things going on here: Tax revenues and other money are being drained out of the United States into tax havens elsewhere, and a flow of foreign (often dirty) money is moving in the other direction back into the country. The United States is estimated to be losing $100 billion annually from offshore tax abuses—a gigantic transfer of wealth from ordinary taxpayers to rich people.[30] And that is not to mention the role the offshore system plays as a giant hothouse for international crime and fraud or its role in undermining financial regulation, which I shall get to.

But the money flowing into tax haven USA does not make up for the money and tax revenues being drained out. The inflows have made matters worse still for ordinary U.S. taxpayers, let alone for foreigners being stiffed by their own wealthy and unaccountable elites. As the following chapters will show, the inflows delivered massive rewards to a small financial elite, while helping Wall Street to gain its too-big-to-fail stranglehold on the U.S. economy and the politicians in Washington. "Tax havens are engaged in economic warfare against the United States, and honest, hardworking Americans," says Senator Carl Levin. He is quite right—but we should add that the United States in its role as a tax haven is conducting economic warfare against honest, hardworking people at home and around the world.

Like the British offshore system, the U.S.-based offshore system operates on three tiers.

At the federal level, on the top tier, the United States dangles a range of special tax exemptions, secrecy provisions, and laws designed to attract foreigners' money into the United States in true offshore style. U.S. banks may, for instance, legally accept proceeds from a range of crimes, such as handling stolen property—as long as the crimes are committed overseas. Special arrangements are made with banks to make sure they do not reveal the identities of foreigners parking their money in the United States.

The second offshore tier involves individual U.S. states. A range of different things are happening, in a number of states. Florida, for example, is where Latin American elites do their banking, and the United States generally does not share banking information with those countries, so a lot of this is tax-evading and other criminal money, protected by U.S. secrecy. Florida's banks also have a long history of harboring Mob and drug money, often in complex partnerships with the nearby British Caribbean havens. On a different tack, smaller U.S. states like Wyoming, Delaware, and Nevada have become specialists in offering low-cost and very strong forms of almost unregulated corporate secrecy, which has attracted illicit money, and even terrorist money, from around the globe.

The third U.S. offshore rung is an overseas satellite network, far smaller than the British zone. One is the U.S. Virgin Islands, a U.S. "Insular Area" and a minor haven used by Bank of America, Boeing, FedEx, and Wachovia, among others.[31] A more interesting haven in the U.S. zone is the Marshall Islands, a former Japanese colony under U.S. control since 1947, now under a Compact of Free Association with the United States. It is primarily the host for a "flag of convenience" service that, *The Economist* magazine recently noted, is "much prized among shipowners for its light regulatory touch." The Marshall Islands registry was set up in 1986 with USAID help by Fred M. Zeder II, a golfing buddy of George H. W. Bush who later ran the United States Overseas Private Investment Corp. (OPIC), and its flag of convenience service is run by a private U.S. corporation out of offices in Reston, Virginia, near Washington Dulles Airport. The Marshall Islands provides the anything-goes, unregulated flag for, among many others, the *Deepwater Horizon,* the BP-operated oil rig that caused environmental chaos off the U.S. Gulf Coast in 2010.[32]

A small, opaque tax haven also grew alongside the Marshall Islands shipping registry, which the GAO reckoned was being used by ConocoPhilips, Morgan Stanley, and News Corp. When Khadija Sharife, a South African journalist, posed as a shipping client pretending to be worried about disclosure, she was told that forming a Marshall Islands company could be done in a day for an initial filing fee of $650 plus annual fees of $450, and

> If the authorities . . . come to our Registry and Jurisdiction and ask to disclose more information, regarding shareholders, directors of the company etc. . . . we are not privy to that information anyway, since all the business organization and conduct of the entity is performed by the entity's lawyers and directors directly. Unless the name of directors and shareholders are filed in the Marshall Islands and become a

public record (which is NOT mandatory), we are not in a position to disclose that information.[33]

In Africa, Liberia was set up in 1948 as a "flag of convenience" by Edward Stettinius Jr., a former U.S. secretary of state, and its maritime code was "read, amended, and approved by officials of Standard Oil," according to the historian Rodney Carlisle. Its sovereign shipping registry is now run by another private U.S. corporation out of Vienna, Virginia, about five miles from the Marshall Islands registry.[34] Sovereignty is, literally, available for sale or rent in such places.

The biggest tax haven in the U.S. zone of influence is Panama. It began registering foreign ships from 1919 to help Standard Oil escape U.S. taxes and regulations, and offshore finance followed: Wall Street interests helped Panama introduce lax company incorporation laws in 1927, which let anyone open tax-free, anonymous, unregulated Panama corporations with few questions asked. "The country is filled with dishonest lawyers, dishonest bankers, dishonest company formation agents and dishonest companies," one U.S. Customs official noted. "The Free Trade Zone is the black hole through which Panama has become one of the filthiest money laundering sinks in the world."[35]

This strange and little-known U.S.-centered pattern, echoing the neocolonial role of the secrecy jurisdictions in the British zone, provides a pointer to the fact that the secrecy jurisdictions have for years quietly been at the heart of neoconservative schemes to project U.S. power around the globe. And almost nobody has noticed.

It should be clear by now that the offshore world is not a bunch of independent states exercising their sovereign rights to set their laws and tax systems as they see fit. It is a set of networks of influence controlled by the world's major powers, notably Britain, the United States, and some jurisdictions in Europe. Each network is deeply interconnected with, and warmly welcomes offshore business from, the others. Wealthy U.S. individuals and corporations use the British spiderweb extensively: Enron, for example, had 881 offshore subsidiaries before it went bust, of which 692 were in the Cayman Islands, 119 in the Turks and Caicos, 43 in Mauritius, and 8 in Bermuda, all in the British spiderweb. The United States returns the favor to wealthy British interests investing tax-free, in secrecy, via Wall Street.

Not only that, but the world's most important tax havens in their own right are not exotic palm-fringed islands but some of the world's most powerful countries themselves. Marshall Langer, a prominent supporter of secrecy jurisdictions, neatly describes the misperceptions that have grown up about tax havens. "It does not surprise anyone when I tell them that the most important tax haven in the world is an island," he said. "They are surprised, however, when I tell them that the name of the island is Manhattan. Moreover, the second most important tax haven in the world is located on an island. It is a city called London in the United Kingdom."[36]

Jason Sharman, an Australian academic, checked how easy it was to set up secrecy structures, using the Internet and those seedy offshore advertisements that infest the back pages of business publications and airline magazines. In his report published in 2009 he records making forty-five bids for secret front companies. Money laundering controls seem to be in operation patchily, but of those 45 bids, 17 companies agreed to set them up without even checking his identity. Only four of these were in the "classic" havens like Cayman or Jersey, while the other 13 were in countries from the wealthy Organisation for Economic Cooperation and Development (OECD), including seven in Britain and four in the United States.

What Sharman was encountering, *The Economist* magazine noted, was not traditional Swiss banking secrecy, where discreet men in plush offices promised to take their clients' names to the grave. "This is a more insidious form of secrecy, in which authorities and bankers do not bother to ask for names. . . . For shady clients, this is a far better proposition: what their bankers do not know, they can never be forced to reveal. And their method is disarmingly simple. Instead of opening bank accounts in their own names, fraudsters and money launderers form anonymous companies, with which they can then open bank accounts and move assets."[37] The United States, Sharman noted, was offering nonresident foreigners all the elements of a tax haven, notably no taxes and secrecy. As he put it, "The United States, Great Britain and other OECD states have chosen not to comply with the international standards which they have been largely responsible for putting in place."

Rich OECD nations have worked hard to persuade their publics that there has been a major crackdown on the secrecy jurisdictions. "The old model of relying on secrecy is gone," said Jeffrey Owens, head of tax at the OECD. "This is a new world, with better transparency and better cooperation."[38] Many people believed him. French president Sarkozy went further. "Tax havens and bank secrecy," he said, "are finished."[39] Yet big OECD member states are the guardians and promoters of the offshore system. It continues to process vast tides of illicit money—yet an OECD blacklist of tax havens is effectively a whitewash, as I will explain later.[40] And to the very, very limited extent that rich countries have tried to address the problem, low-income countries are being left on the sidelines as usual.

When the fox announces that it has done an excellent job of beefing up the security of the henhouse, we should be very cautious indeed.

The offshore world is an endlessly shifting ecosystem, and each jurisdiction offers one or more offshore specialties. Each attracts particular kinds of financial capital, and each develops a particular infrastructure of skilled lawyers, accountants, bankers, and corporate officers to cater to their specific needs.

Yet few people are even aware that such businesses exist. You may well have heard of the Big Four accounting firms KPMG, Deloitte, Ernst & Young, and PricewaterhouseCoopers. But have you heard of the Offshore Magic Circle? Its members are made up of highly profitable multijurisdictional law firms mostly originating in Britain or its Overseas Territories and Crown Dependencies: a smartly dressed regiment of accountants, lawyers, and bankers forming a private global infrastructure that, in league with captured legislatures in the secrecy jurisdictions, makes the whole system work.

Offshore services range from the legal to the illegal, with a huge gray area in between. In terms of tax, the illegal stuff is called tax *evasion,* while tax *avoidance* is technically legal, though, by definition, it also involves getting around the intent of elected legislatures. To distinguish between evasion and avoidance is a slippery business, and it often takes vast, lengthy court cases to find out which side of the law a multinational corporation's tax shelter lies on. Former British chancellor Dennis Healey gave a neat definition of where the dividing line lies. "The difference between tax avoidance and tax evasion," he said, "is the thickness of a prison wall."[41] Even when offshore is not technically illegal, it is often a problem. Secrecy jurisdictions routinely convert what is technically *legal,* but abusive, into what is seen as *legitimate.* Of course what is legal is not necessarily what is right: think slavery, or apartheid.

Illegal offshore services and structures include tax-evading private banking or asset management, sham trusts, corporate secrecy, illegal reinvoicing, regulatory evasion, fraud concealment, and many, many other nefarious possibilities. These are often hidden behind soothing bromides like "tax optimization" or "asset protection" or "efficient corporate structure."

On the tax side, one important matter concerns something known as double taxation. Say a U.S. multinational invests in a manufacturing plant in Brazil and earns income there. If both countries taxed the same income, without giving credits for the other country's taxes, the multinational would get taxed twice. Tax havens do help companies eliminate this double taxation—though you don't need tax havens for this: It can be ironed out with appropriate treaties and tax credits between countries. But when tax havens eliminate double taxation, something else happens too: double *non*taxation. In other words, not only does the corporation avoid being taxed twice on the same income. It also avoids being taxed at all. I will explore this strange and complex area in a little more detail later.

Each jurisdiction tolerates different levels of dirt. Terrorists or Colombian drug smugglers would probably use Panama, not Jersey—though Jersey's trust company sector in particular, handling several hundreds of billions of dollars' worth of assets, continue to make the island a sink for nefarious activity and illicit, tax-evading loot, notwithstanding Jersey's routine claims to be a "transparent, well-regulated and cooperative jurisdiction." Bermuda is a magnet for offshore insurance and reinsurance, frequently for the purpose of avoiding tax; the Caymans are favored locations for hedge funds, frequently for the purposes of escaping tax, legally or illegally, but more often to get around certain kinds of financial regulation. In securitization, the practice of packaging up mortgage loans and other assets to sell on to investors—a major contributor to the latest financial crisis—Wall Street has long favored locating its Special Purpose Vehicles (SPVs) in the Caymans and Delaware; in Europe the preferred locations for SPVs are Jersey, Ireland, Luxembourg, and the City of London. All are, as this book will show, major secrecy jurisdictions.

Tax havens often target specific other large economies, usually nearby. Switzerland's wealth managers focus quite heavily on getting business from tax-evading rich Germans, French, and Italians—corresponding to Switzerland's immediate neighbors and to Switzerland's three main language groups—though they are open to all comers from around the world. Monaco caters especially to French elites, while some wealthy French and Spaniards use Andorra, sandwiched in the eastern Pyrenees between the two larger countries. Rich Australians often use Pacific havens like Vanuatu; a lot of illicit North African money finds itself routed through Malta, another former British outpost in the Mediterranean Sea. U.S. and Latin American corporations and wealthy individuals use Panama and the Caribbean havens for a lot of their business, while wealthy Chinese tend to use Hong Kong, Singapore, and Macau.

Some jurisdictions specialize as conduit havens: way stations offering services that transform the identity or character of assets in specific ways, en route to somewhere else. The Netherlands is a big conduit haven: About €4.5 trillion (US $6.6 trillion) flowed through Dutch Special Financial Institutions in 2008—equivalent to over nine times the Dutch GDP.[42] Mauritius, off the African coast in the Indian Ocean, is a new and fast-growing conduit haven that is the source of over 40 percent of foreign investment into India. It also specializes in channeling Chinese investments into Africa's mineral sectors. Money does not always flow through obvious geographical routes, however: Russian dirty money has favored Cyprus, Gibraltar, and Nauru, all with strong historical British links, as stepping-stones where it can be legitimized before entering the mainstream global financial system in London and elsewhere. A large amount of foreign investment into China goes via the British Virgin Islands.

Offshore financial structures typically involve a trick sometimes known as laddering—a practice also expressed by the French word *saucissonage,* meaning to slice something into pieces like a sausage. When you slice a structure among several jurisdictions, each provides a new legal or accounting "wrapper" around the assets that can deepen the secrecy and the complexity protecting the assets. A Mexican drug dealer may have $20 million, say, in a Panama bank account. The account is not in his name but is instead under a trust set up in the Bahamas. The trustees may live in Guernsey, and the trust beneficiary could be a Wyoming corporation. Even if you can find the names of that company's directors, and even get photocopies of their passports—that gets you no closer: These directors will be professional nominees who direct hundreds of similar companies. They are linked to the next rung of the ladder through a company lawyer, who is prevented by attorney-client privilege from giving out any details. Even if you break through *that* barrier you may find that the corporation is held by a Turks and Caicos trust with a flee clause: The moment an inquiry is detected, the structure flits to another secrecy jurisdiction. Even if a jurisdiction cooperates with inquiries, it can drag its feet for months or years. "Even when they cooperate to eliminate the fraud," Robert Morgenthau, until recently the Manhattan district attorney, said of the Caymans, "it takes so long that when the door is finally closed, the horse has been stolen and the barn has burned down."[43] At the time of writing, Hong Kong is preparing legislation to allow incorporation and registration of new companies within minutes.

In 2010 Luxembourg's authorities pleaded this laddering as an excuse for potentially harboring North Korean money. "The problem is that they do not have 'North Korea' written all over them," a spokesman said. "They try to hide and they try to erase as many links as possible."[44] That is, after all, the point. Magistrates in France only ever saw a limited part of the Elf system because of this *saucissonage.* "The magistrates are like sheriffs in the spaghetti westerns who watch the bandits celebrate on the other side of the Rio Grande," wrote the magistrate Eva Joly, furious about how tax havens stonewalled her probes into the Elf system. "They taunt us—and there is nothing we can do."

Even if you can see parts of the structure, the laddering stops you from seeing it all—and if you can't see the whole, you cannot understand it. The activity doesn't happen *in* any jurisdiction—it happens *between* jurisdictions. "Elsewhere" becomes "nowhere": a world without rules.

I already mentioned some ballpark numbers suggesting how big the offshore system has become: half of all banking assets, a third of foreign investment, and more. But there have been very few attempts to quantify the damage that this system causes. This is partly because it is so hard to measure, let alone detect, secret, illicit things. But it is also because nobody wants to know.

Recently, however, a few organizations have sought to assess the problem's scale. In 2005 the Tax Justice Network estimated that wealthy individuals hold perhaps $11.5 *trillion* worth of wealth offshore. That is about a quarter of all global wealth and equivalent to the entire GDP of the United States. That much money in hundred-dollar bills, placed end to end, would stretch twenty-three times to the moon and back. The estimated $250 billion in taxes lost each year on the income that money earns is two to three times the size of the entire global aid budget to tackle poverty in developing countries.

But that sum just represents the taxes lost on money wealthy individuals hold offshore. A much bigger transfer of wealth is occurring through illicit financial flows across borders from developing countries into secrecy jurisdictions and rich countries. The most comprehensive study of this comes from Raymond Baker's Global Financial Integrity (GFI) Program at the Center for International Policy in Washington. Developing countries, GFI estimated in January 2011, lost a staggering $1.2 trillion in illicit financial flows in 2008—losses that had been growing at 18 percent per year since 2000.[45] Compare this to the $100 billion in total annual foreign aid, and it is easy to see why Baker concluded that "for every dollar that we have been generously handing out across the top of the table, we in the West have been taking back some $10 of illicit money under the table. There is no way to make this formula work for anyone, poor or rich." Remember that the next time some bright economist wonders why aid to Africa is not working. We are clearly talking about one of the great stories of our age.

In a separate study subsequently endorsed by the World Bank,[46] Baker estimated that only about a third of total illicit cross-border flows represent criminal money—from drug smuggling, counterfeit goods, racketeering, and so on. Corrupt money—local bribes remitted abroad or bribes paid abroad—added up to just 3 percent of the total. The third component, making up two-thirds, is cross-border commercial transactions, about half from transfer pricing through corporations. His research underlines the point that illicit offshore flows of money are far less about the drug smugglers, mafiosi, celebrity tax exiles, and fraudsters of the popular imagination and mostly about corporate activity.

And out of this emerges another profoundly important point. The drug smugglers, terrorists, and other criminals use *exactly* the same offshore mechanisms and subterfuges—shell banks, trusts, dummy corporations, and so on—that corporations use. "Laundered proceeds of drug trafficking, racketeering, corruption, and terrorism tag along with other forms of dirty money to which the United States and Europe lend a welcoming hand," said Baker. "These are two rails on the same tracks through the international financial system." We will never beat the terrorists or the heroin traffickers unless we confront the whole system—and that means tackling the tax evasion and avoidance and financial regulation and the whole paraphernalia of offshore. It is hardly surprising, in this light, that Baker estimates that the U.S. success rate in catching criminal money was 0.1 percent—meaning a 99.9 percent failure rate.

And that is only the illegal stuff. The legal offshore tax avoidance by individuals and corporations, which further gouges honest hardworking folks, adds hundreds of billions of dollars to these figures.

Almost no official estimates of the damage exist. The Brussels-based non-governmental organization Eurodad has issued a limited-edition book called *Global Development Finance: Illicit Flows Report 2009,* which seeks to lay out, over a hundred pages, all of the comprehensive official estimates of global illicit international financial flows.[47] Every page is blank.

Eurodad's gimmick underscores a vital point: There has been an astonishing blindness on the part of the world's most powerful institutions to this system that has effected the greatest transfer of wealth from poor to rich in the history of the planet. As the sociologist Pierre Bordieu once remarked, "The most successful ideological effects are those which have no need for words, and ask no more than complicitous silence."

Language itself encourages the blindness. In September 2009, the G20 group of countries pledged in a communiqué to "clamp down on illicit outflows." Now consider the word *outflows.* Like the term *capital flight,* it points the finger at the *victim* countries like Congo or Nigeria or Mexico—which, this language subtly insists, must be the focus of the cleanup. But each flight of capital out of a poor country must have a corresponding inflow somewhere else. Imagine how different that pledge would be if the G20 had promised to tackle "illicit *inflows.*"

Bad tax systems are pushing some nations toward becoming failed states. "Countries that will not tax their elites but expect us to come in and help them serve their people are just not going to get the kind of help from us that they have been getting," Hillary Clinton said in September 2010, to widespread and bipartisan applause. "Pakistan cannot have a tax rate of 9 percent of GDP when land owners and all of the other elites do not pay anything or pay so little it's laughable, and then when there's a problem everybody expects the United States and others to come in and help."[48] Leave aside for a moment the hypocrisy involved when the United States preaches to developing countries about abusive tax systems while welcoming tides of their illicit money and wrapping it in secrecy. Clinton's basic point is still valid. Wealthy Pakistanis are as enthusiastic about tax havens as elites in any other poor country, and their ability to escape from any responsibility to their societies while leaving everyone else to pick up the tab is one of the great factors corrupting the state and undermining its citizens' confidence in their rulers. This is a security issue as much as anything else.

Even this is not all. The global offshore system was one of the central factors that helped generate the latest financial and economic crisis since 2007. Offshore did not exactly *cause* the financial crisis: It created the enabling environment for the conditions underlying the crisis to develop. "Trying to understand the role that offshore secrecy and regulatory havens have in the crisis," Jack Blum explains, "is like the problem a doctor has treating a metabolic disease with multiple symptoms. You can treat several symptoms and still not cure the disease. Diabetes, for instance, causes high cholesterol, high blood pressure, and all sorts of other problems. There are plenty of discrete aspects of the meltdown to talk about and many possible treatments for symptoms, but offshore is at the heart of this metabolic disorder. Its roots reach back decades, in bankers' attempts to escape regulation and taxation and make banking a highly profitable growth business that mimics the industrial economy."[49]

I will explore this in more detail later—but here is a very short summary of some basic reasons why offshore is implicit in the latest economic crisis.

President Roosevelt's New Deal in the 1930s inflicted a lasting defeat on financial capital, blaming it for the horrors of the Great Depression and tying it down with constraints that would ensure that the financial services sector would contribute to economic development, not undermine it. The New Deal was a great success, but it began to unravel properly just before the 1960s, when Wall Street found its offshore escape route from taxes and domestic regulations: first in London (the subject of chapter 4) then further afield in the British spiderweb and beyond. The offshore system provided Wall Street with a "get out of regulation free" card that enabled it to rebuild its powers overseas and then, as the United States turned itself in stages into a tax haven in its own right, at home. The end result was that the biggest banks were able to grow large enough to attain "too big to fail" status—which helped them in turn to become increasingly influential in the bastions of political power in Washington, eventually getting a grip on both main political parties, Democrat and Republican— a grip that is so strong that it amounts to political capture.

Part of this process has involved a constant race to the bottom between jurisdictions. When a tax haven degrades its taxes or financial regulations or deepens its secrecy facilities to attract hot money from elsewhere, other havens degrade theirs too, to stay in the race. Meanwhile, financiers threaten politicians in the United States and other large economies with the offshore club—"don't tax or regulate us too heavily or we'll leave," they cry—and the onshore politicians quail and relax their own laws and regulations. As this has happened, onshore has increasingly taken on the characteristics of offshore. In the large economies, tax burdens are being shifted away from mobile capital and corporations onto the shoulders of ordinary folks. U.S. corporations paid about two-fifths of all U.S. income taxes in the 1950s; that share has fallen to a fifth.[50] The top 0.1 percent of U.S. taxpayers saw their effective tax rate fall from 60 percent in 1960 to 33 percent in 2007, while their share of the income pie soared.[51] Had the top thousandth paid the 1960 rate, the federal government would have received over $281 billion more in 2007.[52] When the billionaire Warren Buffett surveyed members of his office he found that he was paying the lowest tax rate among his office staff, including his receptionist. Overall, taxes have not generally declined. What has happened is that the rich have been paying less, and everyone else has been forced to take up the slack. The secrecy jurisdictions, in partnership with changing ideologies, are the biggest culprits.

The next factor behind the latest economic crisis is the huge illicit cross-border flows of money that have on a net basis flowed very significantly into deficit countries like the United States and Britain, adding very substantially to the more visible macroeconomic imbalances that fostered the crisis. Meanwhile, zero-tax offshore incentives helped encourage companies to borrow far too much, injecting more risk and leverage into the financial system. In addition, financial and other firms have been festooning their financial affairs around the world's tax havens for reasons of tax, regulation, or secrecy—and the resulting complexity, mixed with offshore secrecy, made their financial affairs impenetrable to regulators and investors alike, eventually feeding the mutual mistrust between market players that helped trigger the crisis.

And now, to cap it all, the system is providing our richest citizens and corporations with escape routes from tax and regulation, meaning that it is ordinary people who will have to pay the costs to clean up this giant mess. The harm that stems from all this is incalculable.

Yet this is not a book about the financial crisis. It is about something older and deeper.

Deregulation, freer flows of capital, and lower taxes since the 1970s—most people think that these globalizing changes have resulted primarily from grand ideological shifts and deliberate policy choices ushered in by such leaders as Margaret Thatcher and Ronald Reagan. Ideology and leaders matter, but few have noticed this other thing: the role of the secrecy jurisdictions in all of this—the silent warriors of globalization that have been acting as berserkers in the global economy, forcing other nations to engage in the competitive race to the bottom, and in the process cutting swaths through the tax systems and regulations of nation states, rich and poor, whether they like it or not. The secrecy jurisdictions have been the heart of the globalization project from the beginning.

———————

Finally, a word about culture and attitudes. In January 2008 the accountancy giant KPMG ranked Cyprus at the very top of a league table of European jurisdictions, according to the "attractiveness" of their corporate tax regimes.[53] Yet Cyprus, a "way station for international scoundrels," as one offshore promoter admits, is among the world's murkiest tax havens: possibly the biggest conduit for criminal money out of the former Soviet Union and the Middle East into the international financial system. If Cyprus is ranked as the "best" in an international league table on tax, something is clearly wrong with the world. When transparency rankings list Switzerland and Singapore, two great sinks for illicit loot, as among the world's "cleanest" jurisdictions, then we seem to have lost our way.

Tax is the missing element in the corporate social responsibility debate. Modern company directors face a dilemma. To whom are they answerable—to shareholders only or to a wider set of stakeholders? There are no useful guidelines.[54] Irresponsible players treat tax as a cost to be minimized, to boost short-term shareholder value alone. Ethical directors recognize that tax is not a cost of production but a distribution out of profits to stakeholders, ranking on the profit and loss account alongside dividends. It is a distribution to society, and it pays for the things like roads and education that help the corporations make their profits.

The corporate world has lost its way, and nowhere is this more true than with the Big Four accountancy firms. Paul Hogan, the star of the film *Crocodile Dundee,* put his finger on something important in 2010 when talking about an investigation by Australian tax authorities into his offshore tax affairs. "I haven't done my own tax for thirty years," he said. "They talk about me going to jail. Erm, excuse me: There's about four law firms and about five accounting firms—some of the biggest ones in the world—that'd have to go to jail before you get to me."[55] On this point, Hogan is right—or at least he should be. These firms, responding to their clients' wishes to escape taxes and other duties that come with living in democratic nations, have grown to become steeped in an inverted morality that holds tax, democracy, and society to be bad and tax havens, tax dodging, and secrecy to be good. Serial tax avoiders are made knights of the realm in Britain and promoted to the top of high society in the United States; journalists seeking guidance in this complex terrain routinely turn to these very same offshore cheerleaders, the accountancy firms, for their opinions. Bit by bit, offshore's inverted morality becomes accepted into our societies.

The fight against the offshore system will differ from other campaigns to fix the global economy. Like the fight against corruption, this struggle does not fit neatly into the old political categories of left and right. It does not involve rejecting cross-border trade or seeking solace in purely local solutions. This fight needs an international perspective, where countries try not to engage in economic warfare against each other. And it will provide a rubric for taxpaying citizens in both rich countries and poor to fight for a common cause. Wherever you live, whoever you are, or what you think, this affects you.

Millions of people around the world have for years had a queasy feeling that something is rotten in the global economy, though many have struggled to work out what the problem is. This book will point to the original source of where it all went wrong.

2

TECHNICALLY ABROAD

The Vestey Brothers, the American Beef Trust, and the Rise of Multinational Corporations

ONE WINTER IN 1934 THE ARGENTINE COAST GUARD detained a British-owned ship, the *Norman Star,* as it was about to sail for London. The raid had been triggered by an anonymous tip-off during an investigation into a cartel of foreign meat packers who were suspected of manipulating prices and shipping profits illegally overseas.

Ordinary Argentinians, amid the Great Depression, were furious about just about everything at that time. Their economy was still mostly in the hands of a few hundred landowning families, and British and American meatpacking houses, which engaged their employees under humiliating conditions, had organized a cartel so effective that while the prices they paid locals for their beef had plummeted, the investors' profits actually rose. The beef export industry was a major plank in the growth of the political power of the Argentine elites; in his book *The Rise and Fall of the House of Vestey,* the biographer Philip Knightley argues that the meat packers' cartel had such a crippling effect on the Argentine labor movement and early economic development that "it led almost directly to the formation of militant labour organisations that pushed Peron into power, the subsequent dictatorship of the generals, the terrorism, the Falklands War and the country's economic disasters."[1]

How much profit were these foreigners really making? Nobody could be sure, but London's influence on the Argentine economy was immense. "Without saying so in as many words, which would be tactless, Argentina must be regarded as an essential part of the British Empire," the British ambassador had noted in 1929. But he was not complacent, for he was aware how fast large U.S. companies were penetrating these areas of British influence. "The United States under Hoover means to dominate this continent by hook or by crook," the ambassador had recently noted. "It is British interests that chiefly stand in the way. These are to be bought out or kicked out."[2] The big historical competitors of the British meat packers, though now inside the Argentine cartel, were the Swift and Armour groups from Chicago that until recently had formed the core of the American Beef Trust, an organization founded by the robber baron Philip D. Armour. The trust had sewn up food distribution inside the United States so effectively that a book about it published in New York in 1905, entitled *The Greatest Trust in the World,* described it as "a greater power than in the history of men has been exercised by king, emperor or irresponsible oligarchy . . . here is something compared with which the Standard Oil Company is puerile."[3] Although by the time of the coast guard raid their cartel tactics had been tamed in the United States, the trust was still happily playing the cartel game in Argentina, in partnership with the British.

Argentinians, of course, hated having their economy carved up in informal economic empires run by foreigners. "Argentina cannot be described as an English dominion," said Lisandro de la Torre, the fire-breathing Argentinian senator who led the investigation into the foreign meat packers, "because England never imposed such humiliating conditions on its colonies."[4]

So he was especially pleased with what the coast guard found in the ship's holds, buried beneath a reeking load of guano fertilizer: over 20 crates labeled "corned beef" and bearing the seal of Argentina's Ministry of Agriculture. When his men opened them, they found not corned beef but documents. De la Torre had exposed to public view for the first time the secret financial details of William and Edmund Vestey, founders of the world's biggest meat retailers, Britain's richest family, and among the biggest individual tax avoiders in history. Their story, and their wrangles and deals with their American competitors, provides a remarkable wind down into the emergence of multinational corporations in the early years of the last century and the emergence of a global industry of international tax avoidance alongside them.

William and Edmund Vestey had started out in 1897 shipping meat trimmings from Chicago to their native Liverpool, where they had built cold storage facilities, giving them an edge over their competitors. They branched out into poultry farming in Russia and China in the first decade of the twentieth century, from where they began processing and shipping vast quantities of super-cheap eggs to Europe. They set up more cold stores and retail outlets in Britain, and then in France, Russia, the United States, and South Africa, then moved into shipping in 1911, before expanding out to ranches and meatpacking in Argentina from 1913. At the outbreak of the First World War, they bought up more farmland and plants in Venezuela, Australia, and Brazil,[5] by which time they were involved in the entire supply change of the beef trade, from cattle to restaurant hamburger. They were pioneers of the truly integrated multinational corporation.

The Vestey brothers dressed in dark, sober suits and hats, and perhaps the biggest visible extravagance for each of them was a watch and chain. They had no outside interests beyond business: They did not smoke, drink, or play cards, and despite their fabulous wealth they lived in modest houses and ate cheap meals. Once, while on honeymoon in Ceylon, William heard of a fire at a company packing plant in Brazil and packed his new wife off to sort out the mess there. William returned to London on the next steamer.[6] Frugal and puritan, the brothers refused to trade alcohol and would even inspect their employees' fingers for tobacco stains.

They lived by the maxim that it is not what you can earn that makes you rich but what you can keep. They lived on the interest on the interest on their income. Peers of the Realm, Masters of the Foxhounds, personal friends of the Prince of Wales, and that sort of thing, the extended Vestey family still enjoys so much inherited money today that some have only discovered they are heirs when presented, on their eighteenth birthday, with checks for startling amounts. One distant heir, suddenly presented with a quarter of a million pounds in the 1990s, said, "I can't handle it" and turned it down.

The brothers lived by two business rules above all: first, never reveal what you are up to; and second, never let other people do something for you if you can do it yourself. They were, at heart, monopolists. They gave their different companies different names to disguise their ownership and bought up rivals, and if one resisted they would use their extraordinary market power—derived from their owning the whole supply chain from the grass, via the cows, to the slaughtering houses, the freezers, the ships, and then distribution and retail outlets—to drive them out of business. "If you mention his name near a meat market, people look over their shoulders," wrote one critic. A weaker competitor said bitterly: "We're not doing business with them. They're in everybody's business and they want everybody's business."

As their business grew increasingly multinational, it became ever harder for any-one to even guess what they were up to. "The juggling acts *El Inglés* [the Vestey com-pany] performed with the packing houses were enough to give the best aviator a dizzy spell," an Argentinian businessman wrote. "It is not surprising that the company tax inspector had a difficult job to unravel it all when *El Inglés,* in the end, was left with just one packing house."[7] In partnership with the Americans, the brothers showed the same controlling behavior at the retail ends too.

So when Senator de la Torre's investigation stumbled across the documents on the *Norman Star* he had achieved quite a coup. Top members of the Argentinian gov-ernment were colluding in, and even profiting from, their subterfuges, he alleged, and dirty political brawls broke out. Insults and counter-insults ricocheted around the Argentine political landscape, culminating in an assassination attempt on de la Torre in which an aide died after taking a bullet intended for the senator.[8]

The Vesteys' basic formula for gaining market power—squeeze them at the producer end, squeeze them at the consumer end, and push all the profits into the middle—was a philosophy that they also deployed, with astonishing success, in the area of tax. It is a formula that underlies the size and power of multinational corporations today.

In those early days the tax haven world was in its infancy, and governments were groping in the dark to understand and to tax emerging multinational corporations. (They still are.) Relatively few tax havens existed then, focusing mostly on the finan-cial affairs of extremely wealthy individuals. Rich Europeans looked primarily to Switzerland, while wealthy Britons tended to use the nearby Channel Islands and the Isle of Man. Wealthy Americans were busy too, as a letter from U.S. Treasury Secre-tary Henry Morgenthau to FDR in 1937 suggests.[9] "Dear Mr. President," it begins. "This preliminary report discloses conditions so serious that immediate action is called for." American tax evaders had set up foreign personal holding corporations in places with low taxes and lax corporation laws, he wrote, singling out the Bahamas, Panama, and Newfoundland, Britain's oldest colony. Stockholders were organizing companies through foreign lawyers, with dummy incorporators and dummy direc-tors, to hide their identities. Though extremely rudimentary by modern standards, the basic schemes Morgenthau outlined would be familiar to followers of today's offshore shenanigans. "The ordinary salaried man and the small merchant does not resort to these or similar devices. Legalized avoidance or evasion by the so-called leaders of the business community . . . throws an additional burden upon other members of the community who are less able to bear it, and who are already cheerfully bearing their fair share."

On the corporate side, offshore activity did not initially focus so much on tax. One great historical landmark in this respect emerged in the late nineteenth century when James B. Dill, a New York corporate lawyer, persuaded the governor of New Jersey that the state could get out-of-state corporate managements to incorporate there by passing permissive incorporation laws favorable to managers to the detriment of shareholders. New Jersey passed its first such law in 1889, then relaxed its rules again and again.[10] Corporations, including the Standard Oil Trust, began to relocate out of New York and other large centers and flock to New Jersey. Britain and the Netherlands began to follow the U.S. lead.[11]

Just before the First World War, however, New Jersey's governor Woodrow Wilson decided to check the rampant corporate abuses that had emerged as a result of these permissive incorporation laws and put in place progressive new antitrust laws and rules to make corporate managers more accountable to shareholders, investors, and other stakeholders. So corporations flocked to neighboring Delaware, which had already set the standard to be used by tax havens thereafter, by letting corporate managers effectively write their own corporate governance rules. By 1929 two-fifths of Delaware's income came from corporate fees and taxes, and it led the United States in incorporations, a lead it has never lost. An article in the *American Law Review* in 1899 noted Delaware's efforts to win the race to relax corporate standards and called Delaware "a little community of truck-farmers and clam-diggers . . . determined to get her little, tiny, sweet, round, baby hand into the grab-bag of sweet things before it is too late."

This brief digression into corporate law helps remind us what offshore is all about. It is not just about tax: In this case it is about attracting money by offering rewards to insiders, at the expense of other stakeholders, undermining or undercutting the rules and legislation of other jurisdictions.

And indeed, Delaware seems to have a long historical predilection toward offshore business: At the Constitutional Convention, Delaware's delegation fought aggressively for each state to get the right to send two senators to Congress—putting tiny Delaware on a par with mighty New York. A Delaware delegate[12] threatened that if they didn't get their way, "the small ones would find some foreign ally of more honor and good faith, who will take them by the hand and do them justice." It is easy to see, in light of examples like this, why offshore business is so often described as unpatriotic.

Offshore corporate tax avoidance really started taking off around the time of the First World War: Before that, taxes were mostly too low to worry about.[13] When war broke out, however, a lot of countries needed to raise a lot of money fast, and income taxes rose dramatically. In the United States, the top rate of tax for individuals rose from 15 percent in 1916 to 77 percent in 1918. The nation introduced the corporate income tax only after the Sixteenth Amendment was ratified in 1913, and it rose to 12 percent in 1918, by which time corporation taxes amounted to half of all federal tax revenues. In Britain the standard rate rose fivefold during the war to 30 percent in 1919, the year after the war ended. But in 1914 Britain had done something else that was especially pertinent for the Vesteys: It had begun to tax British companies on all their income worldwide, whether or not they brought this income home.[14] And the Vesteys were furious.

They tried lobbying against being taxed—which, in the new wartime environment, was doomed to look unpatriotic and to fail. As Britain's tax authorities noted, taxes on business profits never *stop* you from earning the profits—they only kick in once there *are* profits.

But William and Edmund Vestey were having none of it. In November 1915, as fifty thousand British soldiers died at the Battle of Loos, the brothers moved overseas to cut their tax bill. Their first stop after leaving was Chicago, where they found they weren't the first wealthy Britons to move for tax reasons. "What's the matter with your people?" a local tax lawyer asked. "You are the third Englishman I've had in here this week in the same business." From there they moved to Argentina, where they paid no income tax at all—and even then, they fought to cut the residual company taxes they still had to pay in Britain.

As the war progressed, however, the brothers increasingly started to wish they could return home, closer to their food empire's real profit center. So they began to hatch up a new scheme to return and *still* escape the tax net.

They put into place a two-stage plan. First they returned temporarily in February 1919, taking careful legal precautions to ensure they continued to be treated as visitors, not taxable residents, and they began lobbying. They wrote an impassioned plea to the prime minister, dressed up with appeals to patriotism and claiming their return would contribute to local employment—arguments that multinational corporations still routinely make today. They also complained bitterly about how unfair it was that their big competitor, the American Beef Trust, faced lower taxes and gained a big competitive advantage from it.

They had pointed to one of the great problems in international tax. Each country taxes its citizens, residents, and corporations in different ways, and different countries' tax systems often clash in unpredictable ways. Multinationals based in these different countries face very different tax bills on similar incomes, enabling one to out-compete another on a factor that has nothing to do with efficient management or real productivity.

U.S. citizens and corporations formed under U.S. laws were taxed on their income from all sources worldwide, and the test of whether one was a U.S. taxpayer was based on citizenship, not on residence—a subtle but important difference. But if the corporation—even a subsidiary of a U.S.-based corporation—was formed overseas, it did not pay taxes to the United States but to the foreign country where it was incorporated. The Chicago-based Beef Trust used this to avoid paying taxes in the United States—and then used various loopholes to avoid tax in Britain, too, where it sold a lot of its meat.

The Vesteys, who *were* paying significant taxes, did not like it, and the British prime minster referred their claims to an official commission. William's testimony to that commission was to become a classic in the tax world, cited in academic tax papers ever since. He posed the question of double taxation that I referred to in chapter 1: When a business is spread across several countries, which country gets to tax which bit of it?

"In a business of this nature you cannot say how much is made in one country and how much is made in another," said William Vestey. "You kill an animal and the product of that animal is sold in fifty different countries. You cannot say how much is made in England and how much abroad." He had put his finger on the central problem with taxing multinational corporations today. By their nature they are integrated global businesses, but tax is national. Taxing a corporation straddling multiple jurisdictions involves gruesome complications, and if each country scrambles to get as large a share as possible of the multinational's taxes, then the corporation risks being taxed twice or more on the same income.

So as taxes rose across the wealthy nations amid the First World War, a new source of economic conflict emerged. Double taxation became a hot issue, and businesses began to complain and to mobilize. An International Chamber of Commerce was set up in 1920, with tax squarely on its agenda from the outset.[15]

From the beginning, the emerging multinationals stayed a few jumps ahead of tax collectors.

Just as the Vesteys and the U.S. meat packers used their market muscle to squeeze their competitors at both the producer end and the consumer end, so they also began to squeeze the tax authorities at both ends. The trick, once again, was the same "transfer pricing" principle used by the banana companies that I described in the last chapter. If you own the ranches, the cattle, the freezers, the docks, the ships, the insurers, the wholesalers, and the retailers, then you can, by adjusting the prices one subsidiary charges another for goods, drive the profits away from the producer and the consumer countries, and instead take your profits at the most convenient place down the line. "And the most convenient stage," notes Knightley, "is naturally where you will pay the least taxation, preferably where you will pay none at all."

By siphoning the profits to a holding company in a tax haven, explains tax expert Sol Picciotto, the multinationals had found a way to avoid being taxed anywhere. They could now out-compete, and grow faster than, smaller, purely national firms. A system designed to avoid double taxation had, via the use of tax havens, turned into one of double *non*taxation. And through this basic formula, the offshore system has become one of the main foundations of the power of multinational corporations today.

———————

William Vestey's testimony to the official commission in 1920 reveals a man accustomed to getting his way. "If I kill a beast in the Argentine and sell the product of that beast in Spain, this country can get no tax on that business," he said. "You may do what you like, but you cannot have it."[16] He wanted to live in Britain, without paying his way, demonstrating an arrogance that pervades the offshore system, underpinned by that same old argument that bankers and other owners of footloose capital wield against our democratic representatives today: don't tax or regulate us too much, or we will move offshore.

Stung by the Vesteys' lack of patriotism after a major war, the commissioners hit back. "Are you not to pay anything for the advantage of living here?" one asked.

William Vestey refused to answer. "I should like to have an answer," the commissioner continued. "It is one that has agitated me a good deal since the witness has been in the chair." In the end, Britain refused to give in to the Vesteys. So they moved to the second stage of their plan, involving a more devious approach, something that helps us better understand the slippery world of offshore.

They set up a trust.

Many people think that the best way to achieve secrecy in your financial affairs is to shift your money to a country like Switzerland, with strong bank secrecy laws. But trusts are, in a sense, the Anglo-Saxon equivalent. They create forms of secrecy that can be harder to penetrate than the straightforward reticence of the Swiss variety. Trusts are powerful mechanisms, usually with no evidence of their existence on public record anywhere. They are secrets between lawyers and their clients.

Trusts emerged in the Middle Ages when knights leaving on the Crusades would leave their possessions in the hands of trusted stewards, who would look after them to provide benefits to the knights' wives and children when they were away or if they never returned. These were three-way arrangements binding together the original owners of the properties (the knights), with the beneficiaries (their families), via an intermediary (the stewards, or trustees). Over the centuries bodies of law grew up to formalize these three-way arrangements, and today you can enforce these things in the courts.

What a trust does, at heart, is to manipulate the ownership of an asset. You might think ownership is a simple thing: you have, say, a million dollars in the bank; you own it, and you can save it, or spend it, or take it out in ten-dollar bills and put it in your bathtub. But ownership can, in fact, be unbundled into separate strands. This happens, for example, when you buy a house with a mortgage: Until you repay the loan, the bank has some ownership rights over your house and you have other rights.

A trust unbundles ownership into different parts very carefully. When a trust is set up the original owner of an asset in theory *gives it away* into a trust. The trustee becomes the *legal* owner of the asset—though this person is not free to spend or consume it—for they must legally obey the terms of the trust deed, the instructions that tell them exactly how to share out the benefits to the beneficiaries. The trustee must obey these instructions, and apart from fees he or she may not receive any of the benefits. So a rich old man with two children might put $5 million into a bank account owned by a trust, then appoint a reputable lawyer as the trustee, instructing him that when the son is twenty-one he should receive half the money, and when the daughter later becomes twenty-one she should get the rest. Even if the wealthy man dies before the money is paid out the trust will survive, and the trustee is bound in law to pay out the money as he is told. It is very hard indeed to break a trust.

Trusts can be legitimate. But they can be used for more nefarious purposes, like criminal tax evasion. When a trust sets up solid legal barriers separating out the different components of ownership of an asset, these barriers can become unbreakable information barriers too, shrouding the assets in secrecy.

Imagine that the assets in a trust are shares in a company. The company may register the trustee—the *legal* owner—but it will not register the beneficiaries—the people who will be getting and enjoying the money—anywhere. If you have a million dollars in an offshore trust in the Bahamas and the tax inspectors come after you, it will be hard for them to even start their inquiries: Trust instruments in the Bahamas are in no official register. Even if the tax inspectors or police get lucky and find out the identity of a trustee, that is likely to be simply a Bahamas lawyer who does this for a living, who may be the trustee for thousands of trusts. She may be the only other person in the world who knows you are the beneficiary, and he or she is bound by professional confidentiality to keep your secrets safe. The tax inspector has hit a stone wall.

You can make this secrecy deeper still, of course, by layering one secrecy structure on another. The assets in the Jersey trust may be a million dollars in a bank in Panama, itself protected by strong bank secrecy. Even under torture the Bahamas lawyer could never reveal the beneficiary because he or she wouldn't know.[17] Such intermediaries merely send the checks to another lawyer somewhere else, who also isn't the beneficiary. You can keep on going: layering the Jersey trust on another trust in the Caymans, itself perched on a secret company structure in Nevada. If Interpol comes looking they must go through difficult, slow, and costly court procedures, in country after country, and face the "flee clauses" that mean the asset automatically hops elsewhere at the first sign of investigation.

The trust arrangement that the Vesteys set up in December 1921, signed in the Paris offices of the British lawyers Hall & Stirling, was fairly simple compared to the great offshore embroideries that are common today. Yet even so, it took Britain's Inland Revenue eight years to know it even existed.

In the meantime, while the Vesteys' secret Paris trust ticked over quietly, a new scandal erupted.

In June 1922, seven years after leaving the country to escape British wartime taxes, it emerged that William Vestey had bought himself a title, becoming Baron Vestey of Kingswood. Plenty of people who had made fortunes in the Great War had done this, craving the respectability of a peerage to mask the taint of war profiteering. Prime Minister Lloyd George had sold off official honors willy-nilly, causing outrage. "Gentlemen received titles," a member of parliament had spluttered in 1919, "whom no decent man would allow in his home." When challenged on his tax-avoiding activities, William Vestey did not endear himself to anyone by stating that "I am technically abroad at present . . . the present position of affairs suits me admirably. I am abroad. I pay nothing." The scandal rumbled on, but in the end nothing was done and the Vesteys returned home to Britain as they had wished. Their secret Paris trust kept the tax authorities at bay.

But even when the British tax authorities found the Paris trust, through patient detective work, they *still* could not get the Vesteys to pay tax on it. For secrecy is not the only subterfuge that trusts provide.

People are sometimes puzzled by one particular thing about trusts. If you must *give the asset away* into a trust in order to hide the asset and dodge your tax bill, is that not an oversize price to pay?

The answer is not straightforward. In part, this is a cultural question. Wealthy classes have grown to feel comfortable separating themselves from their money and leaving it to be managed by trusted strangers. Their education prepares them to recognize those who will respect their claims and whom they can therefore count on to do the right thing by them.

But there is another part to the answer, which offers further insight into the sneaky world of offshore. If you want to evade taxes or hide money through a trust, the trick is to make it *seem* as if you have given your asset away, while *in reality* you retain control of it. You can tell the tax authorities, or the police, that you really don't own the asset anymore—and only your trust lawyer need know that you are still really in control.[18] The preamble to the Paris trust deed hints at exactly that pretence. "In consideration of the natural love and affection of the settlors [the Vesteys] for the beneficiaries," it began, "and for divers other good causes and considerations." The money, it was saying, had really been given away to their dear beneficiaries, their wives and children.[19]

But what the Vesteys actually did was this. First, they leased most of their overseas empire to Union Cold Storage Ltd., a company based in Britain. In any normal arrangement, Union would have simply paid rent to the Vestey brothers. But instead Union paid the rent to two trusted lawyers and a company director in Paris. These trustees were then given very wide powers of investment, to be carried out under the direction of certain "authorised persons." And who were those persons? Why, the Vestey brothers! So the trustees, under the Vesteys' direction, lent large sums to another company in Britain, which the Vesteys also controlled, and which they used as their own personal piggy bank.[20] They had seemed to have given away their money while retaining real control.

And here comes a point about tax havens. Reputable jurisdictions have put in place laws to make it very hard for you to play this trust subterfuge. But secrecy jurisdictions have done the opposite, specializing in providing laws to help you perfect the deceit. Many jurisdictions, for example, allows things called revocable trusts— trusts that can be revoked so that the money is returned to the original owner. If you can do that, then you have not really separated yourself from the asset. Until it is revoked, though, it looks as though you have passed the asset on, and the tax authorities cannot have it. A Jersey sham trust provides a different subterfuge, letting you replace trustees with more pliable ones later, and changing their instructions at will. Or a trust might have a "trust protector" who has influence over the trustees, who acts discreetly on behalf of the person who pretended to give the money away. A Cayman Islands "Star Trust" lets you, the original owner, make the trust's investment decisions—and the trustee is not obliged to ensure the investments are in the interests of other beneficiaries. And so it goes on. There are offshore lawyers who sit in their offices all day, doing little more than dreaming up deviant new flavors of trusts.

Trusts are not only about tax, either. As we shall see, many of the structured investment vehicles that helped trigger the latest economic crisis involved offshore trusts. Most people would be surprised, even shocked, to find out how central they are to global finance.

———————————

In choosing the trust mechanism to protect their vast wealth, the Vesteys had chosen a powerful weapon indeed. And when the Argentinian senator Lisandro de la Torre found those crates of Vestey documents buried under the guano on the *Norman Star* in 1934, he was probably unaware just how crafty his adversaries were in this kind of offshore subterfuge. Soon after the raid, new and incriminating Vestey documents turned up in

Uruguay, and the senator achieved another coup when he got the British Foreign Office, whose diplomats were deeply uneasy with the Vesteys' business practices, to agree to turn Argentina's quest into a multicountry joint committee of investigation.

There was no telling what such a probe might uncover, so the Vesteys went on the offensive. When their local manager died of a heart attack, William Vestey wrote to the committee and brazenly accused Senator de la Torre of murdering him. Argentina's government responded furiously, calling Vestey's letter "an unprecedented piece of insolence."

Things went downhill from there. The committee worked for two more years while the Vesteys pulled strings in London to emasculate it, and despite sixty meetings and a report filled with detail about the Argentine meat trade, they never got to see the Vestey books in London. Senator de la Torre shot himself on January 5, 1939, leaving a suicide note that, as his biographer Philip Knightley notes, "expressed his disappointment at the general behaviour of mankind."

Each time Britain's authorities tried to tax overseas trusts in the ensuing decades, William and Edward, and their descendents, kept refining their tax planning and slipping through the net. "Trying to come to grips with the Vesteys over tax," one tax officer said, "is like trying to squeeze a rice pudding."

In 1980, shortly after one such assault by the Inland Revenue, an investigation by the *Sunday Times,* then one of the world's most respected newspapers, revealed that in 1978, the Vesteys' Dewhurst chain of butchers in Britain had paid just £10 tax on a profit of more than £2.3m—a tax rate of 0.0004 percent. "Here is an immensely wealthy dynasty which for more than sixty years has paid trivial sums in tax," the newspaper wrote. "All that time its members have enjoyed the considerable pleasures of being rich in England without contributing anything near their fair share to the defences which kept those pleasures in being—against foreign enemies in wartime, against disorder and disease in times of peace." Edmund Vestey, the grandson of the original Edmund, put the icing on this particular cake. "Let's face it, nobody pays more tax than they have to. We're all tax dodgers, aren't we?"[21]

The Paris trust loophole was finally closed in 1991,[22] but opportunities for legal tax avoidance for Britain's wealthy remain abundant. When the British Queen finally started paying income tax in 1993 after a public outcry, the latest Lord Vestey smiled and said: "Well, that makes me the last one."

As we shall soon see, he was very far from alone.

3

THE OPPOSITE OF OFFSHORE

John Maynard Keynes and
the Struggle against Financial Capital

IT IS WITH A STRANGELY DEFENSIVE TONE that Robert Skidelsky, the best-known biographer of John Maynard Keynes, prefaces the U.S. edition of volume 3 of his biography of the great British economist. He takes issue with U.S. economist Bradford DeLong's accusation that he has fallen under the influence of "a strange and sinister sect of British imperial conservatives."[1]

Skidelsky's work argues that for Britain the Second World War was in fact two wars, one pitting Britain under Winston Churchill against Nazi Germany, the other lying behind the facade of the Western alliance and pitting the British empire, led by Keynes, against the United States. America's main war aim after the defeat of the Axis powers, he argued, was to destroy the British empire. "Churchill fought to preserve Britain and its empire against Nazi Germany; Keynes fought to preserve Britain as a Great Power against the United States. The war against Germany was won; but in its effort to win it, Britain spent its resources so heavily that it was destined to lose both its Empire and its Great Power status."[2] Keynes himself outlined one of his central aims as he negotiated in Washington: "America must not be allowed to pick out the eyes of the British Empire."[3]

The arguments are complex, not least because Keynes's main negotiating partner in Washington, Harry Dexter White, was almost certainly passing information to the Soviet Union. But Skidelsky's account leaves no doubt that the two countries were quietly locked in a titanic struggle for financial dominance, as the thrusting new American superpower began to displace the old empire.

It was only long after the war that the two economic competitors would eventually work out a suitable arrangement for coexistence. It happened, as I shall explain later, through the construction of the modern offshore system. This chapter, however, explores what came before it: an international arrangement that Keynes helped design, where nation-states cooperated with each other and tightly controlled flows of financial capital between them. This system was, in a sense, the very opposite of today's fragmented, laissez-faire system, where wild, unregulated, and untaxed tides of capital flow across borders with almost no restraint, much of it through offshore centers.

For all its problems, the years of the anti-offshore system that followed the Second World War were a period of tremendous, broad-based growth and prosperity—not just for the American middle classes but for the world as a whole. The collapse of the system in the 1970s and the explosion of global offshore finance after that ushered in a period of lower growth, recurring economic crisis, and stagnation for most Americans, while wealth at the top of the income pile soared.

Keynes was as complex a character as any who have taken the world stage. He crammed the intelligence, and seemingly the lives, of twenty people into one. The aging Alfred Marshall, arguably the leading economist of his generation, once declared after reading a pamphlet from the young economist that "verily, we old men will have to hang ourselves, if young people can cut their way so straight and with such apparent ease through such great difficulties."

Keynes first properly made his reputation in 1919 with his pamphlet *The Economic Consequences of the Peace,* arguing that the vast reparations being heaped on Germany after the First World War would ruin it, with terrible results for the wider world. He was quite right: The stringent demands for reparation helped trigger the rise of Adolf Hitler and the Second World War. Years later, while writing his *General Theory of Employment, Interest and Money,* arguably the most famous economics textbook of the last century, Keynes was building a theater in Cambridge with his own money, drawing graphs of receipts from the theater restaurant, collecting tickets when the clerk failed to materialize, and, improbably, turning it into a huge artistic and commercial success. He became a respected art critic, a towering civil servant and diplomat, a hyperactive editor of economic publications, and a journalist whose articles could make whole currencies swoon. He wrote a book on mathematical probability that the polymath and philosopher Bertrand Russell said was "impossible to praise too highly," adding that Keynes's intellect was "the sharpest and clearest that I have ever known." Russell felt that when he argued with Keynes, he "took his life into his hands."

Opponents of Barack Obama have claimed that his Keynesian attempts to resuscitate the U.S. economy through deficit-financed public works constitute a Soviet-styled takeover of the free enterprise system. Yet Keynes was never the socialist bogeyman of the conservative imagination. He loathed Marx and Engels, he saw government intervention as a temporary fix, and he believed passionately in markets and trade as the best routes to prosperity. He wanted to save capitalism, not bury it.

———————————

For much of the nineteenth century, free traders had dominated policy in the United States and much of Europe: It was self-evident, many people thought, that free trade delivered prosperity *and* brought peace by creating economic interdependencies that made it harder to wage war. It was a bit like an argument memorably made in the 1990s by journalist Thomas Friedman, who said that no two countries with a McDonald's—that symbol of free trade and the "Washington Consensus"—had ever fought a war with each other.[4] Keynes believed this, for a while. "I was brought up, like most Englishmen, to respect free trade," he wrote in the *Yale Review* in 1933, "almost as a part of the moral law. I regarded ordinary departures from it as being at the same time an imbecility and an outrage."[5]

He had begun to see then that finance is different. He learned of the irrationality of markets first hand, spending half an hour each day in bed speculating with his own money in the famously treacherous terrain of international currencies and commodities, diving into company balance sheets and statistics (and declaring of the latter discipline that "nothing except copulation is so enthralling").[6] It made him a fortune, though he nearly bankrupted himself when a gamble against the Deutschmark in 1920 went disastrously wrong. "When the capital development of a country becomes a by-product of the activities of a casino," he famously said, "the job is likely to be ill-done."

Keynes understood instinctively the important differences between trade and finance. When two parties trade goods with each other, it is more or less a meeting of equals. But with finance the borrower is usually subservient to the lender. It is a relationship described years later by James Carville, Bill Clinton's adviser, who famously articulated the borrower's sense of helplessness when he said that if reincarnated he wanted to come back as the bond market because then "you can intimidate everybody." The interests of industrial capitalists and financial capitalists often conflict too. Financiers, for instance, tend to like high interest rates, from which they can derive considerable income, while industrialists want low interest rates, to curb their costs.

And the financiers then, as today, firmly had the upper hand. As is well known, the Great Depression that erupted in 1929 was the culmination of a long period of deregulation and economic freedom for Wall Street and a great bull market built on an orgy of debt, along with mind-bending rises in economic inequality. In the late throes of the boom the richest twenty-four thousand Americans, for example, received 630 times as much income on average as the poorest 6 million families[7]; and the top 1 percent of people received nearly a quarter of all the income—a proportion slightly greater than the inequalities suffered at the onset of the global crisis in 2007. "We have involved ourselves in a colossal muddle," Keynes wrote in the 1930s, "having blundered in the control of a delicate machine, the working of which we do not understand." The similarities with our current situation can hardly be missed.

Though there was no interconnected offshore system in his day—just the few assorted havens I described in the last chapter—Keynes still offered penetrating insights that help us understand the offshore system and are eerily prescient in light of the recent global financial and economic crisis.

When a company or government sells bonds or shares, investors hand over money in exchange for pieces of paper that give the holder title to a future stream of income. When the bonds or shares are *first* issued, savings are mobilized, funds are raised, and they flow into productive investment. This is generally healthy. But the next step is when things change. A secondary market appears in these pieces of paper, where the shares and bonds are traded. These trades no longer contribute to creating new productive investment in the real world: They merely shuffle ownership. Well over 95 percent of purchases in global markets today consist of this kind of secondary activity, rather than real investment. Keynes explained what happens when you start to separate real business operations in the real world from their owners. The holders of paper, the investors, become detached from the real businesses that they are investing in, and incentives change dramatically. When this happens across borders, the problem gets worse still: "When the same principle is applied internationally it is, in times of stress, intolerable," Keynes continued. "I am irresponsible towards what I own, and those who operate what I own are irresponsible towards me."

Shuffling ownership of bits of paper may seem to promote efficiency by helping capital flow to those projects that offer the highest risk-weighted returns, Keynes noted. A little speculative trading in these markets may well improve information and regulate prices. But in the real world, when the volume of this dealing is a hundred times bigger than the underlying volume of real trade, the results can be catastrophic. "Experience is accumulating," he said, "that remoteness between ownership and operation is an evil in the relations among men, likely or certain in the long run to set up strains and enmities which will bring to nought the financial calculation."

His words seem more apt than ever in a world where credit derivatives, asset-backed securities, and other products of financial engineering have placed ingenious but impenetrable barriers between investors and the assets they own, becoming great financial tinsel that is repackaged and resold down chains of investors across the planet, at each step being distanced further from the people and businesses who populate the real world.

Now consider the offshore system in light of this. The secrecy jurisdictions, by applying a sort of super-lubricant to the flow of capital around the world, dramatically widen these chasms inside capitalism. They are the supreme generators of remoteness and artificiality: creating secrecy barriers and generating unfathomable complexity as corporations garland their financial affairs around the world's tax havens to fox the world's tax authorities and regulators, and to shield particular investors against other nations' laws and regulations. As we have discovered since 2007, the system was wildly inefficient: consider the wealth destroyed and the costs heaped onto the shoulders of taxpayers.

Capital no longer flows simply to where it gets the best return but to where it can secure the best tax subsidies, the deepest secrecy, and to where it can most effectively evade the laws, rules, and regulations it does not like. None of this has anything to do with allocating capital more efficiently. Keynes would have viewed the explosion in offshore finance since the 1970s—and the massive capital flight it fostered—with horror.

With all this in mind, we can now turn to one of Keynes's great feats: the construction of a new world order after the Second World War that was the antithesis of the offshore system that would follow.

———————————

As Britain entered into the Second World War, Keynes went to Washington to negotiate the terms on which the nation was to receive U.S. assistance and to discuss what might come after the war. Many Americans, he soon realized, were rather more hostile to Britain than he had supposed. Roosevelt, for example, despised the British empire, mistrusted England's aristocracy, and, Skidelsky notes, "suspected the Foreign Office of pro-fascist tendencies."[8]

Americans had fairly effectively chained and muzzled Wall Street after the Great Depression, and policymakers in Washington saw the far more lightly regulated City of London—the financial heart of the hated British empire—with deep suspicion. Britain was discriminating against American goods in international trade, and Roosevelt's Republican opponents were horrified at the prospect of entanglement in another foreign war. Why help Britain again, many asked, after Britain had snared America into entering the First World War, then refused to pay its war debts *and* hung on to its empire. After the British army was forced into a humiliating retreat from Dunkirk in 1940, some in Washington were also reluctant to back what looked like a lost cause.

Global economic might had already shifted decisively across the Atlantic from London to New York, but Britain still held India by force, along with much of Africa and the Middle East. Keynes's combative and too-clever-by-half style fitted Americans' stereotypes of the British as super-wily imperial puppeteers, ready to bamboozle them. When Keynes first met U.S. Treasury Secretary Henry Morgenthau, who was no lover of technicalities, Keynes spoke for an hour, in great detail—and Morgenthau "did not understand one word," a Washington insider later wrote to a friend.[9] Harry Hopkins, one of Roosevelt's advisers, called Keynes "one of those fellows that just knows all the answers."

But Keynes's problem was more fundamental. America wanted Britain to fight fascism, and it was prepared to give huge military aid under its Lend-Lease Act of

March 1941, but it also saw the war as the chance to dethrone Britain and its empire once and for all. As Keynes wrote later, the U.S. administration took every possible precaution to see that the British were as near as possible to bankrupt before giving any help. "Why do you persecute us like this?"[10] he once asked his American counterparts. In response to the challenge, Britain's chief aim was, as Keynes put it, "the retention by us of enough assets to leave us capable of independent action."[11]

It was a grueling war for Keynes, in a decidedly unequal contest. He was seriously ill, diagnosed with septic tonsils and a "large heart and aorta," and he was representing an empire on its knees. When Keynes disagreed with his American counterpart Harry Dexter White, the American economist Brad DeLong wrote, "he usually lost the point because of the greater power of the United States. And in almost every case it seems to me that Keynes was probably right."[12]

As the war went on, Keynes turned his attention in Washington to negotiating the construction of a new cooperative international monetary order to govern future economic relations among the nations of the world, grounded upon efforts to restrain the international financial freedoms that had preceded and helped cause the Great Depression. The rampant capitalism of that era, founded upon an old alliance between Wall Street and the City of London, had involved freely floating currencies, strictly balanced government budgets, and free flows of capital around the world—a little like the modern global financial system. "The decadent international but individualistic capitalism," Keynes wrote, "is not a success. It is not intelligent, it is not beautiful, it is not just, it is not virtuous—and it doesn't deliver the goods. In short, we dislike it, and we are beginning to despise it." On this broad point his American colleagues were with him: Morgenthau said that the aim must be "to drive the usurious money-lenders from the temple of international finance."[13]

Keynes's negotiations culminated in the Bretton Woods Conference in 1944, the outcome of which would shape the international financial architecture for decades. The conference involved many nations but was an American production: The U.S. Treasury stage-managed the drafting committees and the conference to produce the desired results. U.S. Commission chairmen would prevent a vote on anything they didn't want voted on and would arrange the discussion to stop inconvenient topics from being aired.[14] It was hard to see what the international "monkey house" of delegations from other countries would *do,* Keynes archly commented: "Acute alcohol poisoning would set in before the end."

Keynes had hoped that the IMF would become a depoliticized institution, over-seeing automatic mechanisms to resolve global financing imbalances automatically and remove politics—and raw American power—from the equation as far as possible. He did not get his wishes, and when these matters were decided at a subsequent meeting in 1946, Keynes said acidly that he hoped "there is no malicious fairy, no Carabosse"—a reference to the wicked fairy-tale godmother figure of *Sleeping Beauty*, popularized in Tchaikovsky's and later Diaghilev's ballet—"whom he has overlooked and forgotten to ask to the party." Fred Vinson, a top U.S. negotiator, who felt he was the target of the remark, was heard to say in response, "I don't mind being called ma-licious—but I do mind being called a fairy."[15]

Many people today see the IMF and World Bank—the children of the Bretton Woods Conference—as the handmaidens of globalization, of unfettered trade and capital flows, and the instruments of Wall Street bankers. This was not the original idea. Keynes did want open trade, but finance was to remain tightly regulated: other-wise, surges of flighty capital would generate recurrent crises that would hamper growth, disrupt and discredit trade, and possibly drive fragile European economies into the arms of the communists.

Keynes understood the basic tension between democracy and free capital move-ments. In a world of free capital flows, if you try to lower interest rates, say, to boost struggling local industries, capital is likely to drain out overseas in search of higher re-turns, thwarting your original intent.[16] Investors hold a kind of veto power over na-tional governments, and the real lives of millions of people will be determined not by their elected representatives but by what the Indian economist Prabhat Patnaik called "a bunch of speculators." Freedom for financial capital means less freedom for coun-tries to set their own economic policies: from financial freedoms a form of bondage emerges.

Keynes's answer was simple and powerful: control and constrain the flows of cap-ital across borders and limit the trade in currencies through exchange controls. He be-lieved that financing was usually best when it happens inside, rather than between, countries. Capital controls would give governments more room to pursue objectives like maintaining full employment: Instead of limiting the scope of democracy in the interests of speculators and financiers, the plan was to limit the international mobil-ity of capital: Finance would be society's servant, not its master. "Let goods be home-spun whenever it is reasonably and conveniently possible," he wrote. "Above all, let finance be primarily national." The Bretton Woods plan, for all its faults, was designed to tame the forces of international finance.[17]

Capital controls can be hard to imagine for those who have not experienced them. To get foreign exchange for overseas trips, for example, you needed official permission. Frequent international travelers, for instance, would have a section in their passports, "Foreign Exchange Facilities—Private Travel," that would be filled with official stamps and signatures authorizing access to sums of foreign exchange. Companies had to get permission to shift money across borders.

This short history helps us to see how very far indeed we have now traveled from the system created by Keynes and his American counterpart Harry Dexter White. Dismantling capital controls is one thing. But we have taken a full step again beyond that, to a world where capital is not only free to flow across borders but is *actively and artificially* encouraged to flow, lured by the offshore attractions of secrecy, evasion of prudential banking regulations, tax evasion and avoidance, and more. Once again, Keynes would have been horrified.

———————

There is something else about this episode that is rather less well known.

Many mainstream economists embrace a simple idea that goes something like this. Poor countries lack capital. Foreign investment can fill the gap. So it makes sense to free up flows of capital to let capital flow into these capital-starved countries, where it can get higher returns. This may seem like a sensible idea, but what mainstream theory has failed seriously to address is that if you free up capital flows, money might not necessarily flow in. It might, instead, flow *out*. And the ways in which it may flow out might be unusually harmful.

Keynes understood the problem. "Advisable domestic policies might often be easier to compass, if the phenomenon known as 'the flight of capital' could be ruled out," he said. His words were prescient, for capital flight in his day was nothing when compared to the world-bending amounts that flood out of poor countries into the secrecy jurisdictions today.

He also knew there was a problem: Even in a world of tight capital controls, there would be leakage. Multinational companies needed permission to move investment capital overseas but had much more freedom in moving money for *current* purposes—that is, for financing trade and other day-to-day business. Of course, they could easily disguise a capital payment as a current one. To this, however, Keynes and Harry Dexter White had an answer. "What is often forgotten," the Canadian scholar Eric Helleiner notes, "is that Keynes and White addressed this with a further proposal. They argued that controls on capital would be more effective if the countries receiving that flight assisted in their enforcement."[18] In the earliest drafts of the Bretton Woods agreements, both Keynes and White had required that the governments of countries receiving the flight capital would *share information* with the victims of that flight. In short, they wanted transparency in international finance. Without the lure of secrecy, capital would have far fewer incentives to flee.

Enter Wall Street bankers and their lobbyists. U.S. banks had profited hugely from handling European flight capital in the 1930s, and, fearing that transparency would hurt New York's allure, they gutted the proposals. While early drafts of the IMF's Articles of Association had "required" cooperation on capital flight, the final version that emerged from the Bretton Woods conference saw that word replaced with "permitted." And through that one-word gateway drove a great, silent procession of coaches and horses across the Atlantic, laden with treasure from a shattered Europe. And the capital flight that ensued was as bad as Keynes and White had feared: A U.S. government analysis in June 1947, admitting that it only saw a part of the picture, found that Europeans held $4.3 billion in private assets, an enormous amount in those days, and far bigger than America's jumbo postwar loan to Britain that year.

American bankers were thrilled. And a new economic crisis exploded in Europe. America filled the hole with aid: the giant Marshall Plan of 1948. It is widely believed that the plan worked by offsetting European countries' yawning deficits. But its real importance, Helleiner argues, was simply to compensate for the U.S. failure to institute controls on inflows of hot money from Europe. Even in 1953, the authoritative *New York Times* correspondent Michael Hoffman noted, American postwar aid was *smaller* than the money flowing in the other direction.[19]

Henry Cabot Lodge, a Republican senator, was one of those who raised his voice to object to the stink. "There is a small, bloated, selfish class of people whose assets have been spread all over the place," he said. "People of moderate means in this country are being taxed to support a foreign aid program which the well-to-do people abroad are not helping to support."[20] The comparison with Hillary Clinton's words about Pakistan can hardly be missed. These words would be painfully familiar today to citizens of Argentina, Mexico, Indonesia, Pakistan, Russia, Nigeria, and so many other nations that have watched powerlessly while local elites mount raids on their countries' wealth and collude with Western financiers and businessmen to hide it offshore, avoid paying tax on their income, and then expect Western aid donors to fill the gaps. The Marshall Plan had set the precedent: American taxpayers would foot the bill for policies that delighted Wall Street and its clients. What was presented as enlightened self-interest was substantially a racket, in the precise sense of a fraud, facilitated by public ignorance. As we shall soon see, the rackets have multiplied ever since.

———————

Keynes died in April 1946, less than a year after the Nazis surrendered in Europe. The accolades poured in. "He has given his life for his country, as surely as if he had fallen on the field of battle," said Lionel Robbins, one of his most potent ideological adversaries. Friedrich Hayek, Robbins's former pupil who was just then fathering a new free-market ideology to dethrone Keynesianism, called him "the one really great man I ever knew."

Though Keynes had failed in many ways, many things he advocated were put in place, not least widespread capital controls. And events seem to have proved him right—or at least not wrong. The first two years after the war marked a brief period when U.S. financial interests dominated policymaking, and the restrictive international order was in abeyance. But the disaster that ensued, and the new economic crisis in 1947, discredited the bankers, and from the following year things became more restrictive.

The quarter century that then followed, from around 1949, in which Keynes's ideas were widely put into place, has become known as the golden age of capitalism: an era of widespread, fast-rising, and relatively untroubled prosperity around the world. As Britain's prime minister Harold Macmillan put it in 1957, "Most of our people have never had it so good." From 1950 to 1973, annual growth rates amid widespread capital controls (and extremely high tax rates) averaged 4.0 percent in the United States and 4.6 percent in Europe. Not only that, but as the Cambridge economist Ha-Joon Chang notes, the per capita income of developing countries grew by a full 3.0 percent[21] per year in the 1960s and 1970s, significantly faster than the record since then. And from the 1970s, as capital controls were progressively relaxed around the world, and as tax rates fell and the offshore system really began to flower, growth rates fell sharply. The countries that have grown most rapidly, the top-ranking economists Arvind Subramanian and Dani Rodrik explained in 2008, "have been those that rely least on capital inflows . . . financial globalisation has not generated increased investment or higher growth in emerging markets."[22]

Average growth is one thing, but to get an idea of how well most people are doing, you need to look at inequality, too. In the offshore era from the 1970s onward, inequality has exploded in country after country. According to the U.S. federal Bureau of Labor Statistics, the average American nonsupervisory worker was actually receiving a *lower* hourly wage in 2006, adjusted for inflation, than in 1970. Meanwhile, the pay of American CEOs rose from less than thirty to almost three hundred times the average worker's wage. Nor is this just a story about growth and inequality. Another famous study found that between 1940 and 1971, a period mostly covering the time of the golden age, developing countries suffered *no* banking crises and only sixteen currency crises, whereas in the quarter century after 1973 there were 17 banking crises and 57 currency crises. A major new study in 2009 by the economists Carmen Reinhardt and Kenneth Rogoff, looking back over eight hundred years of economic history, concluded that, as reviewer Martin Wolf put it, "Financial liberalisation and financial crises go together like a horse and carriage."[23]

We cannot infer too much from these very different episodes. Other reasons exist for the high growth rates during the golden age, not least postwar rebuilding and productivity improvements during the war. The 1970s oil shocks go some way toward explaining the subsequent slide into crisis and stagnation.

Still, less drastic but nevertheless powerful conclusions do emerge. The golden age shows that it is quite possible for countries, and the world economy, to grow quickly and steadily while under the influence of widespread and even bureaucratic curbs on the flow of capital, and high taxes. China carefully and systematically restricts inward and outward investments and other flows of capital, and at the time of writing it is growing fast. Clearly these kinds of controls, unfashionable for so many years, ought to be a policy option. Mainstream thinking on this is, at last, shifting a little: In February 2010 the IMF issued a paper[24] outlining what would have been considered heresy just a few years earlier, arguing that capital controls are sometimes "justified as part of the policy toolkit" for an economy seeking to deal with surging inflows. Very often countries can, as Keynes believed, get along perfectly well with their own domestic credit systems and localized capital markets, without exposing themselves to the killer seas of global offshore finance.

What has happened since the golden age ended is not simply a return to the free movement of capital but financial liberalization on steroids. The offshore system that tore financial controls apart from the 1970s has been both an accelerator for flighty financial capital but also a distorting field, bending capital flows so that they end up not necessarily where they can find the most productive investment but where they can find the greatest secrecy, the most lax regulations, and freedom from the rules of civilized society. It would seem sensible to take our foot off the accelerator.

Quite soon after Keynes's death a new ideological insurgency took hold, based on an idea of the near infallibility of free financial markets, which overthrew Keynes's ideas. The Chicago economist Robert Lucas would write in 1980 that "at research seminars, people don't take Keynesian theorizing seriously anymore; the audience starts to whisper and giggle to one another."

The latest financial crisis, which, I will show later, had its roots substantially in offshore finance, has helped resuscitate Keynes's ideas, at least in some circles. "If your doctrine says that free markets, left to their own devices, produce the best of all possible worlds, and that government intervention in the economy always makes things worse, Keynes is your enemy," wrote the economist Paul Krugman. "And he is an especially dangerous enemy because his ideas have been vindicated so thoroughly by experience."

Parallel with the ideological changes, however, something else began to emerge, even before the golden age ended. It first appeared in the City of London, before being embraced by Wall Street and spreading across the globe. Ideology mixed liberally with cash would create the conditions for the construction of a new world of offshore.

4

THE GREAT ESCAPE

How Wall Street Regained Its
Powers by Going Offshore to London

AS THE BRETTON WOODS SYSTEM THAT KEYNES helped design got properly under way after the Second World War, Wall Street was tied down at home with domestic regulations, many dating from the Great Depression. Financial flows across borders were constrained, taxes were high, and the U.S. economy was growing very nicely indeed. Across the country working people were buying refrigerators, televisions, and new cars for the first time.

Wall Street bankers wanted an escape route. They found it in a new offshore market in the City of London, the financial district at the geographical center of the greater London metropolis.

Nobody quite agrees when this new strain of offshore activity first emerged, but it was probably first spotted by a financial regulatory authority in June 1955 when staffers at the Bank of England, the UK's central bank, noticed some odd trades going on at Midland Bank, now part of the globetrotting HSBC.[1] Exchange rates in those days were mostly fixed against the dollar, and banks in London were not supposed to trade in foreign currencies unless it was for financing specific trades for their clients, and they were not allowed to lend against deposits in foreign currencies. Midland Bank was apparently contravening UK exchange controls by taking U.S. dollar deposits that were not related to its commercial transactions, and it was also offering interest rates on these dollar deposits that were substantially higher than those permitted by U.S. regulations. A Bank of England official called in Midland's chief foreign manager for a chat, to ask why the bank was contravening official controls. Afterward he noted down that the Midland official "appreciates that a warning light has been shown."[2] Luckily for Midland, though, Britain was struggling to shore up its shaky foreign exchange reserves, and the Bank was reluctant to snuff out a new area of international business. "We would be wise, I believe, not to press the Midland any further," the Bank concluded.[3]

Regulation in the City of London in those days typically consisted of your being invited to the Bank of England for tea, where an eyebrow would be raised in your direction if you were out of line. The tradition in London then, as today, was to rely heavily on self-regulation by financial firms, in stark contrast to the United States and its regulatory authorities' far more activist, rules-based approach. The City of London proceeded along the lines of a grand British Old Boys network, bound by elaborate rule and ritual. Discount brokers would wear top hats, and every evening in the rush hour a platoon of guardsmen would troop through the City in scarlet tunics and bearskins. "A banker could show his disapproval of sharp practice by crossing the road," wrote Anthony Sampson in the 2005 edition of his book *Anatomy of Britain.* "Behind all the conventions lay the assumption of a club based on common values and integrity. It was a club which could easily work against the interests of the public or outside shareholders, through insider trading and secret deals; and it was based on cartels which could exclude competitors and newcomers. But it was also quite effective."[4] A firm handshake and membership in the right kind of club was often enough to secure a man's credit.

As in the United States, however, finance was still relatively closely tethered, at least when compared to today, and the City of London was deep in a slumber. "By Thursday afternoon at four," one U.S. banker remembered, "one of the senior partners would come across to the juniors and say, 'Why are we all still here? It's almost the weekend.'"[5] Oliver Franks, a chairman of Lloyds Bank, compared it to driving a powerful car at 20 miles per hour. "The banks were anaesthetised," Franks said. "It was a kind of dream life."[6] American banks overseas were similarly quiescent.[7] For much of the time since the turn of the twentieth century they had been, as one account describes them, "courtesy stations where rich aunts could get their checks cashed or have a trust officer keep an eye on investments. Their nephews and nieces on short European tours used the bank, and so did a few vacationing businessmen."[8]

Ambitious U.S. business school graduates would prefer cutting-edge manufacturing jobs than stodgy, old-fashioned banking.

It is hard to imagine those days now: an era when international bankers took a backseat and fumed impotently at politicians' mighty powers. Those few years after the Second World War were, in fact, the only time in several hundred years when politicians had any real control over the banking sector in Britain. And with Midland's funny trades from 1955, and the Bank of England's decision not to interfere to stop it, that control began to unravel.

Just then, Britain's formal empire was starting to crumble too. India had secured independence in 1947, communist guerrillas were attacking British colonialists in Malaya, Egypt had broken free, civil war was breaking out in Sudan, and Ghana was preparing for independence. In July 1956, just over a year after the Bank started noticing Midland's funny trades, Egyptian president Gamal Abdel Nasser nationalized the Suez Canal. Britain and France, trying to adjust to their less magisterial postwar roles in world affairs but still driven by imperial-era motivations and arrogance, joined Israel in a three-sided invasion. It was a colossal mistake: The U.S. forced them to retreat, humiliated. "It marked, with brutal clarity, the end of Britain as a world power," said David Kynaston, historian of the City of London. It was the trigger for the collapse of the British Empire: Within a decade, an empire that had ruled over 700 million foreigners at the end of the Second World War shrank to a population of just five million.

As the empire crumbled, the pound—then fixed against the U.S. dollar at $2.80 per pound—began to totter and with it the whole edifice of solid, dependable imperial finance.[9] Coming less than a decade after Henry Morgenthau, the U.S. treasury secretary, had declared his intention to "move the financial center of the world from London and Wall Street to the U.S. Treasury," it was almost too much for the whiskery old gentlemen capitalists in London to bear.

In 1957 the British authorities, in a last-ditch attempt to rescue sterling's old imperial role, raised interest rates and applied new curbs on overseas lending to protect the pound. But the London banks, having noticed that the Bank of England had decided not to stop Midland's trades, sidestepped the new curbs by shifting their international lending away from sterling and into dollars, in this new market. And here is the crucial part: The Bank of England not only did not *stop* Midland's trades, but it actively decided not to *regulate* the market either. It simply deemed the transactions not to have taken place in the UK for regulatory purposes. Since this trading happened inside British sovereign space, no other regulatory authority elsewhere was allowed to reach in and regulate it, either.

Banks in London began keeping two sets of books—one for their onshore operations, where at least one party to the transaction was British, which was regulated, and one for their offshore operations, where neither party was British.

A new offshore market had been born, which would become known as the Eurodollar market or the Euromarket.[10] It was no more than a bookkeeping device, but it would change the world.

The new unregulated Euromarket that emerged amid the dust and fire of Suez would grow explosively and become nothing less than the heart of a new British financial empire centered on the City of London. It would raise the City to even greater financial glories, provide a new playground for U.S. banks, and prove the key to resurrecting an old alliance between the City of London and Wall Street, helping each break the grip of their governments at home and restore them to their full powers.[11]

"As the good ship Sterling sank, the City was able to scramble aboard a much more seaworthy young vessel, the Eurodollar," wrote P. J. Cain and A. G. Hopkins, the leading historians of British imperialism. "As the imperial basis of its strength disappeared, the City survived by transforming itself into an 'offshore island' servicing the business created by the industrial and commercial growth of much more dynamic partners."[12]

Modern histories of the City of London's growth as a financial center point to the "Big Bang" of 1986—the sudden deregulation of London's markets under Prime Minister Margaret Thatcher—as the moment when London really took off in its modern form. But Tim Congdon, one of the City of London's most experienced spokesmen, spotted the real story. "The Big Bang," he wrote in 1986, "is a sideshow to, indeed almost a by-product of, a much Bigger Bang which has transformed international finance over the last 25 years. The Bigger Bang is—on all the relevant criteria—a multiple of the size of the Big Bang."[13] "An extraordinary situation has arisen where the Euromarket, which has no physical embodiment in an exchange building or even a widely recognised set of rules and regulations, is the largest source of capital in the world."[14]

The scholar Gary Burn put it in a different light. The market's emergence, he said, was "the first shot in the neo-liberal counter-revolution against the social market and the Keynesian welfare state."

The modern offshore system did not start its explosive growth on scandal-tainted, palm-fringed islands in the Caribbean or in the Alpine foothills of Zurich or Geneva. It began its life in the City of London. American banks would soon dominate this market utterly. And, as is usual with so much that has happened offshore, very few people outside the financial sector even noticed.

Before proceeding with this tale, it is essential to understand something peculiar about the City of London.

Few British people, let alone anyone else, know that the City of London is the most important financial center in the global offshore system. Before getting properly into the strangeness of this ancient city, some of its more obvious offshore qualities are worth noting.

London's first claim to be a tax haven is the subject of this chapter: its role as the creator and developer of the Euromarkets, Wall Street's giant escape route from the checks and balances of U.S. financial regulation. Here the subsidiaries and affiliates of U.S. commercial banks have long been allowed to engage in, among many other things, investment banking—"casino banking," as some have called it—something the Glass-Steagall Act of 1933 explicitly prohibited. Over the years, as this business became more integral to their global banking models, Wall Street could increasingly pressure the U.S. government to do away with the original restrictions to allow them to do at home what they already did offshore, and this was arguably the main factor that led to the repeal of Glass-Steagall in 1999. It was the classic offshore pattern: banks find an offshore escape route, then say in Washington, "We can already do this offshore—so why not here?"—and domestic regulations get relaxed.

London provides endless loopholes for U.S. financial corporations, and many U.S. banking catastrophes can be traced substantially to those companies' London offices. The unit that blew up the insurance company American International Group (AIG), putting the U.S. taxpayer on the hook for $182.5 billion, was its four hundred–strong AIG Financial Products unit, based in London. The court-appointed examiner looking into the collapse of Lehman Brothers in September 2008 found it had used a trick called Repo 105 to shift $50 billion in assets off its balance sheet, and that while no U.S. law firm would sign off on the transactions, a major law firm in London was delighted to oblige, without breaking the rules.[15] When the United States introduced the Sarbanes-Oxley regulations to protect Americans against the likes of Enron or Worldcom, the City of London did not follow, and more U.S. financial business flowed to London.

Another important role for London has concerned a seemingly arcane practice known as "rehypothecation,"[16] a way of shifting assets off banks' balance sheets. The U.S. has firm rules to curb the abuses, but London does not—so ahead of the latest crisis, Wall Street investment banks simply went off to London where they could do it without limit. A little-noticed IMF paper in July 2010 estimated that by 2007 the seven largest players in the market—Lehman Brothers, Bear Stearns, Morgan Stanley, Goldman Sachs, Merrill/BoA, Citigroup, and JPMorgan—had shifted $4.5 *trillion* off their balance sheets in this way. So this London-based practice injected trillions more debt into the financial system than would otherwise have been the case.[17] The City of London and Wall Street banks got rich off this—and ordinary Americans will pay for it for years to come.

World oil markets are also affected by the London loophole. In June 2008, as world oil prices soared amid uproar about market manipulation, former regulator Michael Greenberger noted in testimony to a U.S. Senate Committee[18] that the U.S. Commodity Futures Trading Committee (CFTC), the regulator for energy derivatives, had been pursuing a "continuous charade that a U.S. owned exchange (ICE) located in Atlanta and trading critically important U.S. delivered energy products should be regulated by the United Kingdom, whose regulation of these markets is self evidently lacking." Almost every Russian firm listing overseas chooses London, not New York, partly because of Britain's permissive governance standards. The list of London loopholes goes on.

The next component of the City's offshore status is its role in running, protecting, and being fed by Britain's offshore spiderweb. As a reminder, this web of partly British tax havens around the world provides the City with three things. First, it captures passing foreign business and assets nearby and channels them, and the business of handling them, to London, just as a spiderweb catches insects. Second, it is a storage mechanism for assets. Third, it is a kind of money-laundering filter that lets the City get involved in foreign dirty business but at sufficient distance to minimize the stink. In the second quarter of 2009, the UK received[19] net bank financing of $332.5 billion just from its tax havens of Jersey, Guernsey, and the Isle of Man; in June 2009 the British web as a whole held an estimated $3.2 trillion in offshore bank deposits, half the global total, according to data from the Bank for International Settlements.

London's next offshore attraction is secrecy. Britain does not practice Swiss bank secrecy, which would make its violation a criminal offense, but it uses other equally effective mechanisms. The British spiderweb is a big part of this story, as is UK trust law. When Denis MacShane, a former British foreign office minister, criticized bank secrecy at a European seminar, his opposite number from Luxembourg retorted: "Have you ever examined UK trust law? All our bankers and financial lawyers say that if you really, really want to hide money, go to London and set up a trust."[20] Britain offers all manner of other secrecy facilities. Under UK law, for example, offshore companies can be directors of UK companies, and it is usually impossible to know who the real owners are.[21]

Another London attraction is the so-called "domicile" rule, whereby wealthy foreigners can come to live in England and escape tax on all their non-UK income. In pursuit of this tax break, the world's super-rich—from Greek shipping magnates to Saudi princesses—have descended on London in hordes. Having gone out of its way to welcome wealthy Arabs since the 1980s and rich Japanese and oil-rich Africans since the 1990s, the City has more recently aggressively courted Russian oiligarchs, offering them an almost tax-free bolt-hole beyond the reach of Russian law enforcement: Alexander Zvygintsev, Russia's deputy prosecutor-general, describes "Londongrad," as it is sometimes known, as "a giant laundrette for laundering criminally sourced funds."[22]

The contrast between London and New York, in terms of tolerance for criminal behavior, is stark. In January 2009, for instance, U.S. law enforcement fined the British bank Lloyds TSB $350 million after it admitted to secretly channeling Iranian and Sudanese money into the U.S. banking system. Robert Morgenthau, the Manhattan district attorney, explained how Lloyds would routinely strip out identifying features from payments from Iran so that wire transfers would pass undetected through filters at U.S. financial institutions.[23] In the City of London, this business just went on unperturbed.

"In America they send hundreds of people to jail: in this country bankers don't go to jail," explains the British author and publisher Robin Ramsay. "There are no consequences in London." Though Americans may roll their eyes at this, as they consider the financial crimes that have gone unpunished at home in the wake of the latest financial crisis, there is no doubt that London's tolerance for abusive or criminal financial behavior is in a class of its own. The Paris-based investigating magistrate Eva Joly, who broke open the Elf Scandal in Paris, described another view from overseas: "The City of London, that state within a state which has never transmitted even the smallest piece of usable evidence to a foreign magistrate."

The next part of the City of London's offshore armory is the strangest one. It concerns an organization called the City of London Corporation. On the face of it, the Corporation of London, as it is sometimes known, is merely the municipal authority for City of London, a 1.22 square mile of prime financial real estate located at the geographical center of the physical, sprawling metropolis of greater London. But the Corporation of London is far more than a municipal authority. It is a lobbying organization for the financial sector that is so deeply embedded in the fabric of the British nation-state that it has become impossible in Britain, even after the greatest financial crisis since the Great Depression, to confront or even seriously check the power of finance. Without understanding the Corporation of London, one cannot properly understand how Wall Street has become so powerful in the United States.

At its broadest, the term *City of London* refers to the financial services industry based in Britain, mostly located inside the so-called Square Mile that is the City. Smaller clusters of financial services activity exist elsewhere: The hedge funds in Mayfair a few underground stops farther southwest and the newer Canary Wharf, three miles east along the Thames river, are also important, hosting the spillover from the overloaded City. Neither these upstarts nor other small financial poles in places like Edinburgh or Leeds are really rivals to the Square Mile. The Corporation of London spreads a protective mantle over them all.

London hosts more foreign banks than any other financial center. In 2008 the city accounted for half of all international trade in equities, nearly 45 percent of over-the-counter derivatives turnover, 70 percent of Eurobond turnover, 35 percent of global currency trading, and 55 percent of all international public offerings.[24] New York is bigger in areas like securitization, insurance, mergers and acquisitions, and asset management, but much of its business is domestic, making London easily the world's biggest international—and offshore—financial hub.

The head of the Corporation of London is the Lord Mayor of London—not to be confused with the mayor of London, who runs the much larger greater London municipality that contains the City, geographically speaking, but has no jurisdiction over its nonmunicipal affairs. And this separation of powers matters.

When the Queen visits the City, she stops at the boundary at Temple Bar and waits for the Lord Mayor of the City, accompanied by assorted City Aldermen and Sherriffs. This tourist ceremony, in which the Queen touches the Lord Mayor's sword, strikingly highlights the political discontinuity between the City and the rest of Britain. When heads of state visit Britain the Lord Mayor throws more lavish banquets than the Queen. Each year the Chancellor, Britain's finance minister, makes a speech at the Guildhall, the seat of City government, and at the Lord Mayor's Mansion House, in which they justify how they have been serving the interests of finance.

The City's nine thousand–odd *human* residents have one vote each in municipal elections here. But *businesses* in the City vote too, as if they were human, with thirty-two thousand corporate votes.[25] In effect, Goldman Sachs, the Bank of China, Moscow Narodny Bank, and KPMG can vote in a hugely important British election.

The strangeness goes deeper and deeper. In fact the Corporation is so ancient and mystifying that barely any outsiders understand it.

The Corporation's website is a warren of tunneling links and unexpected, bizarre connections. A series of rituals confirm the integrity of the whole. There are 108 livery companies, including the Worshipful Companies of Broderers, and of Cordwainers. The current Lord Mayor, Nick Anstee, is an honorary Liveryman of the Plaisterers' Company.[26] There are the Sheriffs, Aldermen, the Court of Common Council, and the "Rules for the Conduct of Life." There is the Lord Mayor's show, resplendent with arcane ritual, gilded coaches, and elderly men in long satin robes, that is watched by millions on the BBC every November.

The Corporation has existed since what tour guides and historians call *time immemorial,* a term taken to mean that its origins extend beyond the reach of memory, record, or tradition. There is no direct evidence, Corporation officials note, of it coming into being: They say, only half in jest, that it dates its "modern period" from the year 1067. This is the world's oldest continuous municipal democracy, predating the

British parliament and rooted in what the Corporation calls "the ancient rights and privileges enjoyed by citizens before the Norman Conquest in 1066." This, notes the City of London expert Maurice Glasman, means that the City is effectively outside the normal legislative remit.

The City's special privileges stem ultimately from the power of financial capital. Britain's rulers have needed the City's money and have given the City what it wants in exchange. Over the centuries the City has used this magic formula to carve out for itself privilege after privilege, exempting itself from laws it dislikes and turning itself into a state within a state: a true offshore island partly separate from Britain and protected from tides of history that have swept the British nation-state over the centuries.[27] Monarchs, firebrands, and demagogues who tried to roll back the City's special rights and privileges had occasional successes, but most came to a sticky end, and the City vigorously reasserted its rights. It was, one nineteenth-century reformer said, "like some prehistoric monster which had mysteriously survived into the modern world."

In 1937, Britain's then prime minister Clement Attlee became one of few politicians to have raised the issue. "Over and over again we have seen that there is in this country another power than that which has its seat at Westminster [the parliament]. The City of London, a convenient term for a collection of financial interests, is able to assert itself against the Government of the country. Those who control money can pursue a policy at home and abroad contrary to that which has been decided by the people."[28] In 1957 an official commission, which sparked a big shake-up of local government across Britain, opened with the memorable words: "Logic has its limits and the position of the City lies outside them."[29]

The carve-out from Britain's rules and laws has a truly ancient pedigree. When William the Conqueror invaded England in 1066, the rest of England disarmed and gave up its rights—but the City kept its freehold property, ancient liberties,[30] and its own self-organizing militias: Even the King had to disarm in the City. When William commissioned the Domesday Book, a survey of the kingdom's assets and revenues that determined taxation, the City was excluded.[31] In the momentous changes that followed—the Protestant Reformation five hundred years later when the English Church became subject to the Crown, the subsequent civil wars that broke the power of the monarchy, and the broadening of suffrage to include almost all adults—the City held on to its privileges and strengths. The Statute of William and Mary from 1690, "confirming the Privileges of the Corporation," and following

a challenge to the City's authority by the late King Charles II, illustrates the scale of
the City's different status:

> All the charters, grants, letters patents, and commissions touching or concerning any
> of their liberties or franchises, or the liberties, privileges, franchises, immunities, lands,
> tenements and hereditaments, rights, titles, or estates of the mayor and commonalty
> and citizens of the City of London, made or granted to any person or persons what-
> soever . . . be and are hereby declared and adjudged null and void to all intents.

In other words, those claims that infringe the City's ancient liberties are worth-
less. Earlier that century, the British crown had asked the Corporation to extend its ancient legal protections and privileges to new areas of London, outside the City, that were
receiving tens of thousands of refugees from brutal land reforms known as the Enclo-
sures. But the Corporation refused, instead shipping excess populations off to the Ul-
ster Plantation and the Corporation of Londonderry in what is now Northern Ireland,[32]
helping build a large Protestant community there and contributing to bitter future conflict. Glasman calls this the "Great Refusal": the moment where the City turned its back
on London and when London's history properly became a tale of two cities, with a
mayor for the vibrant, troubled, and poverty-scarred metropolis, and a Lord Mayor for
the City: the world's most ancient political institution, at the disposal of finance.

For much of the last century the Labour Party, the party of Britain's working
class, had a pledge into its manifesto to abolish the Corporation of London and fold
it into a unified London government. The pledge would remain in place, unfulfilled,
until Labour Leader Tony Blair undid it in the early 1990s. In exchange for the City's
support in his successful bid for power in 1997, he agreed to remove the pledge to
abolish the Corporation and replace it with one to "reform" it instead. The reform he
eventually delivered reinforced the corporate vote, further diluting the humans.[33]

Today the City has an official named the Remembrancer, the world's oldest institutional lobbyist, who is the only nonparliamentary person working in the parliamentary chamber. Currently a man named Paul Double, the Remembrancer is charged
"with maintaining and enhancing the City's status and ensuring that its established
rights are safeguarded,"[34] and he monitors, and lobbies on, anything in parliament that

might touch on the City's rights.[35] At the time of writing in 2010 its most recent public memoranda included one arguing stridently against efforts to rein in hedge funds,[36] and another largely seeking to absolve over-the-counter derivatives of helping cause the financial crisis, and arguing against restricting them.[37] The City of London Corporation also has a pot of money at its disposal named City Cash, which it says is "a private fund built up over the last eight centuries," earning income from "property, supplemented by investment earnings."[38] City Cash funds many things, including monuments and ceremonies, stakes in the property developments[39] outside the City boundaries, free-market think tanks, and permanently staffed lobbying offices from Brussels to Bombay to Beijing.[40] The City will not provide a detailed list of its assets and holdings: some, but not all, are available on the public record. It admits to owning some of the most valuable part of London's West End bordering the world famous Regent and Oxford Streets.[41] The City's Cash is exempted from British Freedom of Information (FOI) requests, so we cannot find out what it owns. Jason Beattie, a reporter who sought to investigate this money pot, found it to be completely different from any other local authority fund he had ever encountered. "I FOI'd them to hell—and I got nowhere," he remembers. Does it own property around Wall Street, as Glasman suspects? There is no obvious way to find out.[42]

Some law made in the British parliament does apply to the Corporation, but some Acts of Parliament specifically exempt it, either fully or in part. The City is connected to the British nation-state, but it remains a constitutional elsewhere. In this the City resembles Jersey or the Cayman islands, the offshore jurisdictions that are its satellites—each of which, as I will show, has also been entirely captured by the interests of global finance.

For skittish global capital, the City's constitutional foundation matters absolutely. Finance knows that any serious challenge to the City would face the mystique of time immemorial and the extravagant skills and powers of the many servants of finance. This globe-encompassing financial services center, whose influence reaches silently into people's homes from Baltimore to Birmingham to Borneo, is founded upon an ancient constitutional platform that is unique and rather impregnable.

This detour through British constitutional history helps us understand a little more about the power of financial capital and its ability to escape offshore to fortified and deregulated spaces, protected from outside interference. It is no coincidence that the futuristic Euromarkets, this new playground for Wall Street, emerged here in this ancient City. This market and its subsequent spin-offs would, as we shall see, ultimately play a central role in *forcing through* the liberalization of the world economy, whether the world's citizens liked it or not. The City had created a new banking order; a new form of money, a new market in which to trade it, and the means by which the City of London would reemerge, phoenix-like, from the ashes of empire.[43] The project to restore the City to postimperial glory, the academic writer Gary Burn notes, "was pursued unhesitantly and unstintingly, without, it seems, any prior or subsequent debate by the Prime Minister, the Treasury, by Cabinet, Government or Parliament. Central to the success of this project was the Bank of England, which after 1945 set about reestablishing the hegemony of international financial capital."

From those early beginnings the Euromarkets spread like a forest fire, fueled by political events. The Soviet Union did not want to hold too many dollars in New York, where they risked being confiscated if the Cold War turned nastier, and they did not want to invest in Sterling either: the risky money of a collapsing empire. In this new liberated Eurodollar market they found their solution: They could hold the money in dollars in London, under the protection of an ancient, rather unaccountable institution with no qualms about the political origins of money. Starting with a deposit of a few hundred thousand dollars by the Moscow Narodny bank in 1957, the Soviets began to pile in. Karl Marx would have raised his prodigious eyebrows at the irony of avowedly Marxist nations nurturing the emergence of the biggest, most unfettered capitalist system in history.

By late 1959 about $200 million or so was on deposit in the Euromarket in London; by the end of 1960 it had reached a billion, and a year later the total was $3 billion, by which time it was spreading to Zurich, the Caribbean, and beyond.

In 1963 the market received two more major fillips. The first came on July 18 when President Kennedy introduced his so-called Interest Equalization Tax on income from foreign securities, which was supposed to curb U.S. dollar outflows by making it less attractive for U.S. bankers to lend overseas. Wall Street responded by doing their lending out of the offshore, tax-free Euromarkets instead. "This is a day you will remember," said Henry Alexander of Morgan Guaranty bank when the new regulations came into force. "It will change the face of American banking and force all the business to London."[44] The second boost that year was the birth of Eurobonds:

unregulated offshore *bearer bonds,* which are just what the name suggests: whoever bears the pieces of paper in their hands owns them. They are a bit like ultravaluable dollar bills: No records are kept of who owns them, and they are perfect for tax evasion. Bearer bonds feature in villain-infested Hollywood movies like *Beverly Hills Cop* and *Die Hard,* and they are considered so pernicious that many countries have since outlawed them. A Bank of England memo from 1963 crystallizes the cynicism. "However much we dislike hot money, we cannot be international bankers and refuse to accept money."[45]

That year American banks were treated to a display of the Bank of England's political muscle when the Bank's governor Lord Cromer forced Britain's new prime minister Harold Wilson to throw away half his election promises and slash government spending, prompting Wilson to shout in one debate, "Who is Prime Minister of this country, Mr. Governor, you or me?"[46]

Though the Bank of England is accountable to parliament, not to the City of London Corporation, its physical location at the geographical center of the City— just across the road from the Lord Mayor's Mansion House—reflects where its heart lies: in a shared view, established over centuries, that the path to progress lies in deregulation and freedom for financial capital—with the City at the forefront. The Bank's purpose was never defined very clearly, but when the Bank's directors decided in 1991 to work out more explicitly what the Bank is *for,* they came up with three main goals. Two were the usual central bankers' goals: to protect the currency and to keep the financial system stable. The third was, as the Bank's then governor Eddie George put it, to "ensure the effectiveness of the United Kingdom's financial services" and to have a financial system "which enhances the international competitive position of the City of London and other UK financial centres."[47] He was effectively admitting to a Bank goal to do what it takes to protect and promote the City at the center of an overseas, or offshore, empire.

A quick numerical exercise shows how unregulated offshore finance can be so profitable, far beyond the potential merely for eliminating taxes.

Governments require banks to hold reserves against the deposits they take. Let's imagine a bank officially has to hold 10 percent of the value of its deposits in cash, and the going interest rate is 5 percent annually for loans and 4 percent for deposits.

For every $100 deposit, the bank may only lend $90 at 5 percent, earning it $4.50. The bank must pay the depositor 4 percent, leaving it 50 cents. Subtract the bank's operating costs of, let's say, 40 cents, and it has made 10 cents' profit on its $100 in deposits.

Now imagine, instead, a bank in the Euromarkets in London, which has no reserve requirements. The bank can now lend all of its $100 at 5 percent, earning $5. Subtract $4 to pay interest to the depositor, then subtract 40 cent operating costs, and the profit now is 60 cents—six times the "onshore" profits. This is grossly simplified, but it exemplifies a basic principle behind offshore's appeal. On the face of it, this looks like a cost-free benefit for everyone: In a competitive market, the bankers will pass some of those profits on to borrowers and depositors. But this is a false view. First, much of the profit will pass to the bank's wealthy owners, and to the extent that the banks do pass on these savings, offshore customers will almost always be the world's wealthier citizens and corporations. Second, the increased profits come at a cost: increased risk. The latest financial crisis has showed what happens when such risks materialize: ordinary people pay. Free money for bankers and for the world's wealthy—at the expense of everyone else—is a basic leitmotif of the offshore system.

There is another offshore secret at play here too. It hinges around why banks have to hold reserves against deposits in the first place.

Imagine you deposit $100 with an "onshore" bank. Under a 10 percent reserve requirement, the bank may lend out only $90 of that to someone else. That person now has $90 to spend, and that $90 will end up in another bank account. That next bank may then lend 90 percent of that $90 out—so $81 more will end up being lent. And the process goes on. This is a well-known principle of so-called "fractional reserve banking," and if you follow the calculations through you will find that with a 10 percent reserve requirement your $100 theoretically balloons out into $1,000, spread across the economy. Money really is conjured out of thin air like this: This is what banks *do*. Money is created by the act of lending it. "The process by which money is created is so simple that the mind is repelled," said the economist J. K. Galbraith. Money creation is not a bad thing in itself. The question is: how much borrowing, and how much money creation, is healthy? Regulators try to control liquidity—making sure that the amount of money sloshing around the system does not grow out of control—by enforcing reserve requirements.

But in the unregulated London-based Euromarkets, with no reserve requirements, the first $100 deposit theoretically lets the bank lend out the full $100, which
turns into another $100 deposit, leading to another $100 loan, and so on endlessly. Of
course it never happened like that: If it had, we might have drowned in money long
ago. No, there is only so much demand for credit at any time, and if credit grows in
the offshore market it will, up to a point, be reined in elsewhere to compensate. Offshore Eurodollars also leak back "onshore," where reserve requirements will slow
down the money-creation machine again. And prudent bankers hold back reserves
anyway, even when they do not have to. Controversy has, in fact, raged for decades
about how much the Euromarkets contribute to puffing up the amount of money
circulating in the world, boosting risk and building unsustainable wobbly pyramids
of debt.

Yet some things seem clear. An unregulated market allowing potentially endless
and unusually profitable money creation will expand and displace regulated banking, and lending will expand into places where it wasn't previously able to and often
to where it shouldn't be. Credit quality is likely to deteriorate, out of sight of regulators. Just as the world was waking up to the ideas of Milton Friedman, who argued
that governments should focus on money supply as the lever to use to manage their
economies, the new London market was starting to make these levers ineffective.

If the 1960s were thrilling for American bankers in London, U.S. regulators weren't
so happy. The archives from that era show that people were fretting about exactly the
kinds of trouble that brought the world economy to its knees in the recent economic
crisis from 2007—uncontrollable financial flows across borders, and the financing of
long-term lending with very short-term borrowing, risking trouble when short-term
markets dry up. "Is the growth of this market a welcome tonic, or a slow poison to the
international financial system in general?" *The Banker* magazine had asked in the earlier years of the Euromarkets' growth.

In 1960 the Federal Reserve Bank of New York, believing that the Eurodollar
markets were already making "the pursuit of an independent monetary policy in any
one country far more difficult,"[48] sent a team to London to investigate. Bank of England staff charmed the American regulators and doubtless offered them a great number of cups of tea. But they did little to address their concerns, even after the

Americans said the Euromarkets posed a danger to stability—and even though some British officials were nervous themselves. "I did get the impression," one Bank of England official noted in a memo in 1960, "some of them were rather keeping their fingers crossed."[49]

James Roberston, vice chair of the Federal Reserve, started to point to another worry: the emerging Euromarket centers in the City's offshore satellites like Cayman and the Bahamas. "My primary objection is that they aren't branches in any sense of the word," he wrote. "They are simply desk drawers in somebody else's desk. Why make banks go through a sham proceeding to obtain certain privileges?" One enterprising trader at a major U.S. bank, recognizing how artificial this game was, planted a cardboard sign saying "Nassau" on a desk in his trading room in New York and recorded trades at that desk, booking them "offshore" and out of sight of regulators. After someone discovered the ploy the traders continued as before but ensured that a clerk simply copied them into a second set of books in the Bahamas.[50] Soon, a shift to computerized trading removed the need for cardboard signs anyway. As the author Jeffrey Robinson noted, "The horse hadn't merely bolted, it was living in a beachfront condo in the Caribbean."

The Euromarkets rippled outward, driven from the center in London, first to Britain's semi-independent Crown Dependencies of Jersey, Guernsey, and the Isle of Man near the UK mainland, then out to the British-held Caribbean jurisdictions, then to Asia, and finally to British-held Pacific atolls. These satellites of the City were simply booking offices: semifictional way stations on secretive pathways through the accountants' workbooks. The banks might park a person or two on each palm-fringed island while the heavy lifting work—the real business of hammering together big banking syndicates, making the accounting cogs mesh properly, and ensuring that the paperwork was legally watertight—happened in London and New York. But these fast-growing, freewheeling hidey-holes helped the world's wealthiest individuals and corporations, especially the banks, to grow faster than their more heavily regulated onshore counterparts.

By 1963 the U.S. Treasury already was warning that the market had aggravated a "world payments disequilibrium,"[51] and one official suggested publicly that American bankers should "ask themselves whether they are serving the national interest by participating in this sort of activity."[52] That was the year that President Kennedy introduced his Interest Equalization Tax, which drove U.S. banks to London in droves. "It is hardly an exaggeration to say that leading American banks thought little about Europe before 1963," wrote the U.S. economist Richard Sylla, "and thought about little else in the decade thereafter.[53]

Once again the U.S. authorities conveyed their fears to the Bank of England and sent the U.S. comptroller of the currency to London to inspect American banks. The Bank of England's response was, effectively, that the United States could go and screw itself. "It doesn't matter to me whether Citibank is evading American regulations in London," one top Bank official said, epitomizing the City of London approach. "I wouldn't particularly want to know."[54]

As the 1960s wore on, U.S. deficits ballooned. America was overspending overseas, in relation to its earnings, and its foreign payments sent an army of dollars outward from the United States, feeding the Euromarkets and further loosening the shackles on finance—just as Swinging London, as it became known, was breaking the constraints of fashion. Ideas about rebellion against authority percolated far into the fabric of society: James Bond's forays offshore, to Switzerland in *Goldfinger* in 1964 and to Nassau in *Thunderball* in 1965, injected an appealingly subversive frisson into the image of tax havens and uncontrolled offshore finance, the new global hothouse for international crime.

By 1967 Robert Roosa, the energetic U.S. undersecretary for the Treasury, warned that the Euromarkets had hugely amplified destabilizing capital flows, "in magnitudes much larger than anything experienced in the past, massive movements." The response from London always came in two forms: either "This is nothing to worry about" or "Mind your own business."

A bizarre, Alice in Wonderland logic lay behind the Bank's decision not to regulate these markets—the sort of logic that permeates the offshore system. If there were a run on a *regulated* bank in London, the Bank of England, by virtue of being its regulator, would feel some obligation to come in and pick up the pieces. In other words, regulation, as a Bank of England memo put it, "would mean admission of responsibility." Better, then, the logic went, not to regulate them![55]

And the Euromarkets just kept blooming. More and more U.S. banks flooded to open offices in London. The publication *Euromoney*, in its inaugural issue in 1969, described the market as being like a child: "It stuffs itself for some time with whatever goodies take its fancy, refuses to listen to warnings that it will get indigestion, gets it, lies low for a few months, then gets hungry again."

That year the biggest bank in the market was Citicorp (or Citibank), whose CEO Walter Wriston was a single-minded champion of the idea of freedom for financial capital, who delighted in the way that governments were once more being cowed by financial markets. "The Euromarkets are now the greatest mobile pool of capital in the world," Wriston said in one interview. "If the British put on reserve requirements or other controls, Bahrain is waiting. In just a couple of keystrokes, the whole market could be gone." And his love for the Euromarkets was, it seems, matched by his confidence in their resilience. When asked in an interview in 1996 about the Euromarkets whether the world risked financial meltdown on account of increasingly risky financial activities, he said simply, "It can't happen."[56]

By 1970 the London-centered market was measured at \$65 billion in all currencies and still growing fast. Daniel Davison, the head of Morgan Guaranty's London office, gushed about London's minimal regulation and generous tax treatment. It was, he said, "a banking bazaar unrivalled in history. The Moscow Narodny Bank, whether it is appropriate Bolshevik doctrine or not, sits almost cheek by jowl with the Bank of China, and rubs elbows with the capitalist banking institutions of the West. There are about three times the number of American commercial banks in the City as there are in New York. The City of London beats Baghdad as a bazaar by a country mile."

The whole character of the City began to change. City gentleman reeled at the sight of Goldman Sachs's star trader, Larry Becerra, turning up for work on a Harley-Davidson in jeans and cowboy boots, and at the sounds of "holy fucking shit" that began to fill the dealing rooms. Within a few years of Goldman Sachs's opening its first international office in the City in 1970, its London operation was accounting for a quarter of the firm's entire business and its offshore satellites a slice more. "The days of friendly co-operation and friendship changed dramatically in the mid-seventies when it became an ugly business," remarked one British banker, John Craven. "That's when unpleasant practices came in—in terms of paying investors under the table in order to take bonds and even a little bit of improper entertainment of guests in flats in London—and it undermined the whole spirit of the thing."[57]

All the time, the Bank of England quietly kept regulation at bay. In 1973 some German bankers went to see James Keogh, a Bank of England official, to ask what permissions they needed to become an authorized bank in London. "Keogh looked at us," one banker remembered, "and he said 'a bank is a bank if I consider it to be one.'"

And that, pretty much, was it—apart from what the historian David Kynaston calls the "occasional, indispensable afternoon ceremony": that cup of tea at the Bank of England from time to time to explain what you are doing.[58] By that year, over half of U.S banks' foreign business was taking place in London—though a lot of that soon began shifting toward London's satellite tax havens, especially the Bahamas and the Caymans.[59]

By 1975 the invading Wall Street ruffians had fully overtaken the plodding British banks and were beating them in market after market. "There was never any sense that old English bankers were competing with us in any way," said Michael Lewis of Salomon Brothers. "It was much more, 'how much did we have to pay them to clear out of town and do something else with their lives.'"[60]

By then, the Euromarkets had grown to exceed the size of the entire world's foreign exchange reserves.[61] At the same time, a new source of dollars had begun to feed the markets, as the OPEC oil shocks hit in the 1970s, and oil-rich countries' surpluses were re-lent through the Euromarkets to finance deficit-plagued oil consumer countries. This gigantic financial recycling via London and its satellites, to be lent out to Latin America and elsewhere, often amid great secrecy and corruption, laid the foundations for the subsequent debt crises of the 1980s.

As the Euromarket bonfire raged ever more strongly, financial capital began a new assault on the citadels of power and the democratic nation-state. Countries were no longer insulated by exchange controls and capital controls against events elsewhere. The Euromarkets seemed to have connected up the world's financial sectors and economies as if by an electric current: A shock rise in interest rates in one place would switch its effects instantly to anywhere plugged into the system. Tides of hot money once again began to surge back and forth across the globe, with the Euromarkets as a kind of anti-Keynesian global transmission belt making financial markets more sensitive to tweaks and changes elsewhere and allowing enough money to pool together in one place to allow large speculative attacks against currencies.[62] Democratic governments began to retreat in the face of financial capital. "What annoys governments about stateless money is that it functions as a plebiscite on your policy," Wriston said. "Money goes where it is wanted and stays where it is well treated. This annoys governments no end."[63]

The Euromarkets just kept snowballing: $500 billion in 1980, then a net $2.6 trillion eight years later[64]; and by 1997, nearly 90 percent of all international loans were made through this market. It is now so all-enveloping that people hardly notice it anymore.

———————————

It is fairly easy to explain why Britain welcomed the new markets, even at the cost of squeezing out British banks. There was the crude question of money, for one thing. "We, at the Bank, have never seen any reason to place any obstacles in the way of London taking its full and increasing share," one official said. "If we were to stop the business here, it would move to other countries with a consequent loss of earnings for London."[65] Not only that, but Britain was rolling out a new political and economic strategy to make up for its loss of status as the world superpower: It would keep as close as possible to a leadership role in world affairs by hitching itself to the new American superpower through a "special relationship" with Washington, which endures, at least in British minds, until the present day. The economic anchor of this special relationship has been this partnership between Wall Street and the City of London, under a simple offshore formula: give Wall Street banks what they want, and they will come.

Yet if it is obvious that the British would welcome this market, it seems rather odder that the United States would let its banks dive headfirst into this unregulated offshore market, knowing they were undermining American financial controls. Several things help explain why it was tolerated in Washington too.

Wall Street lobbying was obviously a huge part of the story. There is also the classic offshore problem: what goes on overseas, out of sight, gets ignored. Many policymakers and regulators in the United States simply failed to understand this strange new phenomenon or dismissed it as a weird, slightly unclean, but temporary anomaly[66]: a funny money best left to Europeans. "Euro-dollars, indeed!" one U.S. banker told *Time* magazine. "It's hot money—and I prefer to call it by that name." And it *was* hot money.

U.S. banking interests worked hard to keep this offshore playground as quiet as possible too. Bankers deliberately avoided discussing it,[67] and when Hendrik Houthakker, a junior member of the U.S. Council of Economic Advisors, wanted to tell the U.S. president about the Euromarket, he was slapped down by his superiors with, "No, we don't want to draw attention to it." A U.S. congressional committee report in 1975 expressed amazement at how it had flourished so far beneath the political radar for so long.[68] Yet there is a bigger reason why the United States ultimately colluded with Britain in letting Wall Street banks roam offshore.

The U.S. dollar is the world's main reserve currency. Less privileged nations are periodically constrained from spending by shortages of foreign exchange, but the nation with the dominant currency can borrow in its own currency—and it can print money to acquire real resources and live beyond its means for a long time. This "exorbitant privilege" helped America fight and pay for the Vietnam War; more recently it helped President George W. Bush cut taxes, invade Iraq, and rack up huge deficits while investors around the world continued to buy U.S. debt. Countries choose dollars as the main component in their reserves because dollar markets are large and liquid, and the dollar is trusted to be relatively stable. Everyone trades in dollars. When I was the Reuters correspondent in war-ravaged Angola in the mid-1990s, the raucous street money changers plumped up their ample brassieres not with Euros, Swiss francs, or Renminbi—but with dollars. Dollars make the world go round, and if you print the stuff, you've got it made.

To claim reserve status, a currency must have huge, deep, liquid, and sophisticated markets—and a currency subject to capital controls and stringent financial regulations is less attractive. U.S. policymakers wanted these deep markets but did not want to give up their taxes and controls. They thought, let's have our cake and eat it, by preserving the rules and constraints at home while permitting this unregulated dollar market to flourish overseas. What they had not appreciated enough was the extent to which this offshore market would rebound back into the United States, with malign effects.

———————

By the time Margaret Thatcher and Ronald Reagan came to power in 1979 and 1981, the political classes in Britain and the United States were losing faith in manufacturing and genuflecting toward finance. Wall Street and the City of London were at the forefront of a global trend of *financialization:* the reengineering of manufacturing firms as highly leveraged investment vehicles and, soon, the packaging of mortgages into risky asset backed securities for offloading into global markets. Everything was for sale: school playing fields, post offices, army services, and old fish markets. In the offshore centers, the very sovereign laws of nation-states had become available for sale or rent.

After Thatcher's giant deregulatory "Big Bang" of 1986 deepened London's off-shore status as a freewheeling, anything-goes financial center, "light-touch London" broadcast ever stronger antiregulatory impulses around the world, deregulating other economies and their banking systems as if by remote control. The City became a crow-bar for lobbyists in Wall Street and around the globe: "If we don't do this, the money will go to London," they would cry; or "we can already do this in London so—why not here?" Its offshore satellites were deregulating even faster, constantly seeking to stay ahead of the others. This race has an unforgiving internal logic: you deregulate—then when someone else catches up with you, you must deregulate some more, to stop the money from running away. For the City, it was a beautiful, self-reinforcing dynamic: The more countries that opened their financial systems, the more business that would float around internationally, ready to be caught in the nearby nodes of the British off-shore spiderweb and then sent up to be serviced in the City and its allies on Wall Street.

Not content with all this, the Corporation of London actively promotes interna-tional financial deregulation around the globe. With this in mind the Lord Mayor makes 20 or so foreign visits per year.[69] An official report into one such visit to Hong Kong, China, and South Korea in 2007, along with the Lady Mayoress, the Sherriff, and a 40-strong business delegation, gives a flavor of the Corporation's ambition and reach. The delegation's aim, according to the report, was to

Lobby for China to maintain its course of economic and financial liberalisation, and encourage South Korea to adopt more open policies; Promote London as a global financial center . . . ;

Explain the UK's liberal approach to regulation and corporate governance

Lobby for liberalisation and improved market access in China's banking, insurance and capital markets sectors; including highlighting the restrictive implications of ordinance 10 [which is designed to curb illicit financial flows and requires Chinese government approval for companies to list overseas,[70]] and the benefits of closer engagement with international players.

Encourage South Korea to adopt more liberal policies, notably in legal services, and to follow up on Seoul's ambitions to become a regional financial hub

Explain the UK's liberal approach to trade policy and regulation; and to encourage a critical mass of similarly thinking countries.[71]

In a meeting with senior officials from Tianjin, the Chinese city chosen as a pilot for national financial reform, the report noted that Mayor Dai Xianglong had "placed great value on deepening cooperation with the City of London, which he dubbed 'the holy place' of international finance and globalisation."

The Corporation of London is a municipal authority for fewer than nine thousand souls and its job is, *officially*, to promote financial freedom and liberalization around the world. In partnership with the Bank of England, it is one of the most powerful players in global financial regulation today. And almost nobody has noticed it.

———————————

Political theorists have had great difficulty even seeing the Corporation of London, let alone appreciating its significance. With its politics of personal proximity, its bonds of shared identity and principle, and its elaborate ceremonials, the City manages to be at once vastly powerful and barely visible. It fits into no modern analytical framework. Mainstream modern publications about the City gloss over its free-floating status.[72] Globalization has led to whole fields of research into the actions and interactions of companies in markets, but they usually only discuss political institutions on an abstract level. Students of the philosopher John Rawls have focused on the social compact—the relationship between rulers and ruled—but have paid relatively little reference to the role of institutions or history. Even Marxists, primed not to worry much about how financial capital organizes itself, have considered the City in the context of a clash between manufacturing capital and financial capital, misunderstanding its true role. The City is, as Glasman puts it, "an ancient and very small intimate relational institution, which doesn't fit into anybody's preconceived paradigm of modernity. Here is a medieval commune representing capital. It just does not compute."[73]

And it was here in the City, just as Britain's imperial dreams collapsed in the ignominy of the Suez retreat, that the financial establishment in London began piecing together the means by which London would restore its position as the capital of a world ruled in the interests of an elite of financial investors. At the moment of its apparent destruction, the British empire had begun to reinvent itself, back from the dead.

5

CONSTRUCTION OF A SPIDERWEB
How Britain Built a New Overseas Empire

AS U.S. BANKS ENJOYED THE DELIGHTS OF LONDON'S unregulated markets from the late 1950s and 1960s, the City of London began to see more clearly how the partnership might be expanded more deliberately at a global level. I have already hinted at how the City began to use offshore centers around the world as nodes in a spiderweb, which would catch passing capital by getting rid of taxes and rules and regulations and providing safe, secretive new bolt holes for the world's wealthy, and then send much of the business up to the City. Criminal money, far enough distanced from Britain itself to minimize the stink, would be turned to profit, and other money would accompany it. Meanwhile, the more that countries around the world deregulated and opened their economies to international capital, the more business would be flying around, and the more would come their way. Now I will explore the untold story of how it happened.

As I've noted, when Britain's formal empire collapsed, it did not entirely disappear. Fourteen small island states decided not to become independent and became instead Britain's Overseas Territories, with Britain's Queen as their head of state. It is a status that has been preserved until today. Exactly half of them—Anguilla, Bermuda, the British Virgin Islands, the Cayman Islands, Gibraltar, Montserrat, and the Turks and Caicos Islands—are tax havens, actively supported and managed from Britain and intimately linked with the City of London. Accompanying these were the Crown Dependencies near the British mainland—Jersey and Guernsey, in the English Channel off the French coast; the Isle of Man, near the Irish republic; as well as a scattering of other territories—Hong Kong as a gateway to China, still under British control, and a variety of ex-colonial oddities in the Pacific and elsewhere.

The most important part of the modern British spiderweb, from the point of view of the United States, lies in the Caribbean: the City's gateway to the vast markets of North and South America. Visit any of these territories and it becomes clear that they are, while half-British, set up to target the United States first of all. Eat out at an outdoor grill or beach restaurant, and your dinner will likely be overshadowed by a giant television screen fixed on a baseball game, and your food may be served by young American waitresses. Each either uses the U.S. dollar as its official currency or has a local currency called "dollar" that is pegged firmly to the greenback.

Offshore finance in the British Caribbean has old roots: Financial interests in Britain and their selected political representatives had learned the basics of tax havenry long before the British empire fell apart.

Organized crime in the United States began to take a serious interest in the U.S. tax code after the mobster Al Capone was convicted of tax evasion in 1931. His associate Meyer Lansky became fascinated with developing schemes to get Mob money out of the United States and bring it back, dry-cleaned. A slick Mafia operator—the inspiration for the figure of Hyman Roth in the film *The Godfather*—Lansky would beat every criminal charge against him until the day he died in 1983. He once boasted that the Mob activities he was associated with were "bigger than U.S. Steel."

Lansky began with Swiss offshore banking in 1932,[1] perfecting the loan-back technique. This involved first moving money out of the United States—in suitcases stuffed with cash, diamonds, airline tickets, cashier's checks, untraceable bearer shares, or whatever. Next, he would put the money in secret Swiss accounts, perhaps via a Liechtenstein *anstalt* (an anonymous company with a single secret shareholder). The Swiss bank would loan the money back to a mobster in the United States, who could then deduct the loan interest repayments from his taxable business income there. Lansky opened operations in Cuba, outside the reach of the U.S. tax authorities, where he and his associates built up gambling, racetrack, and drug businesses, becoming what the author Jeffrey Robinson called an "anti-Disneyland . . . the most decadent spot on the planet." Lansky's close ties to Cuba's right-wing leader General Fulgencio Batista helped stoke the violent anger that eventually brought Fidel Castro to power in 1959.

When Castro came to power Lansky moved to Miami, from where he plotted to find his next Cuba, with a pliable tyrant. "It would have to be small and close enough to the U.S. mainland to get tourists and gamblers in and out easily," Robinson explained. "It, too, would have to come furnished with a thoroughly corrupt political regime, held together by a despot greedy enough to welcome the Mob with open arms; the tyrant would have to be so firmly in place that the political environment would remain stable no matter what. And the Mob's money would have to be spread so thick and wide that, if some other tyrant seized power, he'd need them to maintain his own stability."[2]

The Bahamas, then a British colony, was perfect. Formerly a staging post for British gun-running to the southern U.S. slave states of the Confederacy, and loosely governed for years by laissez-faire members of British high society,[3] the Bahamas were effectively run by an oligarchy of corrupt white merchants.[4] It would quickly become, through Lansky, the top secrecy jurisdiction for North and South American dirty money.

This much is well known. What is not widely publicized is the British authorities' reactions to this burgeoning criminal activity on its territory. A trawl of the archives reveals a curious pattern involving periodic expressions of concern, followed by a seemingly resolute lack of action. A quaint memo from a Mr. W. G. Hulland of the Colonial Office to a Bank of England official in 1961, just as Lansky began major operations in the Bahamas, gives a flavor of such worries. "We feel that this [lack of provision of an effective regulatory system] might be a grave omission, since it is notorious that this particular territory, in common with Bermuda, attracts all sorts of financial wizards, some of whose activities we can well believe should be controlled in the public interest."

London did nothing. Two years later, a "Dear Rickett" memo[5] from M. H. Parsons, a colonial administrator, to Sir Dennis Rickett, K.C.M.G., C.B., warned that the Bahamas's white, racist[6] finance minister Stafford Sands, who had recently taken a $1.8 million bribe from Lansky[7] mobsters, wanted to make it a criminal offense to break bank secrecy, and warned that this might annoy the United States. The proposed new legislation "will surely bring protests by the U.S. Government to Her Majesty's Government," Parsons wrote. "We would look pretty feeble if we had to say that we could do nothing to influence the course of offensive legislation in a territory for which we still have outward responsibility. I admit the point is a ticklish one."

Stafford Sands had estimated that there was a billion dollars or more of dirty money to be tapped by reinforcing bank secrecy, and he was prepared to anger the United States to get it. It was, as the memo put it, "a calculated risk he was prepared to take." London gave the go-ahead, and Lansky built his new criminal empire.

Some locals in the Bahamas were unhappy about what was going on. In 1965 Lynden Pindling, a populist Bahamas politician, threw the ceremonial Speaker's Mace out of a parliament window to a prepared crowd, in a dramatic power-to-the-people gesture. Pindling was elected prime minister in 1967, ending white minority rule, on a platform that had included railing against the gambling, the corruption, and the ruling elites' mob connections, though several accounts say Lansky—astutely assessing the political winds—backed Pindling too.[8] The casinos, the gambling, and above all the Mob-infested offshore industry continued to boom. But when Pindling led the Bahamas to full independence in 1973, skittish offshore players fled in streams. The veteran lawyer Milton Grundy put his finger on what was going on. "It wasn't that Pindling said or did anything to damage the banks," Grundy said.[9] "It was just that he was black."

It so happened that there was a reassuringly British place, just next door to the Bahamas, where the locals were far more friendly, the British were still in control, criminals and bankers were being warmly welcomed, and offshore finance had recently started up: the Cayman Islands. In 1966, when the Caymans' first trust law was written, cows were still wandering through the town center of the capital, George Town, Grand Cayman. The town had one bank, one paved road, and no telephone system. The year afterward, Grand Cayman was connected to the international phone network and the airport was expanded to take jet aircraft. Money began to pour in.

In 1969 a British government team flew to the Cayman Islands to check on progress. The report notes a "frightening absence of certain types of expertise,"[10] adding that "the civil service still reflects in structure and staffing the out-moded pattern of a bygone age."

The report continued, "The flood of private sector activities, progressively drowning basic government functions, has placed an unsupportable burden on senior staff." Flocks of developers were arriving, "usually backed by glossy lay-outs and declaimed by a team of business-men supported by consultants of all sorts. On the other side of the table—the Administrator and his civil servants. No business expertise, no consultants, no economists, no statisticians, no specialists in any of the fields. Gentlemen vs. Players—with the Gentlemen unskilled in the game and unversed in its rules. It is hardly surprising that the professionals are winning, hands down."

At around this time, the archives show two sets of opinions on Britain's offshore hatchlings starting to emerge within the British Civil Service. On one side sat the British Treasury, and especially its tax collectors, who were virulently opposed to tax havenry and who found the Caymans to be especially obnoxious. The U.S. authorities were getting vexed, too, and in large part because of this the British Foreign Office was broadly opposing havenry, though its position was more nuanced. On the other side of this divide sat the Bank of England, acting as the cheerleader for the new havenry and wishing to see it grow fast—though also trying to make sure that this freewheeling Caribbean offshore expansion did not spin entirely out of control. Supporting the Bank of England, with far less influence, was the British Overseas Development Ministry, which saw offshore finance purely as a trick to get the territories to pay their own way and reduce their demands for British aid without any sign that they had any concern for the inhabitants of developing nations around the world that would suffer vast drains of wealth into the Caribbean sinkholes.[11] Discreetly, within the British establishment, battle lines were drawn. The exchanges were vigorous and at times even acrimonious.

The UK Treasury put together a working party whose report in 1971 said Britain should, in effect, stop encouraging tax havenry in its overseas territories. A worried confidential memorandum from the British Foreign Office in 1973[12] shares some of the same concern: "The Cayman Islands set up as a tax haven in 1967 and passed appropriate legislation which went considerably beyond what the UK Treasury was prepared to wear." One particularly significant Caymans bill, it noted, had quietly passed into law after an unnamed desk officer had failed, through an "administrative error," to submit the new Cayman legislation to London for consent. The effect of this, the memorandum continued, had been to drive a wedge through the Treasury's carefully constructed defenses against abuse of tax havenry. Britain later patched the holes in its own tax code as best it could, the memorandum notes—leaving, of course, elites in the United States, Latin America, and the rest of the world free to take advantage of the Caymans' offshore facilities. Despite the warning, however, nothing was done.

Further research in the archives, however, reveals something rather more deliberate than a supposed "administrative error" in the construction of the Cayman Islands as one of the world's most important tax havens. A letter from the Bank of

England dated April 11, 1969, marked "SECRET," gives us a better sense of the real forces driving the changes.[13] It shows several things.

First, despite Britain's guiding hand, these territories were extremely vulnerable to shady operators—and the smaller such jurisdictions are, the easier it is for their local administrations to be captured by unaccountable financial interests based elsewhere. "The smaller, less sophisticated and remote islands are receiving almost constant attention and blandishments from expatriate operators who aspire to turn them into their own private empires," the Bank letter notes. "The administrations in these paces find it difficult to understand what is involved and to resist tempting offers." The Bank of England letter had identified something generic to offshore centers: They are small states captured by large foreign financial, and often criminal, interests. "We need to be quite sure that the possible proliferation of trust companies, banks, etc., which in most cases would be no more than brass plates manipulating assets outside the Islands, does not get out of hand."

But the Bank of England's concerns did not reflect ethical qualms about the harm these places were wreaking on other countries—the Bank was simply expressing its desire to retain power to influence events, and particularly to safeguard the Sterling Area, the British-linked currency zone that had included most British colonies and dominions and whose members enjoyed relative freedom of payments inside the zone but which were strictly constrained from letting capital flow outside the Sterling Area. Attracting foreign dirty money, by contrast, was keenly appreciated by the Bank. "There is of course no objection to their providing bolt-holes for non-residents," the letter continued, "but we need to be sure that in so doing opportunities are not created for the transfer of UK capital to the non-Sterling Area outside UK rules." In other words: no objections to looting the treasuries of the United States and sucking illicit financial flows out of Latin America—just so long as Britain's tax base and its postimperial financial network was protected. Any harm being inflicted on other countries was deliberately to be ignored.

As time went on, however, the Bank became increasingly worried that these Wild West British offshore centers were becoming weak points in the Sterling Area, allowing leakage outside the zone. In 1972, under the Bank's guidance, Britain shrank its Sterling Area to cover only Britain and Ireland and the Crown Dependencies, excluding the new tax havens. The Cayman Islands, for its part, adopted the Cayman dollar as its new currency, at par with the U.S. dollar, and two years later this was devalued to 1.20 Caymanian dollars to the U.S. dollar—where it has remained ever since.

In the same year that the Sterling Area was shrunk, the officials who were trying to stop the tax havenry suddenly disappeared from the archive files. Taking their place was a new group of officials who seemed to be unaware of the 1971 report warning about the dangers of tax haven activities. They realized that the contraction of the Sterling Area hadn't solved the problem at all. In 1977 the new group appears to have rediscovered, still sitting on a shelf, unimplemented, the 1971 report warning about tax havenry. Again nothing was done. It looks to have been like institutional Groundhog Day within the UK Civil Service: Reports were written, memos were drafted—and nothing changed. History had repeated itself within and between the departments, all in a matter of less than ten years.[14] Each time, we find the Bank of England officials working hard to fight the tax havens' corner.

At the same time, the representative of the Overseas Development Ministry, clearly supporting the Bank of England's line, seems to have been concerned almost exclusively with the ten thousand Cayman Islanders, apparently entirely blinkered to the terrible impact this may be having on, say, the several hundred million victims of capital flight in nearby Latin America. Whatever its motivations—hopeless myopia, or a cynical attempt to privilege its own dependent territories at the expense of the rest of the developing world—the development ministry ends up stoutly defending the legislation of places like the Cayman Islands, legislation designed specifically to undermine the tax authorities and economies of developing nations around the world.

A comment from a Caymanian lawyer in the 1970s highlights where the main beneficiaries of all these illicit financial flows were. His clients, he said, would periodically contact him, worrying about Fidel Castro's Cuba nearby and insisting on special clauses to compensate them should Castro invade. "I have to explain that Castro wouldn't find any [money] in the safe," he said; "they're all really held in New York or London."

A long letter in 1971 from Kenneth Crook, the newly arrived British governor of the Cayman Islands, provides a little more detail on the thinking in London in those days and on Britain's behind-the-scenes controlling role. "You, sir, and the office as a whole," he wrote in his first long report back to his superiors in London, "might find some interest in the first reactions of a pair of Diplomatic Service eyes and ears (two pairs, if you count my wife's) to this basically colonial situation."

Then, as today, His Excellency the Governor, whom the British Queen appoints on the British government's advice, was the most powerful person on the island, presiding over a cabinet of local Caymanians. They do have elections in Cayman, with revved-up political rallies and all the fun of the fair—but the governor sent from London remains responsible for defense, internal security, and foreign relations; he appoints the attorney general, the judiciary, and a number of other senior public officials. The final appeal court is the Privy Council in London. Caymanian dollar notes carry the British Queen's head, and the national anthem is "God Save the Queen."

Governor Crook was running a place with just ten thousand inhabitants: a large, part-English village. A *Time* magazine reporter in George Town, Grand Cayman, at around the same time advised readers that if you did not have the proper cab fare, your driver would tell you not to worry—you could just pay him the next time you happen to see him. A history published in the *Cayman Financial Review* claims that mosquitoes would swarm densely enough to suffocate cows.

"This is no tropical paradise," Crook continued.

I could enlarge, in terms of a magnificent but mosquito-ridden beach; of a fairly new but rather ill-designed and sadly-neglected house; of a pleasant but very untidy little town; of swamp clearance schemes which generate smells strong enough to kill a horse; of an office which will one day ere long collapse in a shower of termite-ridden dust.

This is certainly an odd appointment for a Diplomatic Service Officer. How many of my colleagues, like myself, contemplating the inanities of some Head of State, have said to themselves "If only the fool would do so and so, how easy it would be." But have they really thought how it feels to *be* the fool in question? . . . I might invite my colleagues to try running a Parliament in the best Westminster tradition, in which one Member leaves, and as a result throws the entire Finance Committee into confusion for want of a quorum, because he has to drive the school bus—which he owns.

Sir, I hope I may be forgiven if underlying this despatch so far is a note of perhaps unbecoming levity.

The governor's long letter yields a picture of an amiable and decent enough upper-class British colonial type, trying his best to understand and cope in a strange, fast-moving new environment. In a speech in 1973, Crook told banks to remember that they were not the island's only inhabitants: People lived there too. "If you don't think about that," he said, "you might as well buy an aircraft carrier and operate from that."[15]

But on politics, and the strange relationship between Britain and its little quasi-colony, his tone hardens. "Caymanians don't want independence," Crook wrote. "They don't want internal self-government either—they are very unwilling to trust each other with effective power . . . hence they are delighted to have a Governor around; apart from anything else he's very handy for taking unpopular decisions."

Governor Crook also put his finger on a crucial subtlety of the relationship that underpins the entire edifice of offshore finance: the fact that Britain has effective control, while pretending not to be in control. "They realise that if the Governor is seen to have effective power then the others appear to be essentially cyphers. The elected politicians among them find this bad for their image," Crook wrote. "What they want is to make the Constitution look as if it obliges the Governor to do what they want, even though they know it doesn't. I think we are in the world of semantics here. The more Caymanians we can put in positions of power, the better; they will act as lightning conductors for political dissent."

Very little of substance has changed since then, as a senior Caymanian politician, who asked not to be quoted, explained to me on a visit in 2009. "The UK wants to have a significant degree of control over the jurisdiction, but at the same time it does not want to be seen to have that control," he said. "Like any boss, it wants influence without responsibility; they can turn around when things go wrong and say 'it's all your fault'—but in the meantime they are pulling all the strings. The governor can bring an agent of the crown to come here and do whatever they want," he said. "The hand has always been behind the scenes, in the shadows: it has not shown its face." Keeping the reality hidden from Caymanians is, he said, part of political leadership. "It is like having children . . . it is not necessary to tell them all the burdens and challenges you face. Eighty percent of the masses who turn up at our meetings believe they have control."

The gesture toward elected representation given to Cayman voters, plus all the money, keeps the locals happy, and Caymanians solidly support the link with Britain today. Roy Bodden, a former minister and author of a history of the Cayman Islands, remembers the Falklands War between Britain and Argentina in 1982, when influential

Caymanians, not content with having helped Argentinian generals and their wealthy friends loot their country, launched a "Mother Needs Your Help" fund. Collection tins were rattled in the street, and a million dollars raised, he said, then simply handed over to Britain for the war effort.[16]

Crucially, this remarkable degree of local support for the British connection reassures international finance that locals will not rock the boat and disturb the business of making money. But the true bedrock of this financial center is Britain's controlling role. If the islands became fully independent and were handed fully over to dark-skinned Caymanians, most of the money would flee.

––––––––––––––––––

Something else turned up in the archives too. Dated February 23, 1969, it is a cutting from the *Sunday Times,* written by its financial editor Charles Raw. While it is not unusual to find newspaper clippings in archive files, the presence of this particular one—closing the file, and with no attendant commentary—is intriguing. Might it have been left as a marker for historians? Something that couldn't make it into official documentation or be stated explicitly? The name of the clipping is at the least suggestive: "Why Not Turn the City into a Tax Haven?"

Raw's article, written amid one of the great boom phases of the offshore Eurodollar markets in London, is a piece of unashamed cheerleading for the City. It derides a "notorious" section of the UK tax code that gives tax collectors useful powers to curb offshore leakage, and it says London should let nonresidents get tax-free treatment for certain kinds of funds. "Most of the authorities' energies over the past few years have been devoted to stopping money going out," Raw wrote. "But perhaps it would be more rewarding to pay greater attention to money coming in." As we will see in the next chapter, similar lines of thinking were emerging in the United States.

The same *Times* article contains another oddity. It begins by praising a Geneva-based mutual fund group called Investors Overseas Services (IOS), which Raw says "has done wonders for the U.S. balance of payments by pumping the world's savings into U.S. shares." The article goes on to tout a new Bermuda-based fund that would "like to do the same for the UK balance of payments."

IOS, however, was no ordinary company. Raw went on to write a book about it, the title of which, *Do You Sincerely Want to Be Rich?*, was the line that IOS salesmen pitched around Europe, door-to-door, as they vacuumed up retail investments to channel into offshore funds. The company's founder, Bernie Cornfeld, called it "people's capitalism," and for a short time he made IOS into one of the largest foreign institutional investors on the U.S. stock exchange. His board of directors included a former governor of California, Pat Brown, and FDR's son James Roosevelt, and many of his advisers came from the Bank of England.[17] Cornfeld bought castles in France, sailed a forty-two-foot Corsair, and drove a Lancia Flaminia convertible. He dated the *Dallas* soap opera star Victoria Principal and the Hollywood madam Heidi Fleiss, and his company bought banks in the Bahamas, Luxembourg, and Switzerland. "I had mansions all over the world. I threw extravagant parties," he said. "And I lived with ten or twelve girls at a time."[18]

Cornfeld had originally left the United States "looking for a less competitive market," as one obituary put it, and his company's fragmented national identity—it was incorporated in Panama and headquartered in Switzerland—was the key to its success: No regulator or criminal prosecutor, he hoped, would be able to tie it down. It was a quintessentially offshore company. The U.S. tax authorities considered it European, and others considered it American. When the authorities in France became suspicious of IOS, Cornfeld hopped to Switzerland, where he teamed up with the same secretive bank in Geneva that the mobster Meyer Lansky had been using to deposit the skim from his casinos.

At first, Cornfeld took deposits mostly from U.S. military personnel stationed in Germany. He soon began looking further afield: first targeting an estimated 2.5 million U.S. expatriates around the world, then the British postimperial expatriate networks, then traders in Hong Kong, settlers in Kenya, French rubber-planters in Laos and Vietnam, Belgian miners in Congo, the Lebanese in West Africa, the overseas Chinese, and so on. He took money with no questions asked and an assurance that depositors' secrets would be safe. When he bought his first airline, a joke went around inside IOS that he was starting up "Capital Flight Airlines," and its couriers, according to Tom Naylor's book *Hot Money,* spirited huge sums out of developing countries. "As civil war raged in Nigeria and international relief for the traumatised civilian population rolled in," Naylor wrote, "IOS was on the scene to help: the international aid funds often wound up in the safe in Geneva." Even bigger sums were being bled from Latin America.

This, remember, is the company that was being held up as a model for turning the City of London into a tax haven. Even worse, by the time Raw's article emerged, IOS was already enmeshed in high-profile scandals, including illegal operations discovered in a Brazilian police raid in 1966 and a high-profile *Life* magazine exposé of a joint IOS-Lansky courier operation in 1967. What was Raw thinking?

Naylor notes another curiosity about illegal offshore money, of which Cornfeld's story is a perfect example. Banks take in deposits (which are liabilities of the bank) and make loans (which are its assets), but they also hold capital, which is the safety buffer that investors put in. If loans go bad this capital serves as a shock absorber: It is the investor capital, not the deposits, that take the hit (though if more and more loans go bad and the capital is exhausted, then the bank runs into real trouble, as happened to banks in the latest financial crisis). Prudent bankers will restrict their loans up to a multiple of, say, ten times the capital buffer.

Capital is far more valuable to bankers than deposits: The more capital you have, the more you may multiply your balance sheet. And this helps us understand why banks like secret offshore deposits so much. Investigators who probed IOS said it operated under an assumption that 10 to 20 percent of its *deposits* were, effectively, permanent capital—that is, the owners could not withdraw it, either because it was too risky for them to do so or because they were dead. It is no wonder that Swiss bankers were so reluctant to hand over the deposits of Jews who died in Hitler's concentration camps: The deposits had essentially, the Swiss believed, become permanent reserves of bank capital. Not only that, but depositors willingly accept below-market interest rates in exchange for secrecy—boosting the profits to offshore banking.

By 1970 Cornfeld's IOS was tottering under ever more scandals. Some of IOS's Swiss employees had started complaining that Cornfeld owed them money, and an insider accountant, quietly picking through IOS's international labyrinth, realized that it was a house of cards. The company fell into the hands of a big-time criminal named Robert Vesco, whom one partner called "a sonofabitch who hurt, denigrated or corrupted everyone he had contact with." Another associate said Vesco "could talk you right out of your socks, or blast you out of them, or you would find somebody else owned your socks." Vesco had been a major supporter of the Bahamian leader Lynden Pindling but was forced out in 1973 under U.S. pressure after he was found to have secretly donated $200,000 to Richard Nixon's Committee to Re-Elect the President (CREEP), partially financing the Watergate burglary.

Although the official archives paint this picture of divisions between Britain's various departments over their sponsorship of the growth of the British offshore zone, veterans in the Cayman Islands saw things from a very different angle. Under Britain's benign, hands-off approach to government, offshore lawyers were constructing the new offshore system.

One of the very earliest practitioners was Casey Gill, an ethnic Indian lawyer, author of a book about the Cayman Islands' offshore attractions, and one of the first to arrive at the start of the boom times.[19] "It was a slow, sleepy fishing village," Gill remembered. "The town ended just a half mile up there," he said, gesturing toward a window. "No buildings, just wooden shacks—apart from the Barclays building." In those early years, he reminisced, tax and accounting experts would arrive from around the world to give seminars, helping the Caymans to shape their laws accordingly. "They would come and say, 'These are the loopholes in our system.' Someone would say, 'We are competing with, say, Liechtenstein.' Or in those days the Bahamas was still trying to come through. Panama was there, and Switzerland." With each new piece of information from outside, the Cayman-based lawyers, bankers, and accountants got to work targeting the gaps and addressing the competitive threats from elsewhere.

"There was also the Red Threat: the Russians," continued Gill. "Investors were seeing shadows and ghosts everywhere. We had Castro clauses: If any government tries to expropriate assets, it would turn out they were simultaneously domiciled somewhere else." Many of these assets came out of Latin America. William Walker, a veteran father of the Cayman financial sector, described how the assets were handled in an interview to a visiting journalist in 1982. Most of the fourteen hundred registered companies whose names festooned the walls outside his office, Walker said, "don't require too much work—just signing occasional documents and perhaps holding two meetings a year. We funnel a lot of money from Central and South America. . . . Most of the money coming out of Latin America, of course, is in breach of their governments' exchange control regulations."

Gill said he was a founder member of a body called the Private Sector Consultative Committee—an association representing every branch of the burgeoning financial sector: trust practitioners, accountants, bankers, lawyers, and so on. Any government legislation that impacted on the Caymans' role as a tax haven would go through this committee. "The government has a legal draftsman. We would meet them—he would go and prepare a draft and circulate it back to us. We would come back with suggestions, it would be redrafted and circulated to the PCSS, it would get the OK, then the government would pass it into law. The governor would send it to the Foreign and Commonwealth Office (FCO)—and they would say 'no problem.' Usually business would say 'this is what we want' and the FCO would let you do what you want to do."

I asked Gill if Britain ever said no or raised objections to the new legislation. "No. Not ever. Never." He then qualified those last words a little: There had been a case, "eight or nine years" before, when the legislation had been delayed somewhat. But his basic point was clear. While the gentlemen in London buzzed around like irritable wasps, arguing with each other and writing reports on the offshore phenomenon, the wizards of global finance—not to mention half the world's criminals—were forging their own private Caribbean domains, almost entirely free from outside interference, and under Britain's protection. And so the offshore industry grew.

As an aside, it is worth noting what happens when, for example, the Caymans hatches up a new and ingenious offshore loophole targeting U.S. tax laws or financial regulations. The United States will learn about it sooner or later and take counter measures—and so the Caymans will create new loopholes to get around those. As this battle continues, America's tax code and financial regulations grow ever more complex. Offshore rebounds back onshore, in a constant dance of ever-deepening complexity. The confusions that result create, in turn, yet more opportunities for the wealthy and their advisers to find pathways through the expanding legal thickets. Huge, costly industries grow up to service the avoidance industry.

That is not all. The U.S. tax authorities often find defenses against some of the impacts of the worst offshore schemes. Yet a developing country, blind and inexperienced to the ever-deepening offshore complexity, is all but defenseless. As it slips further behind in the battle, its elites enjoy ever more opportunities for abuse, and local politics, and people's faith in their own rulers, rot a little bit further. As this happens, the message from George Town remains the same: "Not our problem. Fix it yourselves."

One of the more dramatic milestones in this ongoing dance between offshore center and onshore regulator came in 1976 when Anthony Field, the managing director of Castle Bank and Trust (Cayman) Ltd., was served with a subpoena upon arriving at the Miami airport, on suspicion that his bank was facilitating tax evasion by U.S. citizens. They wanted him to testify before a grand jury, but he refused.[20] Fearing that Field would spill his clients' secrets, exposing the Caymans to a major international scandal, an oppressive new secrecy law was drafted, the now infamous Confidential Relationships (Preservation) Law, making it a crime punishable by prison[21] to reveal financial or banking arrangements in the Caymans. You can go to jail not only for revealing information but just for *asking* for it.

It was a giant, fist-pumping "fuck you" aimed squarely at U.S. law enforcement, and it has become a cornerstone of the Caymans' success until the present day.

When the confidentiality law was enacted, Cayman practitioners remember cash literally flying in on private aircraft. "Money was still coming in large suitcases," explained Chris Johnson, a veteran accountant. "People arriving with large amounts of money would get a police escort from the airport to the bank if they requested it." It was happening all across the Caribbean. By the early 1980s, the Colombian Medellin cartel kingpin Carlos Lehder was smuggling industrial quantities of cocaine into the United States from Norman's Cay in the Bahamas, having turned it into an ultimate male libertarian fantasy. One former Medellin cartel pilot remembers being picked up by naked women at the airport. "It was a Sodom and Gomorrah," he said. "Drugs, sex, no police . . . you made the rules."[22] Lehder's goons played hide-and-seek with the U.S. Coast Guard across Biscayne Bay, landing planes on U.S. interstate highways and leaving bodies strewn across Florida. As the cocaine flooded into the United States, money flew out again, in shrink-wrapped bills loaded on wooden pallets; the Cayman Islands monetary authority would then return it to the Federal Reserve. How, the Fed asked, could this tiny island selling trinkets to cruise ships send them such a torrent of money?

The drugs money was, at least, saving Britain's development ministry tens of thousands of dollars in foreign aid. The authorities in the Caymans simply denied there was a problem and wheeled out the old offshore favorite: The scandals merely represented a case of bad apples, and the system had been cleaned up thoroughly ever since. When the next scandal came, the official response would always be the same.

Johnson remembers being involved in one bank audit where his company pointed out questionable activities, which the government simply ignored. "That, coupled with the leather-clad hot-panted secretarial staff strutting through the deep pile carpets in high heels, might also have been construed as a red flag," he said. The bank failed two years later.

The fiascos, he added wearily in an interview in 2009 in his George Town offices, have just kept repeating themselves ever since. He continues to bump up against the confidentiality law today. "One problem we have in trying to recover the assets is that we don't even know who the directors are. . . . As a liquidator, I am following the money. If I want to negotiate with a director I have no way, no clue. If I go and ask someone, 'Are you sitting on half a million dollars of my money?' that's breaking the law, and the penalty is jail. It is preposterous that these directors, some of whom sit on the boards of more than a hundred companies—one sits on over 450 boards of directors—are charging fees of up to £20,000 a company." The confidentiality law, he added mirthlessly, should be shredded.

Johnson also pointed to something else. Company law statutes in the Caymans date back to English law as far as 1862—with certain democratic provisions removed. One of these carve-outs means that directors of hedge funds or mutual funds are often indemnified from litigation. "So you can't be sued for negligence. Suppose I'm liquidating a fund and $200 million is gone. Why shouldn't I be able to sue them? The directors are steering the ship, but when it sinks they can't be sued." Other sources indicate that the companies that provide directors owe no duty of care to the company or its creditors to ensure that the directors they provide perform their functions properly.[23] No wonder directors and companies—not to mention fraudsters—love the Cayman Islands. And no wonder so many Cayman vehicles have come to so much grief in the latest financial crisis, as we shall see.

The era of suitcases of drug money flooding into the Caymans is pretty much over today. U.S. authorities began to ratchet up the pressure during the drug war, plugging some of the worst leaks. The lawyer Jack Blum explained what happened next on the Cayman Islands: "They say, 'We don't do that now.' Each time they were exposed, they would clean up the thing that was exposed. They'd say things like, 'We're in financial deals now; we're in insurance.' You go back to Cayman today, and all the guys are in pinstripe suits."

And yet the crime continues, in different, more sophisticated guises. In March 2001, the U.S. Senate Permanent Subcommittee on Investigations took testimony from a U.S. owner of a Cayman Island offshore bank who estimated that 100 percent of his clients were engaged in tax evasion and 95 percent were U.S. citizens. Dig beneath the Cayman Islands' sunny spin today, and the incentives to mischief are easy to find. "Client privacy," a government website notes,[24] "is protected by the fact that the Registrar of Companies can only release the name and type of company, its date of registration, the address of the registered office and the company's status." You cannot find a list of directors of companies in Cayman, or even a charter that describes what a company is about, without going through a court battle. Trusts do not have to be registered—and there lies another very large and murky tale. The form and the context has changed, for sure, but at root Cayman still does what it always did: finds clever new ways to undermine the rules and laws of other nation-states.

As Britain set up its Caribbean offshore networks, it was doing something else far closer to the British mainland, in the crown dependencies of Jersey, Guernsey, and the Isle of Man. While the Caribbean havens project the City of London's global reach to cover the North and Latin American markets, the Crown Dependencies are focused on Europe. Still, U.S. businesses are highly active here. The U.S. Government Accountability Office in 2008 listed Caribbean subsidiaries of Citigroup, American Express, Bank of America, Goldman Sachs, Morgan Stanley, JP Morgan, and Wachovia, among others. Most are in Jersey and involve private wealth management services for U.S. citizens in Europe, derivatives businesses, private equity, tax avoidance, and cash management. JP Morgan alone manages well over $100 billion worth of business out of Jersey just for private equity and real estate funds. Average annual bank deposits in Jersey in 2007 were over $500,000 per person, compared with less than $30,000 in the United States.

As with the Cayman Islands and other Overseas Territories, the Crown Dependencies have an ambiguous, half-in, half-out relationship with Britain that allows them to retain a controlling hand and say, "There is nothing we can do" when somebody complains. Britain handles Jersey's foreign relations and defense, and his Excellency the lieutenant governor represents the Queen; Jersey financial regulation goes up for approval to the venerable Privy Council in London. Jersey is outside the European Union, though it cherry-picks the European laws it likes and discards the rest.

John Christensen, Jersey's economic adviser from 1987 to 1998 and now a fierce critic of its tax haven status, remembers that when Britain got embarrassed about something Jersey was doing, its civil servants would engage in a kind of theater, to get things to change but without being seen to *force* Jersey to change. "A lot happens around winks and nods," he said. "They would say, 'This is all a bit of a bother, but the

Europeans are putting pressure on us and we don't want to put ourselves in a position where we are required to make you do this.' Forcing Jersey to do something would reveal that Britain has the power to make Jersey change—we all knew it. These are highly intelligent people and these things don't need to be said."

Though Jersey feels exceedingly British, this facade hides an alien political system in which medieval politics combines with futuristic, high-speed offshore finance. There are no political parties, and the government is absolutely captured by global financial services. This ambiguous relationship with Britain dates back centuries. When the Prince of Wales fled via Jersey into exile in France in 1649, he was given refuge by George Carteret, a major landowner. Later the prince became King Charles II and gave Carteret a large tract of land in North America, known today as New Jersey. The original Jersey became a refuge and hothouse for European radicals, many of whom had fled first to England to escape persecution, then were shuffled off to this strange quasi-English place, partly to provide the plausible deniability that enabled Queen Victoria to avoid embarrassment in front of her various cousins in France, Belgium, Russia, Hungary, and beyond. Karl Marx and Friedrich Engels were regular visitors. In the twentieth century, officials returning from the colonies brought new colonial connections to help Jersey bankers build networks in Africa, the Middle East, and the Far East. People either moved to Jersey or kept their money there, in a trusted British environment where they could bank secretly and avoid tax. Expatriates who did not declare their income to their countries of residence, often poverty-racked African nations, knew they would never be caught.

It was not only poor countries suffering, of course. Britain's own taxpayers were too. A letter sent in 1975 to Tony Benn, a well-known British member of parliament, describes the cynicism. "I am somewhat surprised to see a Mr. Gent from the Bank of England giving advice on how to avoid paying tax—I wonder if this is really part of the Bank of England's duties?" Mr. Gent, Benn continues, "suggests that the Bank of England will not be prepared to pass on information required by the Inland Revenue! Does the UK Treasury have no control over the Bank of England? Surely Bank employees should not be working against Government Policy? And just what sort of arrangements and deals are made at these events 'behind the scenes'? It really is just a bit too sordid to be true."[25]

Martyn Scriven, secretary to the Jersey Bankers' Association, illustrated how Jersey's network grew over time.[26] He ran the Barclays operation in Jersey, which he said catered to about one hundred thousand British expatriates. Smaller packets—up to £25,000, say—were saved in the clearing banks, while bigger packets went into the more secretive trust companies. "The biggest business developer is client recommendation," said Scriven. "The client will say, 'I'm happy, and I'd like to introduce you to my friend'—and you build it up like that. You get some seriously interesting people . . . someone who goes abroad as a rigger twenty years ago for Shell may now be in charge of the company's West Africa operations." It seems reasonable, too, to imagine how client recommendation might one day deliver Nigeria's oil minister and his friends, say, or a powerful Indian businessman, or a South African casino operator. The network grows, following old colonial links. "We gather deposits from wealthy folk all around the world, and the bulk of those deposits are sent to London," Scriven continued. "The banks consolidate their balances every day, and surplus funds won't sit here—they either go to another bank or on and through to the City. If I have money to spare, I pass it to the father. Great dollops of money go into London from here." In the second quarter of 2009, the UK received net financing of $332.5 billion just from its three crown dependencies.[27]

Jersey Finance promotional literature makes a similar point. "Jersey," it says, "represents an extension of the City of London."[28]

As the City of London's Caribbean havens and its crown dependencies were developing, something similar was happening in Asia. Hong Kong, which the U.S. economist Milton Friedman called the world's greatest experiment in laissez-faire capitalism, was to be the new Asian offshore jewel, a tax haven gateway to China and the subregion. Britain remained the guiding hand, while giving financiers free rein. The colony's financial secretary, Sir John Cowperthwaite, installed in 1961, had such stridently antigovernment views that he curtailed the publication of official statistics on the grounds that it would help the civil servants. When China introduced its "Open Door" policy of market reforms in 1978, opening up to foreign investment and export industries, Hong Kong was made: It was, as the financial crimes fighter Jack Blum remembered, "an 'anything goes, no-regulation' world." When Britain handed it back in 1997 China kept it as a "special administrative zone" with the same ambiguous offshore status. Hong Kong's Basic Law states that it shall "enjoy a high degree of autonomy" from China in all matters except foreign relations and defense. The close resemblance here with the British offshore arrangements is no coincidence. Chinese elites wanted their own offshore center, complete with political control and judicial separation. "Corporations doing business in China set up Hong Kong companies with secret shareholdings," Blum continued. "Today Hong Kong is where most of the corruption in China is accomplished." When the G20 countries sought to approve a tax haven blacklist at a summit meeting in April 2009, Chinese premier Hu Jintao fought intransigently with Barack Obama to get Hong Kong and Macau, another notorious Asian offshore hub, excluded. He got them relegated to a footnote.

Despite Chinese control, the City of London remains deeply engaged with Hong Kong, as do Wall Street firms—often through their London offices. Hong Kong remains a smallish offshore player: Its nonresident deposits, at $149 billion in 2007, were just one-eleventh the size of the Cayman Islands' $1.7 trillion. One day many years hence, however, it may grow large enough to become a key financial tool in Chinese global imperial strategies.[29]

Singapore set up its financial center in 1968 and soon began to attract hot money.[30] Andy Xie, Morgan Stanley's star Asia economist, described how it had turned out, in an internal email in 2006. "Singapore's success came mainly from being the money-laundering centre for corrupt Indonesian businessmen and government officials," he said. "To sustain its economy, Singapore is building casinos to attract corruption money from China."[31] Xie and two colleagues reportedly had to resign after the email became public.

By the 1980s, the main elements of the City of London's offshore networks were largely in place and being used extensively by Wall Street. But by then the United States, long a victim of offshore erosion, was in the process of turning itself into the world's biggest secrecy jurisdiction.

6

THE FALL OF AMERICA

How the United States Learned to Stop Worrying and Love the Offshore World

EARLY IN 1966 A YOUNG ECONOMIST WORKING at the New York headquarters of Chase Manhattan Bank was riding a company elevator when a former State Department operative handed him a memo. It isn't clear if Chase management knew of the memo: This came from Washington, not from Chase. But the young economist, Michael Hudson, was astonished by its contents.

Hudson had gotten into banking by chance: After studying economics at New York University in 1960 he took a job in real estate banking, and later, when an opening came up at Chase to look at what are called balance-of-payments issues, he was the only applicant. Now a respected (if controversial) American economic commentator, Hudson said his time at Chase—during which, incidentally, he fired a "nasty little twit" called Alan Greenspan[1]—taught him most of what he ever learned about international economics.

In those days Chase was the oil companies' preferred bank, and it had asked Hudson to study the petroleum industry's impact on the U.S. balance of payments to provide ammunition that would help the oil companies claim they were "good for America" and help them lobby for special government perks. One of his tasks on this project was to find out where the oil companies made their profits. At the producing end? At the refineries? In the gas stations? David Rockefeller, Chase's president, arranged for Hudson to meet Jack Bennett, Treasurer of Standard Oil of New Jersey, now part of the ExxonMobil empire.

Bennett gave him his answer. "The profits are made right here in my office," the oilman said. "Wherever I decide."

He was talking about transfer pricing, the practice I explained in chapter 1, where banana companies trailed their accounts around the world's tax havens in order to shift paper profits into the low-tax countries and the costs into the high-tax countries. Bennett showed Hudson exactly how large, vertically integrated multinationals could shift profits around the globe, apparently without breaking the law. The company would sell its crude oil cheap to a shipping affiliate registered in zero-tax Panama or Liberia, which in turn sold it on at a high, nearly retail price to its refineries and marketing outlets. In the high-tax countries where the oil is produced and consumed, the subsidiaries buy at a high price and sell cheap, so they are unprofitable and pay little tax. But in the middle, in zero-tax Panama or Liberia, the subsidiaries buy cheap and sell dear, making vast profits. But these havens levy no tax on those profits.[2]

To this day, accounting standards effectively hide this kind of trickery, letting companies shovel results from different countries into a single category (often called simply "international") that cannot be unpicked to work out who takes what profit where. "Only the immense political power of these extractive sectors," said Hudson, "could have induced their governments to remain so passive in the face of the fiscal drain."

This kind of offshore leakage was relatively restrained in the 1960s if compared to today. Capital flows were strongly regulated, taxes were high, and the offshore system, though alive, was still a fairly modest phenomenon, and the British offshore spiderweb was in its infancy. With the golden age of capitalism in full swing, American households, and particularly the poorest, were seeing tremendous improvements in wealth and welfare; Germans were basking in their *Wirtschaftswunder;* France was in the midst of its *Trente Glorieuses;* Italy was installing the springboard for its *Il Sorprasso* moment, to come twenty years later, when its economy would outgrow Britain's; and Japan was unleashing its own economic miracle. In large swaths of the developing world, infant mortality was falling, economies were growing, unemployment was tumbling, and hungry children were finding food regularly on their dinner tables.

Although change was coming, the United States still harbored major and powerful opponents of the offshore system. After the Great Depression, Wall Street, diluted in a large and diversified industrial economy, had relatively little political clout to veto progressive New Deal–style legislation. By contrast, the City of London's position at the center of the globe-spanning British empire gave it the domestic political heft to sabotage any British version of the New Deal. Not only that, but British finance hadn't been so directly implicated in the excesses of the 1920s. London was perfectly placed to provide American banks with an escape route from regulation at home. They could rebuild their powers offshore.

The brief memo passed to Hudson in the elevator suggested, however, that some Americans were hoping to transform the U.S. approach to the offshore world.

"Like Switzerland, flight money probably flows to the US from every country in the world," the memo started. But then the complaints began. The United States was not following the Swiss lead aggressively enough, it said. "US-based and US-controlled entities are badly penalized in competing for flight money with the Swiss or other foreign flight money centers." One reason the United States lagged in the quest for dirty money, it argued, was "the demonstrated ability of the US Treasury, Justice Department, CIA, and FBI to subpoena client records, attach client accounts, and force testimony from US officers of US-controlled entities, with proper US court back-up." There were also American taxes, plus risks associated with the Cold War and a view among "sophisticated" foreigners that U.S. money managers were "naïve and inexperienced in manipulation of foreign funds."[3] It also criticized investment and brokerage restraints "which limit the flexibility and secrecy of investment activity."

The message was unequivocal and strong. America ought to turn itself into a tax haven.

"They were saying 'We want to replace Switzerland. All this money will come here if we make this the criminal center of the world. This is how we fund Vietnam,'" Hudson remembers. "We wanted foreign criminal money, which was patriotic, but not the American criminal money." The operative in the elevator suggested to Hudson that he might find out how much foreign illicit money the United States might be able to get.

Fast forward 40 years, and it is clear that the wishes of whoever wrote that memo have been realized. A table in Raymond Baker's 2005 book *Capitalism's Achilles Heel* outlines just how far the United States has fallen. By then, it showed, U.S. banks were free to receive the proceeds from a long list of crimes committed outside the country, including alien smuggling, racketeering, peonage, and slavery.[4] Profiting from these crimes is legal, just so long as the crime itself happens offshore. A few of these loopholes have now been closed, and U.S. law addresses *some* of the others, though often only in tangential, incomplete ways. But it remains true that a U.S. bank can knowingly receive the proceeds of a wide range of foreign crimes, such as handling stolen property generated offshore. The United States is wide open for dirty money, just as that Hudson memo anticipated.

Tax havenry has always been contested in the United States. Only a month after coming to power in 1961, President Kennedy called for an end to the abuse of "foreign tax havens" and, as noted in chapter 1, asked Congress for legislation to "drive them out of existence." Barack Obama's cosponsorship of the Stop Tax Haven Abuse Act just before he came to power, and the subsequent evisceration of the act by offshore lobbyists, is merely a recent skirmish in an old war.

The United States, like most countries, already had some tax haven characteristics long before the day in 1966 that Michael Hudson stepped into that Chase elevator. From 1921 the United States has let foreigners deposit money with American banks and receive interest tax-free as long as it isn't connected with a U.S. business.[5] And Wall Street had ensured that the United States wasn't going to tell foreign governments about their citizens' holdings, despite the best efforts of John Maynard Keynes and his U.S. counterpart Harry Dexter White to combat capital flight with financial transparency.

When president John F. Kennedy launched his "Alliance for Progress" with Latin America in 1961—"a vast cooperative effort, unparalleled in magnitude and nobility of purpose," as he put it—he said he hoped to coax Latin Americans into repatriating all the money they had stashed in U.S. banks in order to reinvest it at home. Latin American leaders quickly pointed out that this would not happen unless the United States amended its tax laws, which promoted secret banking. Substantial pockets of secretly held foreign wealth already existed, not just on Wall Street but elsewhere too: in Texas, for example, but also most especially in the Southern District of Florida.

Just as Latin Americans used the United States as a home for tax evasion, immigrant communities in the United States, and especially first-generation Americans, were major U.S. tax evaders. "For various cultural reasons they didn't trust anyone—so they put it offshore," said Mike Flowers, a former U.S. Senate staffer. In addition to the first-generation Latin Americans who live across the nation, Flowers described the large concentrations of first-generation Iranians and Russians in California, "New Asians" on the West Coast, Jewish communities in various locations, and so on. "They tend to come clean after they have kids and have been here a while," he continued. "They get settled and then they think, 'Oh my God, I have all this offshore money and what do I do now? If I get caught, I'm screwed.'"

In an article entitled "Miami, the Capital of Latin America,"[6] *Time* magazine hinted at the city's in-between, financialized, quasi-offshore status: Miami was "Latin America's Wall Street . . . a hemispheric crossroads for trade, travel and communications in the 21st century—a sort of Hong Kong of the Americas." From the 1950s and 1960s, Florida became a pivot for the French Connection heroin route, for Kuomintang drugs flowing into the United States via Hong Kong (which Lansky laundered through Florida real estate), for Latin American flight money, and for Colombian drug money, often routed via the Bahamas, Panama, and the Netherlands Antilles.[7]

Jack Blum, then a Senate investigator, remembers sitting on his veranda in Miami in those days and listening to the gunfire.

"This place was nuts," he said. "The stories in the *Miami Herald* were so fantastic, you'd say, 'Why hasn't any national editor picked up on this?'" The reason, he found, was that the editors simply didn't believe them. Blum tells of one small aircraft coming in from Colombia via the Bahamas, then getting chased by U.S. helicopters. The pilot tried to escape by flying just under a commercial jetliner, then bailing out just before landing, after first hauling overboard the cocaine with the plane on autopilot.

"The first bag goes through the roof of a house—and nobody complains," Blum said.[8] "The second whacks the steeple off the South Miami Baptist church. The third bag falls into a community swimming pool and soaks the audience of a meeting of Crime Stoppers. The plane went down in the Everglades. The last bags probably got dragged off by alligators. He got busted.

"That happened. That happened."

By the 1980s, two-fifths of the money on deposit in Miami banks was reckoned to have originated overseas, particularly in Latin America. After 1976, the Florida region became the only one of the Federal Reserve's regions to show persistent (and huge) cash surpluses.[9] "Half the property in Miami is owned by offshore shell companies, and the largest yachts on the Intracoastal Waterway are registered offshore," said Blum. "Miami is the facility of choice for Latinex–heads of state, generals, and former friends of the CIA."

Washington did not push hard on transparency: It might frighten foreign capital owners, leading to large net outflows, and worsening an already bad balance-of-payments situation. So alternative ways were sought to stop capital from leaking out of the country. A new tax was introduced in 1963, a levy of up to 15 percent on income Americans received from foreign securities, to try to stop them from exporting capital to buy foreign bonds.[10] As we have already seen, banks instead flocked to the offshore Euromarkets to finance their activities: London-based borrowing tripled just between 1962 and 1963. Chase Manhattan and others began to book more and more loans through the Euromarkets, in London and Nassau in particular. The United States continued to bleed capital, and in 1965 the Johnson administration introduced limited controls on outward capital flows, broadening the controls in 1966 and making them mandatory in 1968.[11] "This was the first time in U.S. history there were rules to stop capital flowing out," explained Jack Blum. "And the corporate community went apeshit." In the face of all the lobbying that ensued, a compromise was accepted. Corporations could continue to keep their money offshore, and it would mostly remain untaxed and outside of these controls unless they repatriated it.[12]

In the tax world, this is a concept known as deferral: Companies may legally *defer* their taxes by holding profits offshore, untaxed, indefinitely. U.S. companies are only taxed on the income they bring back to the United States, usually in order to pay dividends to shareholders. Corporations know this is a bit of a game, partly depending on who is in the White House: Every now and then they are allowed to bring this untaxed offshore money back home through amnesties. In 2004, for example, George W. Bush's administration offered his corporate friends a 5 percent tax rate instead of the normal 35 percent for companies repatriating cash. Over $360 billion whooshed back to the country through this Bush loophole, under a claim that this would "provide jobs" as the capital returned home. Instead, however, much of it went into share buybacks, boosting executive bonuses. The nonprofit research organization Citizens for Tax Justice, which studied the amnesty in detail, concluded, "There is no evidence that the amnesty added a single job to the U.S. economy."

Deferred taxes—taxes that a corporation should (in a fair world) pay this year but can choose to delay—are described by Richard Murphy, a UK-based tax expert, as "a tax-free loan from the government, with no repayment date." This sharply reduces multinationals' cost of capital—a very big deal indeed, especially when this is accumulated over many years—and it in turn gives them a huge competitive advantage against smaller, locally based firms.[13] When corporations dodge tax, others—that is, you and me—must pay the taxes that they won't. The writer David Cay Johnston makes an interesting environmental comparison here. "Tax shelters are to democracy what pollution is to the environment."[14] He is quite right too.

This concession to corporations—allowing them to defer their taxes offshore and indefinitely—has been an enormous political boost for the offshore system. "Suddenly," Blum explains, "every major corporation uses an offshore account." Companies focused especially on the London-centered Eurodollar market but also on Panama, then under a right-wing strongman who venerated Adolf Hitler, and on the Bahamas, where Meyer Lansky had the politicians in his pocket. In the United States, Lansky had close links to the Mob lawyer Sidney Korshak, a true American Mafia kingmaker who in turn helped build up the career of several Hollywood actors, including Ronald Reagan. Some large U.S. corporations even opened their own offshore banks.

As this happened, the interests of big-time criminals, the intelligence services, wealthy Americans, and U.S. corporations began to converge ever more strongly offshore. The system was working two transformations simultaneously: helping criminal enterprises imitate legitimate businesses, and encouraging legitimate businesses to behave more like criminal enterprises.

"The trouble is," Blum said, "you can't separate the channels for paying people off from the other purposes." Although it was tax, not criminality, that most interested the corporations (and lax financial regulation that interested the banks), the big American crime families were especially pleased with the political umbrella that the corporations, and the spies, had hoisted over their offshore playgrounds. And the secrecy, in turn, provided the managers of large corporations with fabulous new opportunities for bribery, insider trading, and fraud. A new crime-friendly environment was being created for American capitalism. The scale of this criminality can hardly be guessed at. But secrecy makes criminality possible. And in competitive markets, whatever is possible becomes necessary.

As this offshore expansion accelerated, the erosion of America from the inside gathered pace.

The oil crises of the 1970s led to high inflation: This, plus the legacy of Vietnam-era deficits, sent the dollar spiraling downward. In August 1979, U.S. president Carter appointed Paul Volcker, a renowned hard-money man, to head the Federal Reserve Board and reassure the markets. Carter cut spending, and Volcker tightened monetary policy savagely.

But Volcker had a problem. "Monetarist" theories of tackling economic problems by focusing on the money supply were coming into vogue, just at the time that unregulated Euromarkets, lacking regulation and official checks on banks' abilities to create money out of thin air, were starting to disrupt the Fed's efforts to control that very money supply.[15] Volcker called for a new cooperative international framework through the Bank for International Settlements, in Switzerland, to get other countries to stamp down on uncontrolled money creation in the offshore system. But New York bankers, in an alliance with the Bank of England and the Swiss National Bank, killed the initiative.[16]

The bankers of Manhattan began to wield the offshore system as a weapon to attack the New Deal regulations that had so effectively clipped their wings at home. In the words of Professor Ronen Palan, a leading academic authority on the offshore system, "The New York banking fraternity, led by Chase Manhattan, used the real or imagined threat posed by the Euromarket and the Caribbean tax havens—which the same banks had of course helped establish as large financial centres in the first place—to achieve their aim of more liberal financial laws."[17] If you can't beat the offshore markets, the lobbyists argued, then join them.

In June 1981, less than six months after Reagan's inauguration, the United States approved a new offshore possibility, the international banking facility. The United States was another step closer to becoming the tax haven imagined in the memo to Michael Hudson.

IBFs, as they are known, are kind of offshore Euromarkets-lite: They let U.S. bankers do at home what they could previously do only in places like London, Zurich, or Nassau: lend to foreigners, free from reserve requirements and from city and state taxes. The bankers would sit in the same Manhattan offices as before and simply open up a new set of books and operate as if they were a branch in Nassau. Once the IBFs were in place, the banks could dispense with the subterfuge entirely and book them openly in New York. The United States had moved closer to the British offshore model.

Bankers in New York signed on to the new possibility with gusto, followed by those in Florida, California, Illinois, and Texas. In three years almost five hundred offshore IBFs had popped up inside the United States, draining money out of other offshore markets in the Caribbean and elsewhere.[18] It was a new get-out-of-regulation-free card for Wall Street and another hole in the American fortress. Not only that, but as author Tom Naylor puts it, "The US hoped to use the IBFs as a bludgeon to force other countries to relax restrictions on the entry of US banks into their domestic financial markets."

Japan followed the lead in 1986 by creating its own offshore market, modeled on the U.S. IBFs. This happened just at the start of a massive credit boom, followed by what was at the time the biggest asset market crash in history. That roller coaster had many causes, but the wildfire was stoked by the $400 billion that whooshed into Tokyo within 24 months[19] and showed local bankers what liberalized finance was all about. That year was also, as noted in chapter 4, the year of the fateful Big Bang of deregulation in the City of London, which provided Wall Street with major new escape hatches from financial regulation.

As offshore finance moved onshore, it became ever harder to tell the two worlds apart. And this, crucially, fed the giant blind spot, which persists to this day. Nearly every tax analyst took this blurring between onshore and offshore as a signal to stop trying to measure or analyze the secrecy jurisdictions, or just to focus on a few smaller, more colorful island havens. Palan, in his book *The Offshore World,* explains what was really happening. "Far from signalling the decline of offshore," he wrote, "the process "must be interpreted as the embedding of offshore in the global political economy."[20]

John Christensen remembers noticing this blind spot in 1986. He was working as a development economist in Malaysia and came across some odd local structures known as deposit-taking cooperatives. These were unregulated quasi-banks that took large volumes of deposits from Malaysian widows and orphans and channeled the money offshore. In July 1985, one of these cooperatives offered him a king prawn luncheon at a sumptuous office penthouse in Kuala Lumpur, washed down with Guinness and Courvoisier. As the lunch wore on, it became apparent that the chief financial officer, a leading light in the Malaysian Chinese Association, wanted to steer the conversation toward Christensen's childhood roots over six and a half thousand miles away in the crown dependency of Jersey, and he was especially interested in its status as a tax haven. He wanted to know if it was safe to invest.

Christensen resolved to look into the cooperatives. "The whole thing was a massive scam," he said. "The Central Bank wouldn't regulate it and nobody else would touch it. Everyone said 'keep away.'" Their international offshore dimension made it impossible for anyone locally—whether curious depositors or government regulators—to find out what was really happening: how profits were being shifted to insiders and risks heaped onto the shoulders of ordinary Malaysian depositors or taxpayers. After doing detailed research, Christensen was able to get an article published in the *Business Times* of Singapore in December 1985 before leaving the country as the ensuing scandal broke. Within months the central bank had suspended twenty-four cooperatives amid a massive run by depositors.

Back in Britain Christensen spent a couple of months combing libraries and seeing all the economists and capital markets experts he could find to try to understand where the money was flowing and how the offshore system worked. Nobody knew anything. "I don't think anyone understood how malevolent this thing had become," he said. "There was no useful information anywhere."

———————————

As the Vietnam War heated up, Michael Hudson worked out that the whole of the U.S. balance-of-payments deficit could be attributed to the costs of Vietnam. And the deficits, later worsened by the great Reagan tax cuts of 1981, posed a quandary. American companies needed to borrow money by issuing bonds, but if they borrowed it all at home, they would compete for funds with the U.S. government, pushing up interest rates and crimping economic growth. So it would be best if they could borrow from overseas.

But there was a hitch. A French investor, say, who wanted to buy some bonds faced a simple choice: either invest in American bonds, and pay a 30 percent withholding tax on the bond income, or hop on the "coupon bus" to Luxembourg and earn income tax-free, and in secret, from Eurobonds. Many investors saw this as no choice at all. They shunned American bonds.

So American policymakers had a problem. The United States wasn't a tax haven, they reasoned, and they didn't want to help tax cheats unnecessarily. They wanted

American companies to borrow overseas, but they wanted to keep the 30 percent tax too, for the revenue. How to square this circle?

At first, they settled for a compromise. American corporations could cook up a version of what was known as a "Dutch Sandwich"—set up an offshore finance subsidiary in the Netherlands Antilles, then use it to issue tax-free Eurobonds and send the proceeds up to the American parent. The United States could argue that it did not have to tax this income from the Antilles, under the rules of its tax treaty with this former Dutch colony via its postcolonial relationship with the Netherlands.

The U.S. Internal Revenue Service could easily have decided that the Dutch Sandwich was a sham and taxed the income. But it looked the other way. "These were Eurobonds, bearer bonds, which were virtually impossible to tax," explained Michael J. McIntyre, a top U.S. expert on international tax, who was one of very few people in the United States to have opposed this at the time. "You British people were quite happy about (the tax-free, secretive Eurobond markets). And we wanted in. We wanted to attract the hot money too."

David Rosenbloom, who was in charge of these matters at the U.S. Treasury during the years 1978–80, also remembers how questionable these officially tolerated offshore antics were. "People were very nervous. Those companies wanted access to the Eurodollar market, and they really wanted security," he said. "The Antilles structures were kind of phoney—these were paper entities; they weren't doing anything real. They existed in some *notaire*'s desk drawer down in Curaçao."[21]

In response to the Antilles structures, the Carter administration commissioned a major survey of secrecy jurisdictions that was published in January 1981, the month Reagan came to power.

The Gordon report, as it was called, was probably the first really serious challenge to the havens in history. It condemned tax havenry as a situation that "attracts criminals and is abusive to other countries" and called on America to lead the world to crack down. Published a week before the Reagan inauguration, it quickly sank out of view. Yet the report was an acknowledgment that there was a big problem, and in this, it was new. "I can't remember any overarching 'Let's go after the havens' thing prior to the Gordon report," said Rosenbloom.

While the Bahamas and Switzerland were certainly on the radar screen, he said, the Netherlands Antilles was the big one.

Eventually, the United States told the Netherlands Antilles it wanted to renegotiate the treaty.

"A whole bunch of rulings came down that scared the bejesus out of everybody," said Rosenbloom. "These were the days when people were actually afraid of our tax authorities."

But there was another hitch: Having tacitly encouraged the Antilles loophole, the United States was not in a great position to object. "From the point of view of U.S. tax policy these things were utterly objectionable, but the U.S. government had its hands completely dirty," Rosenbloom continued. "The government was in a bad position to start getting all self-righteous about this.

"The Antilles could have gotten a decent treaty that would have let them carry on doing business in some form. I was prepared to compromise. I didn't think we had the gumption to do this."

Yet the Dutch Antilles overplayed its hand. "They were holding out," Rosenbloom said. "They thought they could push the United States around in treaty negotiations. They wanted more of this and more of that, and this benefit and that benefit . . . they just held tough on all sorts of positions that we couldn't accept."

American corporations grew skittish. And out of the commotion, a new approach was hatched: From 1984, the United States would bypass the Antilles irritant entirely and waive the 30 percent withholding tax under a new loophole.[22] American companies would no longer set up fictional entities in Curaçao but simply issue their bonds at home. Foreign investors would pay no tax on their bond income.

It was a classic tax haven gambit: plug the deficits by exempting foreigners from tax, and watch as the world's hot money rolls in. It was just as the memo handed to Hudson in the elevator had anticipated.

The loophole was supposed to be available to foreign investors only. Unscrupulous wealthy Americans, of course, got around that simply by covering themselves in a cloak of offshore secrecy and *pretending* to be foreigners.

"The Wall Street types were as happy as clams," said McIntyre. "The rules were designed to facilitate tax evasion. It was a very hot business: People in high places liked it and fostered it. They didn't think it was an ethical issue. . . . Nobody seemed to object, except my brother Bob and I."[23]

The effects were immense. Having set up offshore-lite international banking facilities in 1981, America, by 1984, had a thriving homegrown offshore bond market.

"Suddenly," noted *Time* magazine, "America has become the largest and possibly the most alluring tax haven in the world."

From then on, a drip-drip of new laws and statutes nibbled away at America's onshore defenses.

In the late 1990s, Bill Clinton's treasury secretary and former Goldman Sachs cochairman Robert Rubin deepened the offshore corrosion with a devious new piece of legislation, the Qualified Intermediary Program. And here lies another nauseating tale.

U.S. authorities wanted to protect the nation's own tax base by finding out about American accounts at foreign financial institutions. Yet they could not simply request *all* the information—about both foreigners and U.S. citizens—then simply sift out the U.S. tax cheats and ignore the foreigners. If it did receive information about foreigners, the United States would be *obliged* under its tax treaties to tell foreign governments about their citizens' U.S. investments. Those citizens would then take their money out of the United States and park it somewhere else, where it would remain secret. U.S. deficits would widen.

The answer was to outsource the screening to foreign banks. They would tell the United States *only* about U.S. citizens and not pass on any information about foreigners. And if the United States did not have the information, then it would have nothing to exchange with foreign jurisdiction—and it wouldn't be breaking its treaties. "The rules were designed to make it difficult for the U.S. government to learn who the tax cheats were," McIntyre explained.[24] "This evasion was intended to benefit U.S. borrowers by allowing them to borrow from the tax cheats at a reduced interest rate."[25] It was another classic offshore ruse. A tax haven sets up worthy treaties that require the haven to exchange information with foreign jurisdictions. Then they set up the structures to make sure that they never have the information to exchange in the first place. They keep their secrecy, but by pointing to their treaties they can claim that they are a transparent and cooperative jurisdiction.

Next, the banks simply lied to the U.S. authorities about what they were doing. Under cover of the Qualified Intermediary Program, members of the Swiss aristocracy would stalk the America's Cup and Boston Symphony Orchestra concerts for wealthy Americans, then set them up with tax evasion schemes, even smuggling diamonds in toothpaste tubes to help them evade tax. Then they would check the box to confirm they were respecting American banking laws.

Rosenbloom encapsulated the cynicism in a nutshell. "The program was not aimed at identifying Americans," he said. "The program was aimed at protecting the identity of foreigners while allowing them to invest in the U.S." This narrow focus meant that only very clumsy or poorly advised American tax evaders would ever be caught.

A veteran official Washington investigator who asks to remain anonymous described how one American lawyer responded to the Qualified Intermediary Program. "This guy has a wonderful practice teaching people how to game the system," he said. "The first thing he does is put together a PowerPoint to the banks in central European secrecy jurisdictions, on how to get around the reporting obligations."

"That sonofabitch yelled at me down the phone," the investigator continued. "This is such an abuse of part of our legal culture. They fought [the U.S. government] every step of the way."

The Clinton administration, to be fair, issued proposed regulations near the end of its second term that would provide OECD countries with information about their citizens' U.S. bank deposits. U.S. banks, especially those with major deposits in Florida and Texas, lobbied hard against them. George W. Bush's administration dropped them.[26]

The United States sells financial secrecy not just at the federal level but at the state level too. Delaware is the biggest state provider of offshore corporate secrecy, but Nevada and Wyoming are the most opaque: They allow bearer shares, a vehicle of choice for mobsters and drugs smugglers, and they are particularly lax on allowing company directors and other officers to be named, hiding the identities of the real owners. Nevada does not share tax or incorporation information with the federal government and does not require a corporation to report where it does business. The IRS has no way of knowing whether a Nevada corporation has filed a federal tax return. Arkansas, Oklahoma, and Oregon are also routinely used for fraud by eastern Europeans and Russians, and, as noted, Texas and Florida are havens for illicit Latin American wealth.

In the 1990s, the U.S. government gave millions in aid to help the former Soviet Union countries improve the security at their nuclear power plants. Much of it went missing. When the U.S. Department of Justice went looking for the money, investigators finally tracked it to anonymous shell companies in Pennsylvania and

Delaware. Most cases involving financial market manipulations that the FBI has studied have involved U.S. shell companies from these states. The notorious "merchant
of death" Viktor Bout, inspiration for the character played by Nicholas Cage in the
Hollywood film *Lord of War,* alleged arms runner to the Taliban and other murderous organizations around the globe, operated through businesses in Texas, Delaware,
and Florida.[27]

"US shell companies are attractive vehicles for those seeking to launder money,
evade taxes, finance terrorism, or conduct other illicit activity anonymously," said Republican Senator Norm Coleman, then chairman of the U.S. Senate Permanent Subcommittee on Investigations. "Competition among States to attract company filing
revenue and franchise taxes has, in some instances, resulted in a race to the bottom."[28]

A *New York Times* article from 1986 describes the antics of one Delaware lieu-
tenant-general who flew to Taiwan, Hong Kong, China, Indonesia, Singapore, and the
Philippines, clutching a pamphlet boasting that Delaware could "Protect You from
Politics."[29] The official was, the article noted, "looking forward to a rich harvest of
Hong Kong flight capital" after the British pullout in 1997. "You don't have to tell us
the details of your business; you don't have to list who's on your board or who's holding office; and you don't have to use your name and address—just use your Delaware
agent's." For an extra $50, you could get this in 24 hours.

Today, an "aged shelf company" will help you pretend you have been trading for
years, when in fact you've just started up. "It's an effective means to create a percep-
tion of business stability," one registered agent advertises. "Most people won't ask. . . .
There's nothing wrong with immediate gratification, as long as it's affordable!" Behind
the secrecy, nobody can discover the deception. All this, and more, is yours for $299.

A limited liability corporation (LLC) might offer certified copies of the passports
of that company's directors. That looks reassuring, but even with genuine passport
copies you are no closer to knowing who really *owns* the company or its assets: These
directors are probably professional nominees who work for hundreds of such corporations. Typically the nominee director will route all queries via a company attorney
who has contact with the real people, and when crime-fighters come looking, the attorney will hide behind attorney-client privilege and claim he or she cannot reveal the
information. "That's a secrecy jurisdiction right there, in his office," one irate U.S.
government investigator told me. "The lawyers are worse than the bankers. And there
are the securities firms, and accountants. They are all involved."

These LLCs are a *filter* between the assets and the owner, screening out the information. U.S. states cream off a few hundred dollars in fees, and crimes around the world go unpunished.

A Wyoming website boasts that "Wyoming Corporations and LLCs have a tax haven within the United States with no income taxation, anonymous ownership and bearer shares. . . . Shelf Corporations and LLCs: Anonymous entity where YOUR NAME IS ON NOTHING! These companies already exist and are complete with Articles, Federal Tax ID numbers and registered agents. . . . You may have these complete companies by TOMORROW MORNING!"

Yours for $69, plus modest state filing fees.[30]

These places are selling a cheap and very strong form of secrecy.[31] In Switzerland, information is typically retained, but secrecy laws mean locals may not disclose it. States like Wyoming have no such prohibitions on breaking the secrecy: The trick is simply to ensure no information is available in the first place. All company records may be kept outside the state—in North Korea, for instance—so even if the authorities wanted to find out what your company was about, they couldn't. Stock can be transferred instantly and privately without filing a public notice.

With its corporate laws, the United States does not even comply with the transparency requirements of the IMF's rather toothless IMF Financial Action Task Force, which requires countries to be able to identify beneficial owners. When congressional staffers and others have tried to change this, they have met ferocious lobbying from these states and from the American Bar Association.

"When other countries ask us for company owners, we have to stand red-faced and empty-handed," said Senator Carl Levin. "The United States has been a leading advocate for transparency and openness. We have criticized offshore tax havens for their secrecy and lack of transparency. We have pressed them to change their ways. But look what is going on in our own backyard.

"America should never be the mattress corrupt foreign officials use to hide their money."[32]

Secrecy is just one of several lures that individual U.S. states offer to financial capital elsewhere. Tax is another lure, though a fairly minor one. Certain types of state corporations shield residents from state income tax, asset tax, sales tax, stock transfer tax, or inheritance tax, and U.S. corporations push trademarks, patents, and other nebulous things into low-tax states in a transfer pricing game to cut state taxes. World-Com, for instance, shifted nearly $20 billion tied to "management foresight" to a Delaware company before it collapsed in 2002. Tax is never the individual states' top attraction, though: Corporations paying no state taxes owe U.S. federal taxes.

Two further lures have turned certain U.S. states into corporate havens. One involves usury; I will explore this in chapter 10. The other involves corporate governance, which is largely governed in the United States by state, not federal, laws. In both of these, Delaware plays a starring role.

What ties all these different strands together—the tax, the secrecy, the usury specialties, and the corporate governance—is the political establishment of this tiny state, where everyone knows everyone else and Democrats and Republicans alike seem to share a uniform opinion that local laws must be shaped to satisfy corporate desires, to attract business for the state—and the rest of the world can take care of itself. Only a definition of *offshore* like the one I use in chapter 1—focusing on how locals prioritize their own interests explicitly at the expense of others—enables us to tie together the four strands mentioned above and to understand what is going on.

A brief look at the story of Delaware helps bring this historical section of the book up to the present day.

Delaware, the second smallest of the U.S. states, is home to many of the world's biggest corporations. Conventional definitions of tax havens—those that focus on tax—fail to capture Delaware as a part of the offshore system. But something important is clearly happening here: Over half of U.S. publicly traded companies and nearly two-thirds of its Fortune 500—Coca-Cola, General Motors, ExxonMobil, you name it—are incorporated here; the little state hosted over 90 percent of all IPOs in the United States in 2007. These corporations don't have their headquarters here; they are just incorporated there. Being in Delaware gives modest tax advantages over other states, but the killer lure is, as I've said, laissez-faire standards of corporate governance that give tremendous power to corporate managers.

Delaware has long been a refuge for financial capital. In 1899 the state government, influenced by the du Pont family, who wanted to incorporate their chemical industries,[33] adopted a new and permissive corporation law that reflected the laissez-faire spirit of an age of growing corporate power. In Delaware, the message went, company managers gain huge leeway to do what they want at the expense of other stakeholders. Other states began to follow suit. "Even as the starter's gun went off," the Chancery Court's official history puts it, "Delaware was already being accused of leading a 'race to the bottom.'" This classically offshore theme has remained a permanent character of Delaware history. In 1974 William Cary, a former chairman of the U.S. Securities and Exchange Commission, wrote in a landmark article in the *Yale Law Journal* that Delaware law has "watered down the rights of shareholders vis-à-vis management to a thin gruel" and that "necessary high standards of conduct cannot be maintained by courts shackled to public policy based upon the production of revenue, pride in being 'number one,' and the creation of a 'favorable climate' for new incorporations."

To be fair to Delaware, there are healthier reasons for incorporating here. Its Chancery Court has become—because of Delaware's success in attracting out-of-towners—the specialist in corporate law, with unrivaled experience and expertise.[34] And its location halfway between New York and Washington gives Wilmington a fearsome geographical edge too. Who wants to fly to Alaska to litigate?

The Delaware Chancery Court has a "business judgment rule" under which courts should not second-guess corporate managers, provided they have not blatantly violated some major rule of conduct and their decisions are approved by a "neutral" decision-making body. Whatever one thinks of this approach, Delaware has taken it to extreme lengths, granting corporate bosses extraordinary freedoms from bothersome stockholders, judicial review, and even public opinion. As Bernard Black, a professor of law at Columbia University, wrote in 1998, "Shareholders haven't been able to stop managers, and their allies on the Delaware Supreme Court and in state legislatures, from chilling hostile takeovers through poison pills, antitakeover statutes, and judicial decisions that let managers 'treat shareholders like morons' who are incapable of understanding a firm's true value."[35]

In 2003 Delaware passed new legislation expanding the Chancery Court's jurisdiction, and the official synopsis said the aim was to "keep Delaware ahead of the curve in meeting the evolving needs of businesses, thus strengthening the ability of the state to convince such businesses to incorporate and locate operations."[36] J. Robert Brown, a professor of corporate law at Denver University and a leading critic of Delaware courts, said that "Delaware courts have all but eliminated meaningful limits on self-interested transactions."

A Reuters story in May 2010 provided a fascinating insight into one role Delaware's incorporation business played in the latest financial crisis.[37] The story examines the "dean of CDOs," a retired University of Delaware finance professor who became the sole independent director of the Delaware-based corporations behind more than two hundred mostly subprime-backed CDOs, including ones underwritten by Goldman Sachs and Morgan Stanley. Independent directors are supposed to bring unbiased opinions to company boards and ought to be what one expert terms "the cornerstone of good corporate governance."[38] Janet Tavakoli, a Chicago-based structured finance consultant, said these independent directors "are basically there just as a rubber stamp." We will see a lot more of Delaware's role in the financial crisis later, but the point for now is that allowing toothless directors for securitization deals, just like Nevada's tolerance for nominee directors who reinforce corporate secrecy, is offshore business.[39]

Richard Murphy of Tax Research UK captures the artificiality of these arrangements. "Offshore is used to repackage what happens elsewhere," he said. "It is used to change the form, but not the substance, of a transaction." A world-famous totem to this artificiality is Ugland House, in the Cayman Islands, which Barack Obama once criticized for housing over twelve thousand corporations: "either the biggest building," he said, "or the biggest tax scam."[40] When Obama said that, Antony Travers, chairman of the Cayman Islands Financial Services Authority, fired right back. Obama would be better advised to focus his attention in Delaware, where, he said, "an office at 1209 North Orange Street, Wilmington, houses 217,000 companies."

After Travers said that, I had to see the world's biggest building.

This, as it happens, is the office for the Corporation Trust, a subsidiary of the Dutch firm Wolters Kluwer. It is just at the edge of Wilmington's small financial center: a forgettable yellowish brick low-rise with a modest maroon awning: the kind you'd find outside a pizza restaurant. It sits between the scruffy little parking lot behind it and the unsightly six-story parking garage across Orange Street, and it is, legally speaking, the corporate home of Ford, General Motors, Coca-Cola, Kentucky Fried Chicken, Intel Corp., Google Inc., Hewlett Packard, Texas Instruments, and many more global corporate giants, including many of the specialized trusts and Special Purpose Entities (SPEs) that underlay the latest financial crisis. These corporations are not here for secrecy but for the corporate governance. The Corporation Trust will, as part of the service, also help your company serve and receive notices, subpoenas, summons, and the like. Delaware's government website lists 110 registered agents—these, by the way, are not regulated.[41] In 2008 Delaware hosted 882,000 active business entities: one for every man, woman, child, and baby in the state.[42]

Before visiting the building, I called repeatedly to request an interview with the management of the Corporation Trust. Each time I was promised a call back, which never came, until I eventually caught a new receptionist who put me through to the office manager, Cory Bueller. Evidently flustered, she agreed to see me. I turned up ten minutes ahead of time and was buzzed into a reception room about twelve by twelve feet, with an aging, scuffed gray-patterned carpet, two potted plants, and light-colored walls dotted with odd grease smears. Behind a glass window sat the receptionist, a slightly unshaven black man in a baseball jacket, who was replaced soon after I arrived by an attractive, well-dressed young woman in a vivid red coat, who smiled brightly and promised that Bueller would be out shortly.

Bueller came through the door in faded jeans, white sneakers, a white T-shirt, and a gray cardigan and said sheepishly that she couldn't give me that interview after all. I asked if I could have a quick nose around. That would not be possible, she said, wringing her hands. I pressed again. "Just a quick peek?" A flush of color came to her cheeks, and she declined again. She would not give me her own card but instead passed me a piece of headed paper with a phone number for Wolters Kluwer's New York press office. Back outside, I could see long rows of work cubicles through one window. It looked very similar to what I had been able to see of the ground floor of the Caymans' Ugland House. This was clearly a place for secretarial work: Bueller did confess under my questioning that about 80 people worked there, and none were lawyers.

———————

As late as the early 1990s, mainstream development theorists trying to work out why some states were failing, or why poverty was so widespread, all but ignored the issue of corruption. Berlin-based Transparency International (TI), founded in 1993, put corruption on the map, launching its famous Corruption Perceptions Index (CPI) two years later. The *Financial Times* nominated 1995 as the International Year of Corruption; and the World Bank, which had previously been so polite toward developing country elites that it all but banished the c-word from its policy documents, followed TI's lead in 1996 when its president, James Wolfensohn, accepted in a land-mark speech that the bank needed to deal with "the cancer of corruption." The OECD's Anti-Bribery Convention came into force only in 1999, and the UN's Convention Against Corruption was only solidified in 2003. In many OECD countries, bribery was even tax-deductible until just a few years ago.

Even so late, the shift was very good news. But now consider this.

TI's corruption ranking is invaluable to investors trying to assess "country risk." But Nigerians already know that their country is among the world's most corrupt. They want to know where almost $500 billion worth of their oil money has gone. The corruption index gives no clues. After the brutal Nigerian president Sani Abacha died in 1998, poisoned while in the company of Indian prostitutes, it was revealed that he had raked off billions of dollars of oil money from state coffers. Two countries in particular had soaked up his embezzled wealth: Britain and Switzerland. The Nigerian finance minister Ngozi Okonjo-Iweala revealed the problems in an interview with journalist Paul Vallely of *The Independent* in May 2006.[43]

NGOZI: The Swiss have now returned $500 million of stolen resources. Switzerland has set the example.

VALLELY: What about the British?

She gives a long throaty chuckle.

NGOZI: Now heaven help me. It's very hard to condemn the British. On debt relief the UK has set the example.

VALLELY: So why are the British dragging their feet on the repatriation of stolen resources?

NGOZI: It's been more difficult with the British. Our president has raised it many times with Prime Minister Blair. Eventually he returned $3m. We understand there are other monies but while all the discussion was going on those monies left the country and went somewhere else.

TI's rankings suggest that Britain and Switzerland, not to mention the United States, are among the world's "cleanest" jurisdictions. In fact, about *half* the top 20 in the index are major secrecy jurisdictions, while the nations of Africa—the victims of the gargantuan illicit flows—are ranked the "dirtiest."[44]

Clearly, something is wrong here.

In November 2009 the Tax Justice Network published a new index based on two years of work by a dedicated team. Named the Financial Secrecy Index, it ranked countries according to how important they are in providing financial secrecy in global finance. It did this by looking at a range of key secrecy indicators and structures to see how secretive a jurisdiction was, then weighting each according to the scale of cross-border financial services activity that it hosts.

Nothing like this had ever been done before, and newspapers and television stations around the globe published the results, with some of the countries traditionally seen as the "cleanest" being ranked as among the world's *least* transparent.

In fifth place in the Financial Secrecy Index was the United Kingdom. Although it has by far the most important historical role in the emergence of offshore, and it is the center of the British offshore spiderweb, its own domestic secrecy structures in themselves are relatively transparent. Third and fourth most important were, respectively, Switzerland and the Cayman Islands. Luxembourg, a gigantic but hardly noticed haven of financial secrecy, came second. And which country was ranked—by a mile—the world's most important secrecy jurisdiction?

Step forward, the United States of America.

7

THE DRAIN

How Tax Havens Harm Poor Countries

BY THE EARLY 1980S THE MAIN ELEMENTS of the modern offshore system were in place and growing explosively. An older cluster of European havens, nurtured by old European aristocracies and led by Switzerland, was now being outpaced by a new network of more flexible, aggressive havens in the former outposts of the British empire, themselves linked intimately to the City of London. A state within the British state, the City had been transformed from an old gentleman's club operating the financial machinery of empire, steeped in elaborate rituals and governed by unspoken rules about what "isn't done," into a new, brasher, deregulated global financial center dominated by American banks and linked intimately to this new British spiderweb. A less complex yet still enormously important offshore zone of influence had also grown up, centered on the United States and constructed by U.S. banks. The stateless Euromarkets linked all these zones with each other and with the onshore economies, helping free banks from reserve requirements and other democratic restraints on their behavior.

While the old European havens were mostly about secret wealth management and tax evasion, the new British and American zones were increasingly about escaping financial regulation—though with plenty of tax evasion and criminal activity thrown in, of course. Players in each zone were warmly welcomed into the others, in true laissez-faire style, and as the offshore system became more interconnected it grew stronger too, as states competed with each other in races to the bottom on lax financial regulation, tax, and secrecy in order to lure financial capital. This competition also helped force offshore practices steadily onshore, making it harder to tell the two apart.

The Bretton Woods system of international cooperation and tight controls over financial flows had collapsed in the 1970s, bringing to an end the so-called golden age of capitalism that followed the Second World War. The world had entered a phase of much slower growth, punctuated by regular financial and economic crises, especially in the developing world.

And as all this happened, and the offshore system grew and metastasized all around the global economy, a new and increasingly powerful pinstripe army of lawyers, accountants, and bankers had emerged to make the whole system work. Offshore, in partnership with changing ideologies, was driving the processes of deregulation and financial globalization. In particular, the London-based Euromarkets, then the wider offshore world, provided the platform for U.S. banks in particular to escape tight domestic constraints and grow larger again, setting the stage for the political capture of Washington by the financial services industry, and the emergence of too-big-to-fail banking giants, fed by the implicit subsidies of taxpayer guarantees, plus the explicit subsidies of offshore tax avoidance, that continue to hold western economies in their stranglehold today. The emergence of the United States as an offshore jurisdiction in its own right attracted vast financial flows into the country, bolstering bankers' powers even further. The old alliance between Wall Street and the City of London, which collapsed after the Great Depression and the Second World War, had been resurrected.

Many people supposed that by eliminating double taxation and creating nearly frictionless conduits for financial capital, the offshore system was promoting global economic efficiency. In reality the system was rarely adding value, but was instead redistributing wealth upward and risks downward, and creating a new global hothouse for crime.

The U.S. crime-fighting lawyer John Moscow summarized the problem. "Money is power and we are transferring this power to corporate bank accounts run by people who are in the purest sense of the word unaccountable and therefore irresponsible."[1]

Secrecy jurisdictions had penetrated the public consciousness, a little, but still only as marginal, dubious oddities at the exotic fringes of civilization. Under cover of this great misunderstanding, often artfully encouraged by those who wanted to conceal the true nature of the new financial revolution, the offshore system would play out in ways that would become increasingly significant in the 30 years to follow.

What was happening was nothing less than a head-on assault on the progressive New Deal in the United States; on the foundations of social democracy in Europe; and on democracy, accountability, and development in vulnerable low-income countries across the world.

———————

Take any significant economic event or process in the last few decades, and offshore is almost certainly behind the headline and probably central to the story.

Poverty in Africa, for example, cannot be understood without understanding the role of offshore. The world's worst war for years has been the civil conflict in the Democratic Republic of Congo, which is tied in with the wholesale looting of its mineral resources—via tax havens. Large-scale corruption, and the wholesale subversion of governments by criminalized interests, across the developing world? Offshore is central to the story, every time. Nearly every effort to generate large flows of capital to developing countries since the 1980s has ended in crisis because the money has escaped offshore. Towering inequalities in Europe and the United States, not to mention in underdeveloped countries, cannot be understood properly without exploring the role of secrecy jurisdictions. The systematic looting of the former Soviet Union, and the merging of the nuclear-armed country's intelligence apparatus with organized crime, is substantially a story that unfolds in London and its offshore satellites. The political strength of Saddam Hussein had important offshore underpinnings, as does the power of North Korea's Kim Jong-Il today. Prime Minister Silvio Berlusconi's strange hold over Italian politics is significantly an offshore story. The Elf affair, discussed earlier, which helped powerful French elites float above and out of reach of French democracy, had secrecy jurisdictions at its heart. Promoters of frauds such as "pump and dump" schemes to hype up stocks, then dump them on an unsuspecting public, *always* hide behind offshore entities. The death of a Russian oligarch's lawyer in a mysterious helicopter crash? Arms smuggling to terrorist organizations? The growth of mafia empires? Offshore. The narcotics industry alone generates some $500 billion in annual sales worldwide[2]: To put this into perspective, that is twice the value of Saudi Arabia's oil exports.[3] The profits made by those at the top of the trade find their way into the banking system, the asset markets, and the political process through offshore facilities. You can only fit about $1 million cash into a briefcase. Without offshore, the illegal drugs trade would be more like a cottage industry.

Financial deregulation and globalization? Offshore is the heart of the matter, as I will show. The rise of private equity and hedge funds? Offshore. Enron? Parmalat? Long Term Capital Management? Lehman Brothers? AIG? Offshore. Multinational corporations could never have grown so vast and powerful without the tax havens. Goldman Sachs is very, very much a creature of offshore. And every significant financial crisis in the world since the 1970s, including, as noted, the latest global economic crisis, is very much an offshore story. The decline of manufacturing industries in many advanced countries has many causes, but offshore is a big part of the story. Tax havens have been central to the growth of debt in our economies since the 1970s. The growth of complex monopolies in certain markets, or insider trading rings, or gigantic frauds, almost always involves secrecy jurisdictions as major or central elements.

This is not to say that all of these problems don't have other explanations too. They *always* do. Tax havens are never the only story because offshore exists only in relation to elsewhere. That is why it is called offshore.

Without understanding offshore, we will never properly understand the history of the modern world. The time has come to make a start in filling this gigantic hole in our knowledge and to appreciate the gravity of offshore: how it has bent the world's economy into its modern, globalized shape, transforming societies and political systems in its image.

———————

I will now describe a rare episode where offshore's role *is* widely acknowledged: the case of the Bank of Credit and Commerce International (BCCI), arguably the most offshore bank in history. The story is well known, but for one or two crucial features.

The BCCI case broke open after Jack Blum, a lawyer and investigator working for John Kerry's Foreign Relations Committee, began picking up signs of wrongdoing in 1988.

Like most people, Blum initially saw secrecy jurisdictions mainly as centers for drug smugglers and other assorted lowlifes. But on a visit to the Cayman Islands in 1974 for the U.S. Senate Foreign Relations Committee, he remembers seeing a line of well-dressed men waiting to use the phone in his hotel lobby. He learned that they were U.S. lawyers and accountants arranging to meet Cayman bankers to set up bank accounts and trusts for tax-evading U.S. clients. The American bankers were referring U.S. customers to their Canadian colleagues, and the Canadians were returning the favor. Over time, he began to notice more sophisticated tricks and to see that this was far bigger than almost anyone imagined.

"I began to see that drugs were only a fraction of the thing," Blum said. "Then there was the criminal money. Then the tax evasion money. And then I realized—'Oh my God—it's all about off the books, off the balance sheet. Offshore, there are no rules about how the books are kept,'" he continued. "I refer to offshore as a kitchen, where corporate books are cooked."

When contacts started fingering BCCI in the late 1980s, Blum already knew it had a bad smell: He had worked previously in private practice, where he remembers his team meeting the staff of Mellon Bank in Pittsburgh and telling them about BCCI. "The entire senior international staff at Mellon just about threw up on the table," Blum said. They would not, under any circumstances, accept letters of credit from BCCI.[4]

The bank was set up in 1972 by an Indian-born banker, Agha Hassan Abedi, who got backing for his venture from members of the Saudi royal family and from Sheikh Zayed Bin Sultan Al-Nahayan, the ruler of Abu Dhabi. BCCI grew superfast under a simple business model: create the appearance of a reputable business, make powerful friends, then agree to do anything, anywhere, on behalf of anyone, for any reason. BCCI larded politicians with bribes and served some of the twentieth century's greatest villains: Saddam Hussein, the terrorist leader Abu Nidal, the Colombian Medellin drug cartel, and the Asian heroin warlord Khun Sa. It got involved in trafficking nuclear materials, in sales of Chinese Silkworm missiles to Saudi Arabia, and in peddling North Korean Scud-B missiles to Syria. Its branches in the Caribbean and Panama serviced the Latin American drug trade; its divisions in the United Arab Emirates, then amid an oil boom and an offshore banking bonanza, serviced the heroin trades in Pakistan, Iran, and Afghanistan; and it used Hong Kong to cater to drug traffickers in Laos, Thailand, and Burma. It also got into the U.S. banking system, getting around the concerns of U.S. regulators by using offshore secrecy structures to make its ownership invisible. It paid off Washington insiders and built up a solid partnership with the CIA. This gave it fearsome political cover and made Blum's investigations extraordinarily difficult from the outset.

"There was an army of people working in Washington on all sides trying to say this bank was a wonderful bank," Blum said. Friends in law enforcement warned him that his life was in danger, but he pressed on. He took the case to the Manhattan district attorney Robert Morgenthau, who shared Blum's outrage and put a team together to take BCCI down. Fighting against what must have seemed like half the political insiders in Washington, Morgenthau helped shut it down in 1991 and charged BCCI and its founders with perpetrating "the largest bank fraud in world financial history."

But the most interesting thing about BCCI was its offshore structure.

Abedi split his bank between jurisdictions, registering holding companies in Luxembourg and in the Caymans, so that no regulator could see the whole thing. Different auditors were used for different parts of the bank too.[5] Yet he also wanted the credibility of being in a world-famous financial center, though it would need to be lax enough to ask few questions. That meant only one place: the City of London. In 1972 BCCI set up its headquarters in luxury offices in Leadenhall Street, at the heart of the City, and began making generous contributions to Britain's Conservative Party.[6]

A rule of thumb was that banks should lend no more than 10 percent of their equity capital to a single borrower—but BCCI was making loans to some clients worth *three times* its capital or thirty times the accepted ratio. In 1977 the Bank of England tightened these rules further. To get around this, Abedi dumped shaky loans in the Cayman Islands, where, as a BCCI official noted at the time, there was "obviously more flexibility in record-keeping" and which bank officials called "The Dustbin."[7] Neither the British regulators, nor those in Luxembourg or the Caymans, assumed responsibility.

BCCI also constructed an audacious but simple offshore trick: to manufacture equity capital—the foundation and safety buffer of any bank—out of thin air. The Luxembourg bank would lend money to a BCCI stockholder—one of Abedi's friends—who would then invest this money in the Caymans bank, building up its capital there. Likewise, the Caymans bank lent money to a stockholder who would use it to create capital in the Luxembourg bank. From just $2.5 million in equity capital at the beginning, BCCI had raised nearly $850 million by 1990, with the help of this offshore bootstrap.[8] Abedi also wrote off his friends' debts but kept expanding by operating a Ponzi scheme: milking the staff pension fund and taking in more deposits simply to pay its outgoings. Many of its eighty thousand depositors were relatively poor people from the developing world who had no idea that this apparently London-based bank, backed by wealthy Arab Sheikhs, was a fiction piled on a fiction.

"There is no way to learn banking from books: it is bullshit," said Blum, highlighting the make-believe possibilities that emerge in the liberated offshore environment. "Nothing tells you how money-laundering generates products."

When Morgenthau tried to probe the bank, the Caymans authorities refused to cooperate. "We subpoenaed BCCI Overseas—they told us, 'Sorry: the laws of Cayman don't permit us to do this,'" he said, expressing particular irritation with the attorney general, a "crotchety British guy" named Alan Scott.[9] "We tried again. Finally, they said we had to go through the (U.S.-Cayman tax information exchange) treaty. We went through the treaty. Then they said, 'The treaty doesn't include local District Attorneys: go through the Justice Department. We can't show this to you.' The Justice department wasn't overly cooperative either."[10] Morgenthau and his deputy John Moscow went to the Bank of England. "We had no cooperation from the Bank of England," Morgenthau said. "We tried to get financial records out of London; they didn't provide us with anything."

With the help of Senator John Kerry, Morgenthau threatened to raise a public storm if the Bank of England did not act. Only then, finally, the Bank agreed to shut BCCI down.

In the British parliament, the scandal caused an uproar. The Bank, forced onto the defensive, claimed it had left BCCI running until 1991 because there had been no "solid evidence" of fraud until then.

It isn't clear what other evidence the Bank needed. Indictments in the United States implicating BCCI in fraud dated back two and a half years; one stated that money laundering was part of its "corporate strategy."[11] Price Waterhouse had issued a qualified audit report on a BCCI subsidiary in 1989; and in 1990 BCCI employees had written to the Treasury, the Bank of England, and British ministers to warn of fraud inside the bank. That same year, Britain's intelligence services had told the Bank of England that Abu Nidal controlled 42 BCCI accounts in London; the Bank for International Settlements in Basel had expressed concern; and in mid-1990 Price Waterhouse had discovered the so-called Naqvi files, revealing widespread fraud, fictitious companies, unrecorded deposits, manufactured loans, and evidence of stealing from depositors, findings that were passed along to the Bank of England. Still there was no action, even though BCCI headquarters were only a few minutes' stroll down the road from the Bank

"It is difficult to see," wrote Michael Gillard in Britain's *Observer* newspaper, "how the required high ethical standards [for BCCI to be allowed to operate in Britain] fit with BCCI pleading guilty to conspiring with its own officials and two representatives of Colombia's Medellin drug cartel to commit tax fraud and launder the proceeds of cocaine sales."

Robin Leigh-Pemberton, the Bank of England governor, neatly encapsulated London's see-no-evil offshore ethic. The present system of supervision, he added, "has served the community well. . . . If we closed down a bank every time we found an incidence of fraud, we would have rather fewer banks than we do at the moment."[12] That statement should have been evidence enough that the City of London was already the world's premier offshore center.

The full Price Waterhouse report on BCCI remains confidential today, on the grounds that this will disturb Britain's "international partners." It is a clear defense of tax haven London.[13]

Ever since then, Morgenthau has struggled to wake people up to offshore crimes, personally pressing four U.S. treasury secretaries to pay more attention, with little result. "I remember giving a speech a couple of years ago to talk about offshore banks. It put everyone to sleep,"[14] Morgenthau said. "Start talking about offshore money and their eyes glaze over."

———————

Just as the BCCI scandal quieted down, another offshore tale was emerging in the oil-rich African state of Angola, where I was the Reuters correspondent. Jonas Savimbi's UNITA rebels had surrounded major towns in murderous sieges, pouring in mortar fire and trying to starve them into submission. In the city of Kuito desperate defenders were eating dogs, cats, and rats to survive, and bloodied patients were crawling from hospital beds to join armed raiding parties who would sneak out to search nearby fields, often mined, for cassava and other crops, sometimes having to fight their way back into town with provisions. The United Nations was calling it the world's worst war, and the government was under an international arms embargo, so in 1992 it turned to secretive French Elf networks—related to the ones I would later encounter in Gabon, as described in the prologue—to help secure arms supplies. A wealthy Russian-born Jew named Arkady Gaydamak put together some $800 million in financing to help Angola procure weapons from a Slovak company, repaid in Angolan oil money, via Geneva, and get around the embargo. Later, French magistrates probing these oil-for-arms deals heard from a participant that the arrangements were "a gigantic fraud . . . a vast cash pump," generating a 65 percent margin on the biggest arms contracts."[15] The financing trails, of course, involved many tax havens.

I tracked Gaydamak down in Moscow in September 2005, where he was under an international arrest warrant for his so-called "Angolagate" deals.[16] He was eager to set the record straight and to discuss his efforts to—as he put it—bring peace to Africa and the Middle East[17] (just then he was embarking on what would be an ill-fated foray into Israeli politics).

Gaydamak had left the Soviet Union as a twenty-year-old in 1972, moving first to Israel, then to France, where he built up a translation business, mostly servicing Soviet trade delegations. "'Translator' means go-between," he explained. "If you are active in electronics, your position in the business world is usually with people in electronics. If you are a banker, you have relationships with bankers . . . but when you are a translator—a go-between—you know everybody."

In those early post-Soviet days Angola's leaders still looked to Russia as their big-power patron, but they had lost their bearings in a fast-changing Moscow. "I began to be an intermediary," he explained. "Russia was changing so quickly, everything was new: you should know where to go, how to go, how to organize. I was the so-called organizer of everything." Gaydamak became Angola's trusted man in Moscow. He knew that the big money lies in the "elsewhere" zone between jurisdictions, and in this context he gave me what must be one of the most "offshore" quotes of all time.

"In the so-called market economies, with all the regulations, the taxation, the legislation about working conditions, there is no way to make money," he said. "It is only in countries like Russia, during the period of redistribution of wealth—and it is not yet finished—when you can get a result. So that is Russian money. Russian money is clean money, explainable money. How can you make $50 million in France today? How? Explain to me!"

In other words, because Russian and international law is so full of holes, the money "redistributed" to a small oligarchy must be clean.

Some have compared the vast upward redistribution of wealth in Russia after the fall of the Soviet Union to the era of the robber barons in the United States in the nineteenth century. But there is a crucial difference. The U.S. robber barons didn't have a huge offshore network in which to hide their money. In spite of their many abuses, they concentrated on domestic investment. While they fleeced unwary investors and subverted the political process, they also built the country's industrial prosperity. In time, the state was able to rein in their worst excesses.

But in the case of countries like Angola and Russia, the money simply disappeared offshore forever. African governments have grown weaker and more dependent on aid from the very states that are also strengthening the offshore system. It was Africa's curse for her countries to gain independence at precisely the time that the purpose-built offshore warehouse for leaders' loot properly started to emerge. For many of these countries, "independence" really meant independence for African rulers from bothersome societies. In a sense independence was a pyrrhic victory: The colonial powers departed but quietly left the financial mechanisms for exploitation in place.

After the Cold War, Angola was in debt to Russia for about $6 billion, and in 1996 Gaydamak inserted himself into a deal to restructure the debt. The debt was shaved down to $1.5 billion and sliced into thirty-one promissory notes that Angola would pay back in oil, via a private company called Abalone, set up by Gaydamak and his business partner Pierre Falcone, with a UBS account in Geneva.[18] UBS was uncomfortable about the arrangements. "Any possible mention of one of the representatives of one or other of the parties," an internal UBS memo said, "in a newspaper article, even if a posteriori this is judged to be unfounded or indeed libellous, would not prevent, in the first instance, a Swiss or particularly Genevan judge taking an interest in the people mentioned."[19] But the deal went ahead.

Unfortunately for Gaydamak, a Swiss judge intervened in February 2001, after Angola had paid off just over half the promissory notes. The judge had found vast, mysterious flows of money out of Abalone, including over $60 million to accounts in Gaydamak's name, tens of millions more to accounts in the names of senior Angolan officials, and almost $50 million to a former Yeltsin oligarch.[20] But most of it flowed to an array of accounts in Switzerland, Luxembourg, Israel, Germany, the Netherlands, and Cyprus. Little or none of it seemed to have flowed to Russia's treasury. Gaydamak claimed that the Russian treasury got paid indirectly, via these mysterious accounts,[21] and added that this was a "classic trading operation, extremely favourable to us."

Because of the offshore secrecy, it is impossible to tell whether what Gaydamak said is even partly true. What is certain is that Angola's leaders, in partnership with

Russian interests and private offshore intermediaries, cooked up a curious deal, routed offshore, with vast profits for some insiders, and with absolutely no chance of accountability to the people of Angola *or* Russia. The African insiders had used offshore to enrich themselves not from Angola's assets but from its *debts*.

The Swiss judge was later promoted away from the post, and his replacement unblocked the notes in October 2003, arguing that neither Angola nor Russia had complained about the deal, and accepting the argument that the accounts held by the Angolan dignitaries amounted to "strategic funds, placed abroad in a time of war."

I could have chosen any number of murky African offshore episodes to explore, but I chose this one to illustrate a particular point about the scale of the draining of Africa's wealth. Gaymadak's deals represent only a tiny fraction of what the offshore system has drained from Africa. Two recent studies point directly to the sheer scale of the problem.

In March 2010 Global Financial Integrity (GFI) in Washington authored a study on illicit financial flows out of African countries.[22] Between 1970 and 2008, it concluded, "Total illicit financial outflows from Africa, conservatively estimated, were approximately $854 billion. Total illicit outflows *may be* as high as $1.8 trillion." Of that overall conservative figure, it estimates Angola lost $4.68 billion[23] between 1993 (when Gaydamak's main "Angolagate" deals started) and 2002, the year after his Abalone debt dealings ended. My personal belief, based on years of investigating Angola's economy and its offshore-diving leadership, is that Baker's estimate—equivalent to just over 9 percent of its $51 billion in oil and diamond exports during that time[24]—simply *has* to be a gross underestimate of the losses. Many billions have disappeared offshore through opaque oil-backed loans channeled outside normal state budgets, many of them routed through two special trusts[25] operating out of London.

GFI's shocking estimates complement the figures I mentioned in the prologue about the global scale of illicit financial flows: Developing countries lost up to a *trillion* dollars in illicit financial outflows just in 2006—that is, ten dollars out for every dollar of foreign aid flowing in.[26]

Another study emerged in April 2008 from the University of Massachusetts, Amherst, using different methodologies to examine "capital flight" from forty African countries from 1970 to 2004.[27] Its conclusions are similarly striking: "Real capital flight over the 35-year period amounted to about $420 billion (in 2004 dollars) for the 40 countries as a whole. Including imputed interest earnings, the accumulated stock of capital flight was about $607 billion as of end–2004." Yet at the same time, the total external debt of these countries was "only" $227 billion. So, the authors note, Africa is a net *creditor* to the rest of the world, with its net external assets vastly exceeding its debts. Yet there is a crucial difference between the assets and the liabilities. The University of Massachusetts study concludes, "The subcontinent's private external assets belong to a narrow, relatively wealthy stratum of its population, while public external debts are borne by the people through their governments."

Having watched people die before my eyes in Angola; having seen an otherwise pretty six-year-old Angolan girl who, without access to basic medicine, was losing a fight with an infection that had rotted a hole in her cheek the size of a golf ball, I am seared by having witnessed some of the ways Africa's people bear their public debts, in the forms of poverty, war, a hopeless lack of real opportunities, and the regular physical and economic violence perpetrated against them by corrupt and predatory offshore-roaming elites who float free and unaccountable above their societies. Raymond Baker, the director of GFI, was quite right to call the emergence of the offshore system "the ugliest chapter in global economic affairs since slavery."[28]

In February 2003 Phil Gramm, a former Republican Texan senator who became vice chairman of the Swiss investment bank UBS Warburg, wrote to U.S. treasury secretary John Snow, arguing against a plan to increase international financial transparency. "This proposal will limit economic freedom," he wrote, "and reduce the pressure that potential capital flight imposes on high-taxing countries worldwide."[29] Illicit flows are good, Gramm was effectively saying, because it disciplines the victims.

Anyone who understands that there is a difference between wealthy rulers, who are the beneficiaries of illicit flows, and ordinary citizens, who are the victims, can see through Gramm's position. Yet in whole sectors of the Western economics profession, such thinking has become almost an article of faith founded on the ageless blame-the-victim accusations that the losers are stupid, are corrupt, or just didn't flagellate themselves hard enough.

Jim Henry, a former chief economist for McKinsey's who is almost alone in having investigated this globally since the 1980s, sees the conventional roots of the global development crisis as "an economist's fairy tale. . . . It leaves out all the blood and guts of what really happened." Henry's 2003 book *Blood Bankers* explores a number of shocking episodes where offshore banking led to crisis after crisis in low-income countries. First, bankers lent these countries far more than they could productively absorb; then they taught local elites the basics of how to plunder their countries' wealth, then conceal it, launder it, and sneak it offshore. Then the IMF helped bankers pressure these countries to service their debts under threat of financial strangulation. Capital markets were deliberately opened up to foreign capital, according to Henry, "whether or not there were adequate security laws, bank regulations or tax enforcers in place."

He tracked down an American banker from MHT Bank who took part in a friendly private audit of the Philippines central bank in 1983. "I sat in a hot, little room at the Central Bank, added up what the Central Bank showed it had received from us on its books, and compared it with our disbursements," the banker told Henry.[30] "And nearly $5bn was just not there! I mean, it had just not come into the country. It had been disbursed by us, but it was completely missing from the Central Bank's books. It turned out that most of these loans had been disbursed to account numbers assigned to Philippine offshore banking units or other private companies. Apparently, the Central Bank gave MHT the account numbers, and we never questioned whether they were Central Bank accounts—we just wired the loans to them. And then they disappeared offshore."

Philippine officials realized what he was up to, and the following morning the banker got a big breakfast in his hotel room, courtesy of the management. Fortunately for him, he only had time to grab a bite of toast before heading to the airport. By the time he reached Tokyo he was sick, and on the flight home he went into convulsions and spent three days in a Vancouver hospital recovering from what the doctors said was "an unknown toxin."

Later, he told the New York Federal Reserve, and a friend at the National Security Council. "But apparently they just kept it to themselves," he said. "So the Philippines is still servicing all those Central Bank loans." Henry was able to confirm the banker's story on a later trip to the Philippines. He also dug up details on at least $3.6 billion of identifiable government-swallowed foreign loans that ended up with then-president Ferdinand Marcos and his closest associates.

Walter Wriston, the chief executive of Citibank from 1967 to 1984, described the thinking of many of the parties involved as private offshore banking emerged as a global force. Sitting before a picture of himself with President Marcos and his wife,

Imelda (the picture, he said, "caused so much uncontrollable laughter among my colleagues that I've kept that picture on my wall all these years"), he described the pervasive lack of understanding of, or perhaps the deliberate blindness of many toward, what was really going on. "In hindsight, the corruption and the amount of money bled off from those companies was a lot more than anybody knew about, including the United States government, Citibank, and the CIA," he said. "We based our loans on economic analyses—will the power plant supply enough kilowatts to pay back its loan?—without realizing that we also had to account for the fact that the head of the power plant was the dictator's brother."[31]

As all this happened across the developing world, a pinstripe army of bankers, lawyers, and accountants lobbied inside the United States to make it increasingly attractive to these rising tides of dirty money, successfully turning it into a secrecy jurisdiction in its own right, just as the memo Michael Hudson received in 1966 had suggested. Meanwhile, they continued to capture the legislatures in small tax havens to perfect the global dirty-money system. Playing all three corners of the dirty-money triangle—the source countries being drained of illicit wealth, the increasingly offshore-like economies receiving the wealth, and the offshore conduits handling its passage—turned global private banking into one of the most profitable businesses in history. "The rise of Third World lending in the 1970s and 1980s," in Henry's description, "laid the foundations for a global haven network that now shelters the world's most venal citizens."

Henry's calculations suggested that at least half of the money borrowed by the largest debtor countries flowed right out again under the table, usually in less than a year, and typically in just weeks. The public debts were matched almost exactly by the stock of private wealth their elites had accumulated in the United States and other havens, and by the early 1990s there was enough flight wealth in Europe and the United States to service the *entire* debt of the developing world—if only its income were taxed modestly. For some countries, like Mexico, Argentina, and Venezuela, the value of the elites' offshore illicit wealth was worth several times their external debts. Today the top 1 percent of households in developing countries owns an estimated 70 to 90 percent of all private financial and real estate wealth. The Boston Consulting Group reckoned in 2003 that over half of all the wealth owned by Latin America's wealthiest citizens lay offshore. In June 2010 Henry reckoned that the total stock of flight capital financial wealth from developing countries in 2007 had reached *$7–8 trillion*—more than half under the custody or management of the world's top 50 banks.

One U.S. Federal Reserve official noted: "The problem is not that these countries don't have any assets. The problem is, they're all in Miami."

In 1982 Mexico's President José Lopez Portillo gave a speech to parliament, outlining the offshore challenge facing his continent. "The financing plague is wreaking greater and greater havoc throughout the world," he said. "It is transmitted by rats and its consequences are unemployment and poverty, industrial bankruptcy and speculative enrichment." He blamed "a group of Mexicans . . . led and advised and supported by the private banks that have taken more money out of the country than the empires that exploited us since the beginning of time."[32]

Lopez Portillo vowed to ignore the IMF, nationalize the banks, and introduce exchange controls, and within ten days an alliance of bankers, businesspeople, and conservative Mexicans had made him back down. The IMF and the Bank for International Settlements, in Switzerland, ignoring Mexico's offshore flight wealth, ordered Mexico and other debtor nations to "put your house in order."

The economist Michael Hudson describes how he was hired in 1989 by a Boston money management firm to organize a sovereign debt fund investing in the government bonds of developing nations.[33] Huge risk premiums then meant that Argentine and Brazilian dollar bonds were yielding almost 45 percent, while Mexican bonds were yielding 25 percent. In its first year the fund, incorporated in the Netherlands Antilles, became the world's second best performing fund of its kind.

Hudson found out what was happening. "The biggest investors were political insiders who had bought into the fund knowing that their central banks would pay their dollar debts despite the high risk premiums," he said. Some of the biggest investors were people in top positions in central banks and presidencies. "We realized who has all the Yankee dollar claims on Latin America," he said. "It was local oligarchies with offshore accounts. The dollar debt of Argentina in the early 1990s was owed mainly to Argentineans operating out of offshore banking centers. The major beneficiaries of foreign debt service were their own flight-capitalists, not bondholders in North America and Europe."

This kind of simple trick is routinely practiced by so-called "vulture funds." Wealthy foreign investors buy up distressed sovereign debt at pennies on the dollar—typically at a 90 percent discount—then reap vast profits when those debts are repaid in full. The trick is to make sure that influential local government officials are secretly part of the investor group buying the discounted debt—ensuring that these local investors will do battle inside the developing country governments to make sure the debts get paid. Their involvement, of course, is hidden behind a shield of offshore secrecy, so an impoverished nation's citizens need never find out about the wealth that has been stolen from them or how the investors did it.

Economists have not ignored these issues entirely, but they almost always break them down into discrete, country-level local problems that only blame corrupt local elites. These matter, of course, but such analyses obscure what all the disasters have in common: offshore.

And when offshore erosion *has* been considered, it has been taken as an inconvenience, to be addressed with Band-Aids. As one IMF report put it: "Offshore banking has most certainly been a factor in the Asian financial crisis. A special effort is therefore needed to help emerging economies . . . to avert financial crises through dissemination of internationally accepted prudential and supervisory standards."[34]

The IMF is arguing here in an illogical circle. By helping local elites effectively place themselves above the law and creating new temptations to mischief, the offshore system entirely neuters the chance of prudent regulation and supervision that is needed to protect those countries against that very same offshore system. Imagine if those elites had to keep their money bottled up at home, or at least account for their wealth, pay appropriate taxes on it, and submit to appropriate laws. Very soon they would understand why good government is directly in their interest.

Perhaps the saddest part of all this is that it should have been obvious to anybody who gave it a moment's thought.

———————————

The stories in this chapter have been mostly about illicit financial flows drained from developing countries and into tax havens, undermining incentives for local elites to strive for better government by allowing them to remove themselves from the problems of their home countries, building safe offshore stashes that insulate and protect them against the turmoil and poverty that surrounds them. There is one more element to consider that is related to, but not the same as, the illicit offshore money. That element is tax.

Tax is the most sustainable, the most important, and the most beneficial form of finance for development. It is not just a question of revenue: Tax makes rulers accountable to their citizens, not to donors. As Kenya revenue commissioner Michael Waweru put it: "Pay your taxes, and set your country free." Tax helps countries build good government in two broad ways. First, as citizens bargain with their rulers over tax, a social contract develops between them, helping foster representative democracy. Second, the imperative to raise tax revenue stimulates the building of institutions to do so. It strengthens state capacity.

This "no taxation without representation" formula is never perfect or even close to perfect, but historians recognize it as a cornerstone, over the very long term, of the development of democracy and representative government in the developed world. Until very recently, almost nobody spent time wondering whether this formula might work in developing countries too. The answer, instead, has been to send foreign aid.

Developing countries, by and large, have very low tax revenues, and the dynamics of tax and state-building have often been weak. Where tax revenues are high, it is often because the country is a mineral producer: These kinds of revenues make rulers accountable more to oil companies than to their citizens and fail to build accountability. Yet Africans today increasingly understand the importance of tax in their developing countries. "I have made revenue collection a frontline institution because it is the one which can emancipate us from begging," said Yoweri Museveni, the president of Uganda, which collects taxes worth only about 11 percent of GDP. "If we can get about 22 percent of GDP we should not need to disturb anybody by asking for aid; instead of coming here to bother you, give me this, give me this, I shall come here to greet you, to trade with you."[35]

Tax havens, of course, overturn the healthy dynamics by providing escape routes for their elites. It is worth briefly exploring some of the ways in which poor countries are drained of tax money through operations that, even when of questionable legality, are rarely challenged. This brings us back to the story about how countries allocate taxing rights between them.

Since the 1920s, when the League of Nations tried to get countries to agree how they would divide up the tax revenues on incomes from the various operations of multinationals, a big question has been at play. Do most of the taxing rights go to the "source" country that hosts inward investment from a multinational based in another country, which is the source of the income in question? Or do they go to the "residence" country—the multinational's home country, where it is resident?

Capital-rich countries like Britain that hosted a lot of multinationals investing overseas wanted rules giving most taxing rights to "residence" countries, while the "source" countries receiving inward investment—often poorer countries—wanted to tax the investors' income locally, at the source. The agreements were eventually laid out in bilateral tax treaties between countries, but these treaties were heavily influenced by the prevailing models. The rich countries, led by the OECD today, have pushed for a model skewed in favor of themselves, while the United Nations favors a model that shifts taxing rights toward "source" countries, typically poorer ones.

No prizes for guessing which model has come to dominate the field of international tax. When the United Nations produced a draft model tax treaty in 1980 that was supposed to shift the balance back in favor of "source" taxation and developing countries, the OECD intervened aggressively to stop this: not only by ensuring that its own model treaty benefiting rich countries remained the preferred standard, but also by interfering at the United Nations to weaken its model. John Christensen, a former economic adviser to the British Crown Dependency of Jersey, remembers a meeting of the United Nations Tax Committee in Geneva in 2008 when Britain's representative suddenly stood up and began speaking, in what looked like an intervention coordinated with the representative from Liechtenstein. "He kept on interrupting," Christensen said. "It was a general assault on developing countries being better able to represent their interests, about providing more resources to the UN Tax Committee. He was the cheerleader. Twice the chair had to tell him 'please let us speak.' People there were *really* angry with him: we could all see he was blocking progress to protect the UK's and the United States' interests."

The rich countries' model is dominant today. Not only has this problem of double *non*taxation of multinational corporations been allowed to happen, but billions of dollars in tax that would in a fairer world be paid in poor countries is paid in rich countries instead, quite legally.

It is worth briefly examining another role played by tax havens in the weird and wonderful world of international tax that enables companies to knock out their tax bills. Let's say a German bank or company invests in Tanzania. Under a tax treaty between Germany and Tanzania, the African country may well agree not to tax the company's local earnings for fear that otherwise German companies will simply invest elsewhere. But now even with this treaty in place, the German corporation has not solved its problem yet. The treaty may have knocked out the Tanzanian tax charge on the company's earnings, but if it sends these untaxed earnings straight back to Germany they will still be taxed there. So it sends the earnings to a so-called conduit or treaty haven, which will have a wide network of treaties, including one with Tanzania. The treaty haven also agrees not to tax these untaxed earnings: What has happened here is that the haven serves as a stepping-stone for these profits to emerge, along carefully constructed tax-free pathways, out from Tanzania and into the wider world, often via yet another haven where the income will not be taxed at all.

"Like two closely marked football players passing the ball to a third one who is unmarked," explains Professor Sol Picciotto, a tax haven expert, a conduit haven "can create major gaps in the defenses of tax authorities." In this case both Tanzania and Germany are deprived of tax revenues, courtesy of offshore. And this is quite legal. Many tens, and potentially hundreds, of billions of dollars of tax revenue are at stake in this game, vastly increasing the hunger for foreign aid among the world's poorer nations. South Africa's finance minister Trevor Manuel put the problem neatly. "It is a contradiction to support increased development assistance yet turn a blind eye to actions by multinationals and others that undermine the tax base of a developing country."[36]

Over twenty-five hundred tax treaties are in place around the world—an extensive but very poorly understood counterpart of the global trading and investment regime.

The Netherlands, with a wide network of tax treaties, is a good example of a treaty haven. The two biggest sources of foreign investment into China in 2007 were not Japan or the United States or South Korea but Hong Kong and the British Virgin Islands.[37] Similarly, as of 2009 the biggest source of foreign investment into India, at over 43 percent of the total, is not the United States or Britain or China but the treaty haven of Mauritius, a rising star of the offshore system.[38] And here lies another odd tale.

Mauritius illustrates how the British spiderweb is no imperial relic but a modern and self-renewing system. Although French-speaking, the country has a long history of British colonial involvement.[39] Mauritius set up its offshore center in 1989 under the tutelage of experts mostly from the City of London, Jersey, and the Isle of Man. Rudolf Elmer, who worked as a senior offshore practitioner in Mauritius from

2006 to 2008 for Standard Bank, says he trained in Jersey and the Isle of Man before being sent to Mauritius. "There is a lot of British influence," he said. "Major banks like Barclays and HSBC have built up major operations and multistory buildings in Cyber City south of Port Louis [the capital]. Six years ago there were only five. Today, I estimate about 40. It is a hot spot: it will become very prominent."[40]

Though formally independent, Mauritius is a member of Britain's Commonwealth, and its final appeal court is the Privy Council in London. Having gotten over a shaky period in the 1980s, Mauritius is now politically stable and boasts a cheap, well-educated, and multilingual labor force, and it is in the perfect time zone to serve Europe, Asia, and Africa. With over 40 tax treaties with countries in those three continents, Mauritius is a fast-growing conduit haven for investment into India and for investment into Africa from China and the City of London.

Mauritius also specializes in "round-tripping." In this practice a wealthy Indian, say, will send his money to Mauritius, where it is dressed up in a secrecy structure in order to disguise it as foreign investment before it is returned to India. Because of the treaty, the wealthy Indian can avoid Indian withholding taxes on local earnings and use the secrecy to do nefarious things—such as constructing a local market monopoly by disguising the fact that a seemingly diverse and unrelated array of competitors in a market is in fact controlled by the same interests. The construction of secret monopolies via offshore secrecy seems pervasive in certain sectors and goes some way toward explaining why, for example, mobile phone charges are so high in some developing countries.

Local elites lobby for these treaties despite the harm they can cause. "The India treaty with Mauritius is a pure treaty-shopping treaty," said David Rosenbloom, a U.S. tax expert. "Why do the Indians tolerate it? We, the United States, have a treaty with Bermuda, which is ridiculous: Bermuda doesn't even have a tax system. Countries do bizarre things. A lot of it is political. It defies rational thought."[41]

8

RESISTANCE

In Combat with the Ideological Warriors of Offshore

IN APRIL 1998 THE ORGANISATION FOR ECONOMIC Co-operation and Development, a club of rich countries that includes the world's most important secrecy jurisdictions, made an astonishing admission: Tax havens cause great harm. Tax havens and associated offshore activities, an OECD report acknowledged, "erode the tax bases of other countries, distort trade and investment patterns and undermine the fairness, neutrality and broad social acceptance of tax systems generally. Such harmful tax competition diminishes global welfare and undermines taxpayer confidence in the integrity of tax systems."[1]

Offshore is not only a place, a system, and a process, but it can also be considered as a collection of intellectual arguments. Through the OECD's new project—the first serious and sustained intellectual assault on the secrecy jurisdictions in world history[2]—I will explore the main arguments made by the defenders of the offshore system.

At the time the OECD project got under way, worldwide protests were rampant against the obvious failures of globalization. Yet campaigners, who focused many of their arguments on trade, all but ignored the offshore system. The OECD's new initiative, which contained a lot of baffling discussion about international tax, hardly registered on the protesters' agendas.

The new report was allowed to emerge for several reasons. First, the evidence had become impossible to ignore: The use of tax havens was "large, and expanding at an exponential rate," as the report put it. Second, the report was aimed mostly at small Caribbean islands that were not OECD members, and it glossed over the role of OECD countries in offshore.[3] Also, several OECD countries that were not tax havens pushed the report hard inside the OECD. But there is another important reason why the OECD report got through: Tax havens are so steeped in indifference to big inter-governmental bodies that although the OECD had flagged the report for two years, almost nobody offshore had paid it enough attention to mount a serious effort to stop it from emerging.

John Christensen was in Jersey when the 1998 report came out. "Virtually nobody there took it seriously except me," he said. "Bankers were saying 'OECD who? Isn't that some sort of customs organization?'" Daniel J. Mitchell of the right-wing Her-itage Foundation, in Washington, D.C., one of the secrecy jurisdictions' most vocal supporters, had a similar reaction to the Paris-based OECD. "I thought 'Ah, just a bunch of crazy European socialists.'"[4]

Still, Mitchell decided to write a couple of things on it for the Heritage Founda-tion and began to see that this mattered. And the OECD's follow-up report in 2000 contained a primed bomb: a blacklist of 35 secrecy jurisdictions, and a threat of "de-fensive measures" against havens that did not shape up. More alarming for Mitchell, it was not only the "European collectivists" who backed the OECD, but the Clinton administration too.

"Our side was caught with our pants down," Mitchell said in an interview in Washington, D.C. "Heritage, a big full-service think tank, doesn't focus on just one thing. I thought we ought to have a group to have a go at this." So he got together with Andrew Quinlan, a friend from college, and Veronique de Rugy, a Paris-educated libertarian academic, to create a small outfit called the Center for Freedom and Pros-perity (CF&P) with a subgroup, the Coalition for Tax Competition, whose aim was to protect "the cause of tax competition." They lodged it at the Cato Institute, a well-funded free-market think tank in Washington.

The antitax atmosphere in Washington in those days was poisonous. A Delaware senator, William Roth, had been whipping up a hate storm against the U.S. Internal Revenue Service under a declared Republican strategy to "pull the cur-rent income tax code out by its roots and throw it away so it can never grow back."[5] In an effective piece of political theater, Roth, a manic supporter of tax cuts for the wealthy, got IRS agents to testify at hearings behind screens like mobsters, with their voices electronically distorted. His people regaled the hearings with stories about IRS agents in flak jackets storming houses and forcing teenage girls to change clothes at gunpoint—and the IRS had no right of reply. No matter that most of these claims were untrue.[6]

Mitchell began to bombard politicians with emails about the OECD reports, to write scary op-eds in national newspapers with headlines such as "Global Tax Police," and to insult the OECD publicly. Hostilities had begun in the offshore world's first big battle of ideas.

To understand the intellectual underpinnings of offshore finance, it seems appropriate to start with Mitchell, one of the secrecy jurisdictions' noisiest and most active defenders.

He is a man of striking warmth and great personal charm. In his blog "International Liberty: Restraining Government in America and around the World," he declares, "I'm a passionate Georgia Bulldog," in reference to the mascot of the University of Georgia's gridiron team, "so much so that I would have trouble choosing between a low-rate flat tax for America and a national title for the Dawgs. I'm not kidding." In his blog he notes that Britain's left-of-center *Observer* newspaper called him a "high priest of light tax, small state libertarianism" and that this was "the nicest thing anyone's ever said about me."

Mitchell began to take a serious interest in politics in the Reagan era, emerging from George Mason University fascinated by conservative economists such as James Buchanan and Vernon Smith, who explored a branch of economics known as Public Choice Theory, which rejects notions that politicians act on behalf of people or societies and instead looks at them as self-interested individuals. Its followers' distaste for government dovetailed with Mitchell's budding libertarian outlook and his love for Reagan. He worked with Republican Senator Bob Packwood, then for the Bush/Quayle transition team, before joining Heritage.

His libertarian vision is of a world where government is pared back to just a few core roles, such as providing security, leaving the rest to the market. "Some people fantasize about supermodels," he said. "I fantasize about having government at five percent of GDP." (This is quite an ambition: Currently, most OECD governments take in tax revenues equivalent to 30 to 50 percent of GDP.) During our interview he retreated several times behind a personal disclaimer along these lines: "I just work with theories; I have not worked in the real world of business."

Mitchell's specialty is a tone of calculated, arched-eyebrows incredulity when discussing people or ideas that he disdains, and his sound bites are carefully crafted to appear utterly reasonable. His short, peppy little Internet videos are clear, simple, and striking in their directness, and he sprinkles them with homespun wisdom, along with repeated references to freedom and liberty and digs at his adversaries—"international bureaucrats," "intrusive governments," and "Europeans" (especially the French, his particular bogeys)—uttered in tones of theatrical horror.

"Let me give you some frightening numbers," Mitchell said in a bouncy presentation to a "Freedom Conference" at the antitax Steamboat Institute in Colorado in August 2009. Citing a seventy-five-year projection that raised the specter of whopping tax increases, and reeling off statistics about the free-spending habits of George W. Bush (whom he dislikes), he predicted that "we will have a bigger government than any European welfare state—even France and Sweden. . . . I don't know if that means we have to stop using deodorant and train our army to surrender if there's a war, but we are going to be a European welfare state."

Before the OECD report emerged, Mitchell said he did his best to avoid international tax. "My bread and butter was fiscal policy issues: tax cuts versus tax increases; that kind of thing," he said. "For me, international tax—transfer pricing, interest allocations, and so on—was almost as bad as excise taxes on milk in Mongolia."

In those days there was no real ideology for tax havenry: Few people understood how important the offshore system was becoming, and in the age of rapid globalization, almost nobody questioned it. Fortunately for Mitchell, the OECD had tried to avoid looking like it was victimizing smaller jurisdictions by couching its initiative not so much as an attack on tax *havens* but as an attack on harmful tax *competition*—the race to the bottom between states to attract footloose capital by offering zero taxes and other lures. This focus gave Mitchell an immediate advantage in Washington, letting him complain that the OECD was a big bureaucracy that opposed competition.

This question of "competition" is one of the main arguments that tax havens deploy to justify their existence, and it is well worth exploring. Mitchell articulates these arguments as well as anybody.

"International bureaucracies and politicians from high-tax nations are launching a co-ordinated attack against these jurisdictions. The high-tax nations of the world want to set up something equivalent to OPEC," he thundered, flashing up pictures of sinister-looking men in Arab headdresses. "It is an effort by high-tax nations to form a cartel that will enable the politicians to put in place worse tax policies."[7]

"Say you only had one gas station in a town," he continued in a recent presentation.[8] "That one gas station could charge high prices, it could maintain inconvenient hours; it could offer shoddy service. But if you have five gas stations in a town, all of a sudden those gas stations need to compete with each other: They have to lower prices, they have to be attentive to the needs of consumers. We see the same thing internationally, with governments."

He went further. "Imagine you are a governor of Massachusetts. You'd love to shut down New Hampshire—because it's competition. Obama and the rest of the collectivists on the left hate tax havens because they are outposts of freedom. Because of globalization, labor and capital are a lot more mobile than they used to be. If governments are trying to impose high tax rates, [people] actually have options to move either themselves, or their money, across borders. Just like if you have one monopoly gas station in town, and all of a sudden new gas stations open up, you can decide, 'I'm no longer going to shop at that gas station that was ripping me off; I can shop at the gas station that is actually giving me a better deal for my money.'" In other words, the argument goes, tax competition is beneficial, and you can't fight it anyway.

At first glance, these arguments seem reasonable. But look closer, and they collapse in a puff of nonsense. Here's why.

Competition between companies in a market is *absolutely nothing like* competition between jurisdictions on tax. Think about it like this: If a company cannot compete it may fail and be replaced by another that provides better and cheaper goods or services. This "creative destruction" is painful, but it is also a source of capitalism's dynamism. But what happens when a *country* cannot "compete?" A failed state? That is a very different prospect. Nobody would, or could, as Mitchell put it, "shut down New Hampshire." What does it actually mean for a country to be "competitive"? Governments obviously do not "compete" in any meaningful way to police their streets. They do, perhaps, compete to educate their citizens better, but this kind of "competition" points to higher taxes to pay for better education.

The Geneva-based World Economic Forum (WEF) provides a more comprehensive answer, defining competitiveness as "the set of institutions, policies and factors that determine the level of productivity of a country." It uses 12 competitiveness "pillars," including infrastructure, institutions, macroeconomic stability, education, and efficiency of goods markets. One could quibble with the categorizations, but taken together they form a sensible enough selection. Most of them require raising appropriate levels of tax.

It turns out, in fact, that the most "competitive" countries on the WEF's measure are the higher-tax countries. There is plenty of variation, of course: Sweden, Finland, and Denmark, the world's three highest-taxed countries, were ranked fourth, fifth, and sixth most competitive in the 2009–10 index, while the United States, with lower (but still not very low by world standards) taxes, is second. But the *really* low-tax economies like Afghanistan and Guatemala are the least competitive.

Dig further into the data, and other interesting facts emerge. Countries that spend a lot on social needs—something Mitchell opposes—score best on the competitiveness scale."[9] Higher taxes help countries spend more on education, health, and other things that help their workers "compete."

What applies to tax applies to laws and regulation too. What does it mean for a jurisdiction to have a "competitive advantage" in being a heroin smuggling entrepôt or offering lax enforcement on child sex tourism? It may bring in revenue, but in the sense that countries do "compete" with others, it can clearly bring great harm.

Mitchell's world of beneficial tax competition emerges from a sub-school in economics that clings to a 1956 paper by the economist Charles Tiebout, who explored what happens (only in theory, you understand) when markets are perfect and free citizens flee in hordes from one jurisdiction to another at the drop of a tax inspector's hat. This is not, of course, how the world works—but libertarians and defenders of tax competition stretched Tiebout's ideas like rubber to make their intellectual shield for the havens. Mitchell also points to lists of secrecy jurisdictions, claiming they tend to be wealthier than other jurisdictions, and takes this as evidence that offshore is a good thing. This is like an argument that points to the private jets, yachts, and palaces owned by a rich dictator and his cronies as evidence that corruption generates wealth. Well, it does, in a way, but "generating" this kind of wealth is not exactly what we should aim for.

Yet there is one area where Mitchell is probably right. Tax rates have been tumbling for years around the world: Average corporate tax rates, for example, fell from nearly 50 percent in 1980, Mitchell says, down to just over 25 percent today. This is, in large part, the result of tax competition between jurisdictions and with tax havens as the sharp edge of the ax. "When I go in for my salary review, I always say it's because of the great papers I write for Cato that is forcing governments all over the world [to cut taxes]," Mitchell says. "But the real story is tax competition . . . and tax havens are the most powerful instrument of this tax competition."

It is a hard point to prove, but it is reasonable to think that while the world has fixated on ideas and ideologies as the driving force behind global tax-cutting and financial deregulation, tax competition may have been the bigger force.

Many economists see this as a nonstory, though. Although tax *rates* have fallen, tax *revenues* have been fairly steady. Since 1965 personal income taxes in rich-world OECD countries have remained remarkably stable at 25 to 26 percent of the total tax haul,[10] and total corporation taxes have even risen slightly, from 9 to 11 percent. Some say this proves that tax competition does not matter. But look behind the numbers, and an unhappier picture emerges.

Though rich countries have preserved their *overall* tax revenues, corporations and rich folk have paid much less as a share of revenues. Corporate profits, on which their tax liabilities are assessed, have increased sharply.[11] Meanwhile, the rich have not only seen their wealth and income soar, but they have shifted their income out of "personal income tax" categories and into "corporation tax," to be taxed at far lower corporate tax rates. For example, the richest four hundred Americans booked 26 percent of their income as salaries and wages in 1992 and 36 percent as capital gains. By 2007 they only recorded 6 percent as income and 66 percent as capital gains.[12] The same has been happening across all high-income categories and in all OECD countries since at least the 1970s. So falling corporation taxes are being masked by rich people's tax dodges.[13] The working population has seen its personal income taxes and social security contributions rise over the last 30 years, as their wages have stagnated. Mitchell is right to say that tax competition is real, and it bites.

Look at how tax competition smites developing countries, and a bigger story emerges.

One of the only studies ever made was a short IMF paper in 2004[14] that notes how little attention has been paid to how international tax competition has been affecting developing and emerging-market economies and takes what it calls a "first look at those issues."

Its results are remarkable. Tax *rates* have fallen at least as fast as in rich countries, if not faster, and furthest of all in sub-Saharan Africa. But tax revenues fell sharply too:

Just in the short 11-year period from 1990 to 2001, corporation tax revenues in low-income countries fell by a quarter. This is especially troubling because developing countries find it much easier to tax a few big corporations than to tax millions of poor people, so corporate taxes are a bigger deal for them.

One reason for the falling corporate tax revenues has been special tax incentives. In 1990, only a small minority of poor countries offered these incentives; by 2001 most of them did. The IMF's first detailed study on this in July 2009 concluded[15] that these tax incentives, which are supposed to attract foreign investors, slash tax revenues but do not promote growth.[16]

As I have mentioned, tax, not aid, is the most sustainable source of finance for development. Tax makes governments accountable to their citizens, while aid makes governments accountable to foreign donors. Tax competition is destroying developing countries' tax revenues and making them *more* dependent on aid. Brazilians talk about tax competition in terms of a *guerra fiscal*—a tax war—a term that reveals far better what is really happening here and echoes the words of U.S. Senator Carl Levin when he says tax havens are "engaging in economic warfare against the United States and honest, hardworking Americans."

Mitchell has another presentation he likes to make: what he calls "The Moral Case for Tax Havens."[17] A video from October 2008 gives a flavor.

"The vast majority of the world's population lives in nations where governments fail to provide the basic protections of civilized society," says Mitchell (cue pictures of Kim Jong-Il, Robert Mugabe, and Vladimir Putin, looking sinister). "Tax havens protect these people from venal and incompetent governments by providing a secure place to hide their assets.

"One reason why Switzerland has such an admirable human rights policy of protecting financial privacy is that they strengthened their laws in the 1930s to help protect German Jews wanting to guard their assets from the Nazis." (Cue grainy pictures of Hitler saluting from a staff car and a Gestapo officer rounding up frightened women.) "And what about the Argentine family," he continues, "and the risks that their life savings are wiped out by devaluation?" Put it offshore, he says, and the money is safe.

Again, his arguments are persuasive—right up to the point where you stop to think about them.

First, the story about the origins of Swiss bank secrecy is no more than an appealing fiction. The argument about it being set up to protect Jewish money first appeared in the November 1966 *Bulletin* of today's Credit Suisse. It wasn't true. The reason bank secrecy was strengthened in 1934 was a scandal two years earlier when the Basler Handelsbank was caught in flagrante facilitating tax evasion by members of French high society, among them two bishops, several generals, and the owners of *Le Figaro* and *Le Matin* newspapers. Before that, there was professional secrecy (such as exists between doctors and their patients), and violation of this secrecy was a civil offense, not a criminal one as it is today.[18] The law had nothing to do with protecting Jewish secrets.

Next, if a country is misruled, why should it only be the wealthy elites who get to protect their money by going offshore? If a country has unjust laws, then providing an offshore escape route for its wealthiest and most powerful citizens is the best way to take the pressure off the only constituency with real influence for reform. Keep their money bottled up at home, and pressure for change would come fast. Even then, there is no need for offshore secrecy to protect your money. If I am a Tanzanian with a million dollars in London earning 5 percent, and I ought to pay tax on that income at 40 percent, then I owe my government twenty thousand dollars in taxes for that year. I should pay that. Britain could tell my government all about my money, but that would give Tanzania no power under any international agreement to "confiscate" my million dollars. An Argentine family can protect its money from hyperinflation by shifting it to Miami—but secrecy plays no part in this protection. Put it in a normal bank account, exchange the information on the income, and pay tax on it. The principal remains quite safe.

On the question of people needing to protect their cash from tyrants, Mitchell might like to answer this. Who uses secrecy jurisdictions to protect their money and bolster their positions? The human rights activist, screaming in the torturers' dungeons? The brave investigative journalist? The street protester? Or the brutal, corrupt, kleptocratic tyrant oppressing them all? We all instinctively know the answer.

Ah, but, Mitchell then retorts. "Your personal data may be sold to kidnappers who then grab one of your kids." Transparency threatens homosexuals in Saudi Arabia and Jews in France "victimized by corrupt and/or despotic governments. Without the ability to protect their assets in so-called tax havens, these people would be at even greater danger." The answer, he says, is to "place your money in a bank in Miami, since America is a tax haven."[19]

This one carries a shading of truth—but no more. Kidnappers don't need tax data to know that someone has money. And the very wealthy have bodyguards and are relatively rarely kidnapped: The lower and middle classes are usually the victims. More importantly, though, good tax systems promote better governance (and hence less kidnapping), as all the research indicates. By helping elites loot their countries, secrecy jurisdictions are causing exactly the problems Mitchell says he is worried about.

And then we get to the question of freedom. Mitchell is quite clear about his views. The high-tax welfare state, he says, is "a prison for the human soul. It's making pets out of all of us. It's going to put us in a little cage, control our freedom, control our lives—that's what we need to fight against." Tax is bad, and tax havens are the answer.

In this worldview personal property is inviolable, and tax is theft. "It makes sense," Mitchell says, "to protect your family's interest by putting your money someplace like Hong Kong, where the politicians from your country can't find out about it. And if they can't find out about it, they can't steal it."

Leaving aside the question of whether or not this is a general incitement to criminal tax evasion, it is worth asking if tax *is* theft.

Property rights, as the philosopher Martin O'Neill points out, emerge from a general system of legal and political rules that *includes* the rules of taxation. To say tax is theft, then, is to use a system of which tax is a central part as your weapon against taxation. It is to argue in an illogical circle.

Corporations, too, emerge from states, legally speaking. "The state is the only institution in the world that can bring a corporation to life," explains Joel Bakan in his best-selling book *The Corporation*. "It alone grants corporations their essential rights, such as legal personhood and limited liability. . . . Without the state, the corporation is nothing. Literally nothing."[20] To say that corporation tax is theft is, again, simply illogical.

You can find any number of other illogical eddies, ironies, and contradictions in the world of offshore. Secrecy jurisdictions routinely say their role is to promote efficiency in financial markets—but the cloak of secrecy they provide directly contradicts the idea of efficient markets, which require transparency. In an article entitled "Why Do I Have to Deal with People Like Dan Mitchell?"[21] the University of California, Berkeley, economist Brad deLong points to several of Mitchell's articles—

including one praising Iceland for its tax-cutting, deregulated economic policies, just before Iceland's economy collapsed, and one entitled "A Better Way to Chastise France," urging the United States to eliminate withholding taxes on all dividends paid to foreigners, so as to suck tax-dodging capital out of "oppressive high-tax nations." So Mitchell contradicts himself: Tax havenry does "chastise" other nations after all.

Monetary policy is another case where offshore cheerleaders find themselves confused. Generally, these cheerleaders have supported the Monetarist doctrine, which argues that you tackle inflation and unemployment by managing the quantity of money. Yet it is ironic that this doctrine began its rise with a paper by Milton Friedman in 1956, the very year when the offshore Eurodollar market and the offshore system properly took off. But the offshore system directly undermined monetarism: In a world where capital flits effortlessly to unregulated offshore worlds, and where banks can create money willy-nilly, governments struggle to control their money supplies. "The use of quantity of money as a target," Friedman himself finally conceded in 2003, "has not been a success."

Tax avoidance is another case in point. Tax havens endlessly promote themselves as delivering "tax efficiency" to corporations—but this tax avoidance is inefficient. "If tax abuse is needed to ensure an investment is viable," notes the accountant Richard Murphy, "it's a misallocation of resources to do it."

Another offshore antitax favorite is the old claim that tax cuts actually raise revenue partly because people will be less inclined to dodge taxes. Therefore tax competition, driving down tax rates, must be a good thing. This has been bundled together in many Republican minds with another big idea embraced by the antigovernment libertarian world of offshore: It is essential to cut taxes to starve the beast of big government. Or, as the antitax zealot Grover Norquist memorably put it, government should be cut "down to the size where we can drown it in the bathtub."[22] There is a problem with all of this, of course. Many people think tax cuts boost revenue. Starve-the-Beast-ers think tax cuts are useful ways to cut revenue. They can't both be right. Bob McIntyre of Citizens for Tax Justice explains how he thinks the two conflicting theories have thrived side by side for over a quarter of a century. "It's simple," he said. "On Mondays, Wednesdays and Fridays Republicans say that cutting taxes raises revenues. On Tuesdays, Thursdays and Saturdays they say cutting taxes reduces revenues so much that it forces government to cut back—to starve the beast. And on Sundays they rest." In truth, most serious analysts don't believe that tax rates, on their own, make all that much difference. Obviously, real businesspeople invest and hire workers where there is demand for their products, strong infrastructure, and a healthy and educated workforce. Most studies show that corporate tax rates are a relatively minor factor in business location in most areas of business. Tropicana won't grow oranges in Alaska just because it is offered a tax break there. In the golden age of 1947–73, the U.S. economy grew at nearly 4 percent a year—while the top marginal tax rate varied from 75 to over 90 percent.[23] I am *not* arguing that those tax rates caused that growth. But high taxes clearly don't need to choke off growth.

And if tax cuts are the answer to reducing tax evasion, as Mitchell suggests, then he might like to explain the great global eruption of international tax evasion, not to mention the sudden plague of capital flight, from the 1970s onward—just as tax rates went into freefall worldwide.

Here is the real story: As tax havenry exploded and finance became freer, tax evasion and capital flight followed.

By 2000, as the OECD project on tax havens' harmful tax competition rolled forward, Mitchell and his allies began to firehose Washington with letters, emails, and presentations. Almost nobody was articulating the counterarguments.

The OECD was soon on the defensive. Then the havens themselves began to mobilize. In January 2001 the secretary general of the British Commonwealth invited the OECD to set up a joint working group, with equal representation for small member states (that is, the tax havens). This group began to festoon the OECD in red tape, and the whole project got bogged down in arcane haggling. The havens also set up a body called the International Tax and Investment Organisation to coordinate defenses, and they linked up with Mitchell and the Center for Freedom and Prosperity.

Then George W. Bush came to power.

Until then, President Clinton's treasury secretary, Larry Summers, had backed the OECD, even proposing sanctions against the havens in his last budget. Bush's first treasury secretary, Paul O'Neill, initially seemed unsure about the issue, even saying, to Mitchell's alarm: "I support the priority placed on transparency and cooperation."

The Center for Freedom and Prosperity ramped up the pressure. They organized eighty-six congressmen and senators, including big hitters like Jesse Helms and Tom

DeLay, to urge O'Neill to ditch the OECD's project. Milton Friedman, James Buchanan, and other conservative economists signed on. Letters flooded into the treasury. Mitchell thundered about the "Parisian monstrosity," and a Cayman Islands official popped up at the United Nations to rail against "Big Brother" and the "big bully syndrome." The lobbyists neglected to mention that the Caymans were effectively governed from London. The British Commonwealth repackaged the havens' critiques in Washington and lambasted the OECD as a bullying, coercive bureaucracy.[24]

The Caribbean havens also persuaded the powerful U.S. Congressional Black Caucus to act, and to send O'Neill a letter warning that the OECD initiative "threatens to undermine the fragile economies of some of our closest neighbors and allies." The caucus made no mention of the effects these havens had on vastly bigger African nations, of course, or of the fact that the main Caribbean beneficiaries from offshore activities were rich white bankers, lawyers, and accountants.

Mitchell pounced on something else. No OECD country—not Switzerland, not Luxembourg, and certainly not the United States or Britain—was on the blacklist.

"The OECD, a rich man's club of industrialized nations, is launching this anti-tax haven jihad, but they omitted to blacklist their own members," he said. "They are a bunch of racist hypocrites. Powerful white-governed nations in Europe are targeting less powerful nations in places like the Caribbean. Somebody needs to tell the bureaucrats in Paris that the era of colonialism is over."[25]

This time, Mitchell had a point. And he soon got his breakthrough. On May 10, 2001, O'Neill wrote in the *Washington Times,* a conservative newspaper set up by the Reverend Sun Myung Moon that is a regular supporter of tax havens, that the OECD's mission was "not in line with this administration's priorities."[26] The United States, O'Neill continued, "simply has no interest in stifling the competition that forces governments—like businesses—to create efficiencies." The article looked almost as if Mitchell had written it himself.

The United States, O'Neill added, "does not support efforts to dictate to any country what its own tax rates or tax systems should be."[27] It was the offshore contradiction to end them all. "Don't interfere with our rights as sovereign states!" the havens cry—while interfering merrily in other nations' sovereign laws and tax systems.

The OECD's project was dying. As Marty Sullivan of TaxAnalysts put it, the initiative "slowly dissolved into a series of toothless pronouncements, a mixture of cheerleading and scorekeeping. The OECD started to abandon its confrontational approach."[28] The OECD watered down its blacklist criteria; tax havens were now "participating partners" and escaped the blacklist merely by *promising* to shape up—and they need only shape up if everyone else—including the hard nuts like Switzerland or Britain or the United States or newly independent Hong Kong—did too. In other words, it would never happen.

Two months after O'Neill's letter, Senator Carl Levin, fighting a lonely rearguard action, estimated that the United States was losing $70 billion annually from offshore evasion: "a figure so huge that if even half that amount were collected it would pay for a Medicare prescription drug program without raising anyone's taxes or cutting anyone's budget." When Levin noted that fewer than six thousand of more than 1.1 million offshore accounts and businesses were properly disclosed to the IRS, O'Neill's response was simple and clear.

"I find it amusing."[29]

A July 2001 OECD deadline to avoid defensive measures came and went, and the organization later publicly said it had no intention to pursue them in the future. Mitchell's colleague Andrew Quinlan subsequently warned, for good measure, that just ten days of lobbying could shut down the OECD's U.S. funding.

The end result is neatly summarized by Jason Sharman, who wrote a well-researched book about the episode. "The OECD," he wrote, "had to give up its ambition to regulate international tax competition."[30] The tax havens had won.

A lot of the tax havens' arguments hinge on the rightful scope of state power. Democracies have long supported the principle of progressive taxation, as outlined by the Scottish economist Adam Smith: "It is not very unreasonable that the rich should contribute to the public expense, not only in proportion to their revenue, but something *more than* in that proportion." In the United States, as in many countries, the principle of progressive taxation has evaporated. It may not seem like that at first glance: The richest 1 percent of Americans paid just over 40 percent of all federal income taxes in 2009. The right-wing Tax Foundation claimed this "clearly debunks the conventional Beltway rhetoric that the 'rich' are not paying their fair share of taxes." Yet in 2009 the richest 1 percent owned almost half of all financial assets in the country—and the proportion was rising. This is not a story about high taxes on the wealthy but about stratospheric wealth and inequality. And the 40 percent refers only to *income* taxes—as exemplified by the income reporting of the four hundred richest Americans noted earlier in this chapter, rich people usually convert most of their income into capital gains, which is taxed at far lower rates than income; then there are payroll taxes and state taxes, the burden for which tends to fall on low- and middle-income people more heavily than the rich. For the four hundred richest Americans, their effective tax rate was far lower: just 17.2 percent and falling. Count offshore tax evasion by wealthy Americans, which income statistics don't see, and the picture skews further. "A quarter century of tax cuts," wrote the tax author David Cay Johnston, "has produced not trickle down—but Niagara up."[31]

During my long interview with Mitchell in Washington, we went out to a modest eatery near the Cato offices, where we bumped into Richard Rahn, a Cato staffer and a former chairman of the Cayman Islands Monetary Authority. Rahn is a gruff, serious man who wears an eye patch, and when Mitchell introduced us with great bonhomie, Rahn scowled back at him, declined to shake hands with me, muttered something about "European Commies," and stalked out. A year or so later I looked Rahn up, and this time he agreed to talk. This time he was more personable: After first hawking me around the Cato offices as a crazy European curiosity, he then handed me a little maroon passport-sized booklet containing the text of the U.S. Declaration of Independence and the U.S. Constitution. "It looks like an EU passport, doesn't it?" he rasped, twinkle-eyed. "One, of course, is an instrument of oppression. The other is a document of freedom."

"I have ancestors who fought in the American Revolution," he said, sitting me down in his own rather Spartan office. "Genetically I don't like foreign governments." After making me buy Mitchell's book for $20 (I already had a copy but didn't want to spoil Rahn's mood), we began to talk.

Rahn is not a shill for wealthy interests but someone responding, at least in part, to deep personal conviction. "You people upset me . . . I often wonder if you people are evil, or just ignorant," he declared. "Tax oppression is causing misery around the world." He said this was well established in the literature and cited some recent Bulgarian studies to back his case. "When international bureaucrats want to attack places for not imposing bad taxes," he continued, "well, I think that fits into my definition of evil." He described a "conspiracy of the international bureaucratic class" to raise taxes: not so much an organized plot but a constant effort to raise revenues to feed the bureaucrats' own well-being and privileges.

Perhaps there is a *little* truth in this. But his next point is worth tackling, for it is a foundation for the intellectual edifice of offshore.

"Capital is the seed corn of economic growth. Without capital, there is no growth. It is suicidal to tax your own seed corn." Along with this argument comes the tax havens' Exhibit A in their own defense: that they help smooth and promote international flows of capital, channeling it efficiently to capital-hungry developing countries, where it can grow productively and benefit everyone.

Rahn's seed corn contention contains a kernel of truth: Capital certainly can and does promote investment and economic growth. Helping it flow efficiently, at first glance, seems like a good idea. But here is where the arguments fall apart.

First, financial capital isn't the only kind of capital. Social capital—an educated and experienced workforce, a trustworthy business climate, and so on—matters more. Having seed corn is just one factor in achieving a good harvest, along with rain, good soils, fertilizer, and the human capital, knowledge, and confidence to put it all together. "Access to capital is not, in fact, the decisive constraint on economic growth," wrote the economist Martin Wolf. "It is social and human capital, as well as the overall policy regime that matter."[32] These, of course, need tax dollars.

Second, tax isn't only about *revenue,* the first of four "Rs" of taxation. The second "R" is *redistribution,* notably tackling inequality. This is what democratic societies always demand, and as the painstakingly researched book *The Spirit Level* attests, it is inequality, rather than absolute levels of poverty and wealth, that determines how societies fare on almost every single indicator of well-being, from life expectancy to obesity to delinquency to depression or teenage pregnancy. The third "R" is *representation*—rulers must bargain with citizens in order to extract taxes from them—and this leads to accountability and representation. The fourth is *repricing*—changing prices to do things like discourage smoking. Secrecy jurisdictions directly undermine the first three, if you think about it, and possibly the fourth too.

Then there is the small matter of the evidence. One might think that capital should flow from rich countries, where it is plentiful, to low-income countries, where it is scarce, promoting productive investment, growth, and better lives for all. In the real world, this has not happened. The low-income countries that have been growing the fastest, like China, tend to be those that have been exporting capital,[33] not importing it. Countries need, above all, sound institutions, good infrastructure, and the effective rule of law—exactly what the offshore system undermines.

This is not such a surprise. A country can only absorb so much capital, just as an acre of land can only take so much seed corn. Capital loans to low-income countries haven't found their way into productive investment, but instead they have washed back into private bank accounts in Miami, London, and Switzerland, leaving public debts behind. Waves of financial capital, processed "efficiently" offshore, have led to financial crisis after crisis. In many low-income countries, as the economist Dani Rodrik puts it, "capital inflows are at best ineffective, at worst harmful."

And that is not all. Much of the world's wealth derives from what economists call rents: the kind of unearned income that flows effortlessly to oil-rich rulers. "Oil is a resource that anaesthetizes thought, blurs vision, corrupts," as the Polish writer Ryszard Kapuscinski put it. "Oil expresses perfectly the eternal human dream of wealth achieved through lucky accident, through a kiss of fortune and not by sweat, anguish, hard work. In this sense oil is a fairy tale and, like every fairy tale, it is a bit of a lie."[34]

Nearly every sane economist since Adam Smith has agreed that it is very good, and very efficient, to tax rents at very high rates. One kind of rent comes from market monopolies or oligopolies, such as those enjoyed by pharmaceutical patents and Big Pharma; by the government-sanctioned licenses afforded to the Big Four accounting firms identified in chapter 1; by taxpayer-guaranteed international banks; or by the one-and-only Fédération Internationale de Football Association (FIFA), the super-wealthy international governing body of world football.

The global headquarters of most major players in all these highly profitable industries are located offshore, most especially in Switzerland—directly against every notion of economic efficiency. FIFA, for example, used its monopolistic position in 2010 to force poor South Africa to place it in a special "tax bubble" for the 2010 World Cup, shifting its revenues from a poor African nation to that of the company whose luxurious $200 million Zurich headquarters happens to lie just a few hundred meters from where I am writing this chapter.

———

Offshore is not only about tax, of course. When it comes to failures of regulation, the simplest, and commonest, argument that tax havens make is to deny responsibility and use the "just a few rotten apples" defense: The system is basically clean, but occasionally bad ones get through. Immediately after the collapse of BCCI the president of the Cayman Islands Bankers Association, Nick Duggan, said: "BCCI, is a unique world-wide situation and does not reflect on the local banking community at all."[35]

Another argument is like the one on tax: Offshore promotes "efficiency" by driving financial innovation and being what the offshore writer William Brittain-Catlin calls a "seller of novelties on the financial market, a sweetshop for capitalism, developing new flavours." The financial crisis exposed what most of this financial "innovation" really involves. Innovative forms of abuse are to be resisted, not encouraged.

The next offshore regulation argument involves deflection. Anthony Travers, chairman of the Cayman Islands Financial Services Authority, uses this technique widely. In a 2004 article in *The Lawyer* entitled "Framing Cayman,"[36] he sought to explain why some of the biggest economic scandals in world history—BCCI, Enron, and Parmalat, in each of which Cayman played a pivotal role—were in fact not the Caymans' fault at all.

Parmalat was brought down by its Cayman-based finance subsidiary Bonlat Financing, which had fraudulently claimed to hold nearly 4 billion euros in assets. According to Travers, the missing Bonlat billions "never existed at all, save in a document forged in Italy by a corrupt Parmalat executive. If that is the nature of the fraud in relation to Bonlat, how precisely is the 'part' of the Caymans 'substantial'?" In other words, though the Caymans was central to the fraud, it is blameless because the fraudsters were actually elsewhere. He said a similar thing about BCCI. "Had BCCI not been so licenced [as a deposit-taker] by the Bank of England, at a time when the Caymans banking regulator was on secondment from the Bank of England," Travers wrote, "its subsidiary would not have been licenced in the Caymans." As for Enron's 692 opaque Caymans subsidiaries: "These were on balance sheet consolidated subsidiaries which owned the overseas Enron operating assets, thereby lawfully deferring US taxation," their profits "properly accounted for and audited." Enron's Caymans limited partnership LJM No. 2, Travers continued, was "a victim and not a perpetrator"—the perpetrators were Delaware limited partnerships. In other words, the frauds were carried out elsewhere. And he added, "None of the financial recklessness that has brought about much of the current global crisis occurred in or involved the Cayman Islands."[37]

The breathtaking chutzpah of Travers's claims is leavened by the fact that his arguments contain a truth: The frauds could not have happened only in the Cayman Islands. They required culprits elsewhere too. "The charlatans responsible for this type of behaviour," Travers notes, "are far closer to Westminster than the Caymans."

Quite so. But he is deliberately missing the point: *This is how the offshore system works.* Offshore structures always serve citizens and institutions elsewhere—so the beneficiaries are always elsewhere. This is why it is called "offshore." Plausible deniability is the whole game. The fraudsters may well *be* elsewhere, but offshore is what makes the fraud work. Secrecy jurisdictions are to fraudsters what fences are to thieves. These arguments from the Caymans are like those of one who is caught fencing stolen property blaming the police for not stopping the thieves who stole the property in the first place.

The Caymans is a place "which has pledged to meet the highest and quite new international standards of tax transparency," Travers continued, then added a more menacing note. "If it were not for a quirk in the laws of defamation," he said (noting that jurisdictions cannot sue for libel), "comment of this sort would be actionable."

On September 11, 2001, two months after the OECD's tax haven project died, with Al-Qaeda's attack on the United States, a new tale of hypocrisy and deception began that continues up to today.

After the attacks the George W. Bush administration suddenly wanted better cooperation and transparency from the secrecy jurisdictions on terrorist financing, though it wanted to leave offshore tax evasion alone. The problem was how to do this, given that the two practices involve exactly the same jurisdictions, structures, and techniques.

The answer came in the form of one of the slyest offshore tricks ever devised.

The best way for countries to share information with each other is through so-called "automatic" exchange of information—where they tell each other about their taxpayers' financial affairs as a matter of course. This happens routinely inside Europe and between a few other countries, and although the system is leaky—it needs shoring up to cover all sorts of loopholes—it works well enough. Privacy is not invaded: Tax authorities keep the information to themselves, just as doctors keep details of their patients' hemorrhoids and venereal diseases confidential. Doctors and tax authorities *need* the information and can share it with others who need it, but they don't publicize it.

But there is another way of sharing information, known as "on request": A country will agree to hand over information about another country's taxpayers—but only on a case-by-case basis, only when specifically asked, and only under very narrow conditions: You must be able to demonstrate exactly why you need the information. In other words, when you request the information you must already know, more or less, what it is. No "fishing expeditions," or general trawls to find tax cheats, are allowed.

You can't prove criminality until you get the information, and you can't get the information until you can show the criminality. *Catch–22*'s Captain Yossarian would have appreciated the double bind. "On request" information exchange is a fig leaf. It lets tax havens claim they are transparent while continuing business as usual.

The "on request" model, of course, is the one that got the Bush administration's endorsement. Instead of transparency, we got a very conditional transparency: only when there is permission to be transparent. The "on request" standard has become the OECD's model too.

It is hard to know how much information is exchanged "on request" globally, but Geoff Cook, chief executive of Jersey Finance, confessed in March 2009 that in the seven years since Jersey signed a tax agreement with the United States, it exchanged information with American investigators on just "five or six" cases.[38] Compare that to the million-plus U.S. offshore accounts and businesses Senator Levin identified, and clearly the system is a joke. Requests for information can take months or years to process—and the assets under investigation can be shifted elsewhere in hours or even minutes.

It gets worse. After the financial crisis struck in 2007, the OECD, by now at the mercy of the secrecy jurisdictions, set up another piece of sleight of hand to respond to public pressure. At the urging of G20 leaders the OECD set up a blacklist for tax havens, and the way to get off the blacklist was to sign 12 agreements to share information with other countries, using the OECD's hopeless "on request" standard.

The OECD began to claim that a major crackdown was under way. "What we are witnessing is nothing short of a revolution," boomed the OECD secretary-general, Angel Gurría. "By addressing the challenges posed by the dark side of the tax world, the campaign for global tax transparency is in full flow." Newspaper articles ran headlines like "Bank Secrecy Is Dead," and British prime minister Gordon Brown declared the aim of the blacklist was to "outlaw tax havens."

As the new OECD push got under way, tax havens rushed to negotiate new agreements in order to sign the requisite 12 that would get them off the blacklist. At the latest count a third or so were with Nordic states, especially with such global economic giants as Greenland, San Marino, and the Faroe Islands—and another third or so were with other tax havens. The havens did sign a few with larger economies, though as usual, nobody bothered about the developing countries, which suffer most from offshore abuse. India, China, Brazil, and most of Africa were entirely absent from the list. Five days after the G20 had declared that the era of banking secrecy was over, the OECD's blacklist was empty.[39]

"The blacklist has been a sad joke," said Professor Michael McIntyre of Wayne State University Law School, who knows this area better than almost anyone. "The OECD program has provided a patina of respectability to countries that are actively assisting taxpayers in evading taxes in their home country."[40]

The blacklist, in short, was a whitewash.

After a temporary setback during the financial crisis, the offshore system is now growing again at ferocious speed. And the OECD insists to this day that its next-to-useless "on request" form of information exchange is "the accepted international standard."

As with tax, so it goes on regulation. International authorities have long recognized the problem that the global patchwork of fragmented financial regulation offers seamlessly integrated global banks vast opportunities to play the game of arbitrage between different jurisdictions, especially offshore. So world leaders are pretending that something is being done to constrain bankers' impulses. The Bank for International Settlements, in Switzerland, is the biggest of these, along with the Financial Stability Forum that it hosts, set up in 1999 to deal with financial risks and crises. Between them, they have presided over the biggest global financial crisis since the Great Depression.

"Whenever the cops come calling the banks have a ready response for the particular regulator in each country," explained Jack Blum. "No one sees the whole picture and it's really no one's job to even try. When the big and scary stuff happens, the bankers and their friends trot out the Bank for International Settlements and the Financial Stability Forum as proof of effective coordination and regulation. But these things are glorified fig leaves. They have produced absolutely nothing of real value beyond a few minor process quick fixes."

Rich governments cannot be trusted to do the right thing on tax havens and transparency. Many will demand more transparency and more international cooperation, even as they work to frustrate both. They will call for reasoned debate as they engage in character assassination, secret deals, and worse. They will talk the language of democracy and freedom, the better to defend unaccountable, irresponsible power and privilege.

Civil society is, thankfully, beginning to stir. The current thought leaders are Global Financial Integrity in the United States and the Tax Justice Network (TJN) in Europe, whose expertise has been invaluable for this book. John Christensen, TJN's director, remembers holding an expert briefing on offshore for staff in the Senate buildings, in Washington D.C., and seeing a senior congressional staffer with tears in her eyes as she described her happiness at seeing civil society at last begin to engage, after spending so long battling to get any traction on offshore issues, in the face of the ferocious Washington right-wing counter-lobbies. "She said she had waited for years for civil society to take an interest in this." A much greater mobilization is now required.

How do all these shaky doctrines—the OECD's information exchange standards, the contradictory double act of tax-cutting increasing tax revenues, and tax-cutting acting to Starve the Beast, and Mitchell's offshore incoherences—continue to thrive? The author Jonathan Chait provides a good answer.

"The lesson for cranks everywhere," he wrote, "is that your theory stands a stronger chance of success if it directly benefits a rich and powerful bloc—and there's no bloc richer and more powerful than the rich and powerful." But the last word here goes to Bob Mcintyre of Citizens for Tax Justice, who has spent much of his life battling with the armies of lobbyists in Washington. "There are so few of us," he sighs wearily, "and so many of them."

9

THE LIFE OFFSHORE
The Human Side of Secrecy Jurisdictions

IN 2009 I MET UP WITH A FORMER PRIVATE BANKER, Beth Krall, in attempt to understand a question that had been nagging me: How do private bankers who shelter the wealth of gangsters and corrupt politicians justify what they do?

We met in the bustling café at Kramer Books, off Dupont Circle, in Washington, D.C., where she was living, one Sunday in 2009. She had left private banking and had joined the nongovernmental sector. Dressed in a striking black and white coat, she still looked very much the stylish international financier.

Aged 47, and with nearly 24 years in the banking business, Krall (which is not her real name) was still coming to terms with her past life. She hated what she had seen and was clearly unsettled by exposing the horrors she had experienced, but she adamantly refused to reveal any of the client details she had sworn to protect. She was wary of disrupting the many friendships she had made in the industry and was careful about what she would and would not say.

Krall's last offshore posting was in the Bahamas, the island archipelago with over three hundred thousand residents that has been an important offshore center since the golden age of American organized crime in the early decades of the last century. A few months earlier, a practitioner in the Caymans had warned me to watch for my personal safety if I go "asking all these questions" in the Bahamas. Krall said she was unsure what might happen to her if she went back, as she was partly breaking the private bankers' code of silence. "I don't want to have concrete shoes put on me," she said, without smiling. One reason for her fear was something that had angered her in the first place: that so many of the people she dealt with were powerful members of society in their countries. One case involved "very prominent people in world politics."

Unusually, for a foreign banker in the Bahamas, Krall became closely involved in local Junkanoo cultural celebrations, a mixture of Latin American and Caribbean carnival traditions that a dedicated website calls "the greatest cultural event of not only The Bahamas, but also the world at large." She seemed distressed, while we talked, at the thought that fellow members of her Junkanoo group—not to mention many other friends she had left behind in Nassau—might judge her criticism of the country's offshore industry "anti-Bahamian." When we spoke she was still working up the courage to tell them why she could not go back. She was still redefining her relationship with the offshore values within which she had made her career: that secrecy is good, whatever brings in the money is good, and if you break the code of silence you are sloppy or treacherous.

People want to do the right thing, and it is easy, offshore, to be seduced into the idea that what matters is doing the right thing by your peers—and the rest of the world can take care of itself. In the rush to make a career, one can only make progress by ignoring the structural implications of what one does. She is one of very few to recognize the full moral weight of what she was doing and to step away.

Krall was born in Leicester, England, and took her banking exams straight after school, starting in Britain's Midland International bank in 1980 before moving to a partly state-owned Swedish bank and then, in 1987, to Chase Manhattan in Luxembourg to work in its "back office"—the administrative side, where Chase was a paying agent for certain Eurobond issues. She moved to a Brazilian bank, Banco Mercantil de São Paulo, then to Cititrust in the Bahamas, where she ran evaluations and accounting for their mutual funds business. From this point onward, Krall declines to identify her employers precisely.

She became a client relationship manager with the private banking arm of a well-known British bank in the Bahamas. They worked with what were euphemistically called "managed banks" or shell banks, an offshore specialty. These have no real presence where they are incorporated, so they can escape supervision by responsible regulators. A shell bank will typically be operated through an agent in the tax haven jurisdiction, perhaps a famous global bank, which provides a reassuringly solid name and address to back the shell but will otherwise carry no responsibility or even real knowledge of what the shell is actually up to. So a shell bank might be incorporated in the Bahamas, for example, but its owners and managers could be anywhere.

Shell banks handle business that many banks will not touch. U.S. senator Carl Levin notes that they are generally not examined by regulators, and virtually no one but the shell bank owner really knows where the bank is, how it operates, or who its customers are. The bank Krall worked for provided a well-known name to reassure the Bahamas regulator. I asked Krall how much due diligence her British bank did on these entities. "Ha ha. Yeah," was her initial reply. "These banks would send quarterly statements to the Bahamas Central Bank—but it wasn't our job to monitor them."

There would literally be brass plates in her British bank's reception area saying "Banco de X"—perhaps an Argentinian bank using the Bahamian address and phone number of the British bank on their headed notepaper. The Bahamas regulator could not find out what was going on back in Argentina, and vice versa: the classic offshore "elsewhere" technique. Predictably, some of these banks failed, despite being audited and passed by Big Five accounting firms,[1] and Krall remembers taking calls from angry depositors. "People were on the phone in tears, with their life savings gone, and I was saying to them, 'There is no point coming on a plane to look for the money because there is no money here.'" The money never *was* there.

With the terrorist attacks of September 11, 2001, prompting the United States to legislate against shell banks, a bank in the Bahamas now had to employ two senior bankers and keep its books and records there to be judged real enough to do business. "That means a bank maybe with a room or suite in a building, with two people in it— that's a bank now," Krall said. She pointed me to the current website of a Bahamas-based trust company that will provide you with exactly that: the appearance of being a real bank, including two staff members as directors of your bank and a place to keep the books and records. Such a set-up can allow business almost as usual, yet still check off the regulators' boxes.

Krall moved to a big European bank, again as a client relationship manager— in effect, someone who finds wealthy clients and keeps them happy. Trawling for business, she was routinely pointed toward Latin America, where she traveled frequently. "On the immigration form you would write that you are going for pleasure— though your suitcase would be full of business suits and portfolio evaluations, or marketing materials and presentations explaining the advantages of a trust in the

Bahamas." The client's name would be absent from the portfolio evaluations: In fact, the bank would not even record it as the account name. "You'd cut off the account name and number so it was just a list of securities and holdings: you could never attach it to anyone." It was nerve-wracking, sometimes, going through airports, but she always got through unchallenged.

Apart from the anxiety about getting caught, Krall said there was rarely, if ever, a feeling you were doing anything wrong, despite often helping clients break the law. Part of what she called "managing not to check into your conscience" was that there were always cases where you could believe you were helping someone. For example, countries like Brazil have "forced heirship" dictating who in a family gets the assets after the parents die—and an offshore trust may be a way to get around this. Krall cited a case she knew of in another country where forced heirship would have granted the assets to a playboy son instead of to the family's preferred beneficiary, a daughter with special needs. As I explained in the last chapter, human stories like this are commonly used to justify oceans of wrongdoing in the offshore world.

Krall would cold-call top lawyers and asset managers, hoping to get into what is known in the trade as the "Beauty Parade," the lineup of obliging banks that clients and their representatives will look for to manage their riches. The key is to build a relationship of trust, mixing the good and the bad. With the good trust you offer a solid, safe return on the assets; the bad trust is a confidence that you will keep their identities secret and will break laws on their behalf. In pursuit of these elusive relationships, Krall went to polo games, the opera, orchestral concerts in Rio de Janeiro, and umpteen working breakfasts, lunches, and dinners in the most expensive restaurants in town.

Despite her growing qualms, Krall ended up working for a Swiss private bank in the Bahamas. This was no ordinary bank: It had only a hundred or so clients. It was also the only bank where she actually saw a suitcase full of cash. "My bank never once had a client walk through the door," she said. "The bankers and their clients go on big game hunting trips, or to the ballet in Budapest. That is where it happens." From her tone, she made the "it" sound like some sordid sexual act.

Her bank was run out of Switzerland, and the Bahamas was purely a "parking space" or transit point for money: an extra layer of secrecy. A major driver was, of course, the imperative to receive and store the proceeds of crime. "I felt I was prostituting my personality, just to get money in the bank," she said. "I came to realize that the system I was involved in contributes to the perpetuation of poverty in the world." She thought a bit, then added, "But I did enjoy the adrenaline. When it fuels you, you don't question what you otherwise would."

Her colleagues hailed from old European aristocratic circles. While Krall was perfectly good at her job and had close working relationships with top lawyers, asset managers, and so on, a gap remained. "They went to parties with royalty, with ambassadors," she said. "I wasn't in their circle."

At the time, laws in the Bahamas were being tightened a bit, following a feeble global crackdown, and she moved sideways in the bank to work as a "compliance officer." These days, offshore bankers make a big show of their "Know Your Customer" rules, to keep out the bad money. Depositors may have to supply a certified copy of a passport, for example, and divulge where their money came from. Jurisdictions like the Bahamas and the Cayman Islands put these requirements into their statutes, and banks must comply; they employ compliance officers like Krall to enforce this.

That, at least, is the theory.

In her new job Krall began to learn of the many devious avenues around the rules. "You would ask for the source of funds—and they could tell you anything," she replied. "You didn't ask for documentation." Another compliance officer Krall knew was expressly forbidden from seeing certain files. A loophole in Bahamas law let institutions waive due diligence checks on clients if they were referred from a financial institution in a jurisdiction where the legislation is supposed to be good. Once in a while a bank would uncover a money-laundering case to show it is enforcing the law: They were happy to do this, Krall said, provided it did not expose anyone the bank would not want to upset. Legal frameworks that distinguish between the criminal and the legitimate have eroded away offshore, replaced by networks of trust that distinguish between the well established and respectable, on the one hand, and the unknown and dispensable, on the other.

Individuals with sums to launder or invest with minimal taxation want to know that they are dealing with people who can be trusted not to have moral qualms. If the bankers don't know you, you will have to jump through many hoops; if you are a long-standing and trusted client, the rules fall away. These trust-based networks, deferential to the aristocracy of wealth and privilege and resistant to formal laws, are the ultimate source of comfort for the banks' wealthy clients. The similarities with unspoken Mafia codes of behavior are no coincidence at all.

"These banks are competing with each other, but they also scratch each others' backs," Krall said. "The heads of these banks are part of a circle of friends and business associates, where the whole social circle revolves around it: a social structure intertwined with a business relationship. They will pass business between each other."

"The law says you must report suspicious activity to the Financial Intelligence Unit [FIU] or the police," she continued. "But in a very small place, everyone knows everyone and their cousin. I couldn't trust a report being handled confidentially or through proper channels. There is a huge chance that someone in the FIU or the police will be close to people in the bank where you work . . . and this could cause me harm for raising the issue."

Krall was supposed to check for suspicious movements through the accounts—of which there were plenty. She raised many red flags. Her managers "would say, 'This was a commission' [on a contract]." Were these bribes? Commissions on what?

"I went back, and never got an answer."

One Swiss-based trust company that had a relationship with her bank displayed almost no information on their website, bar some photos of a nice fountain in Geneva. "The crap they brought to us was unbelievable—there is no way a responsible trustee should take this on. You would have no idea who the trust settlors were; what the assets were or where they came from. I objected strongly—but the bank took them on."

Over time her qualms grew, and she began to find herself in a very lonely place. "I couldn't even tell my boyfriend. I was supposed to abide by bank secrecy," she remembered. "It wasn't easy for him, with someone walking through the door at the end of the day, pale, drained, and sick, with stuff going on he can never know about." Other compliance officers whom she chatted with also felt their powerlessness. "There was a fear abroad," she remembered. "You have this dilemma: the difficult news you will give to directors may not be appreciated. Most people want to do their job, protecting the bank and country from the taint, as well as doing their ethical, moral, and legal duty. You go into the job with that mind-set."

I chatted to Krall about my own recent experiences in the Cayman Islands: about what happened when I revealed to one of my first interviewees in the Caymans that I had links to an organization that had been critical of tax havens. That meeting ended in minutes. I had been referred to this interviewee by a mutual friend, and after our meeting my friend got emails stressing how "uncomfortable" she felt, and requesting promises on promises that I would never identify her.

People I met in the Caymans almost always seemed to find it distasteful, or changed the subject, when I asked questions such as whether or not one might balance the prosperity of the fifty thousand–odd islanders against the interests of 350 million North Americans, 600 million Latin Americans, and the same number again in Africa. Even more surprising to me was that despite the confidence with which I hold my own views, I found myself feeling shy, almost ashamed, expressing them on the Cayman Islands, from the first day.

Krall recognized this shifty feeling immediately. "When I was planning to leave the Bahamas friends were kindly introducing me to other private banking opportunities," she said. "The thought of continuing in that profession made me feel disgusted to the point of being physically nauseous, yet here were my dear friends, working in exactly the same industry, being helpful. How could I say to them directly there was no way I could do that work anymore, while they were still in it?"

"I felt that 'unclean' feeling from every direction: unclean for having done that kind of work and yet unclean with feeling as though I was being, somehow, not truly and openly honest with my friends."

Stephanie Padilla-Kaltenborn, an American mother of two and an old friend of mine who lived until recently in the Cayman Islands, recalled soon becoming aware of unspoken limits of curiosity and candor in the secrecy jurisdiction. "It's a feeling when you live there that there's something under the surface and I did *not* want to look," she said. "I knew the answers would be more complicated than I could deal with. You cannot talk to people—it's a strange invisible line you can't cross. It's a semi-chosen state of mind—a self-censorship."

———————————

Krall's experiences, and her treatment, are echoed in the widely publicized case of Bradley Birkenfeld, the gregarious old Bostonian UBS director who recently helped the U.S. Internal Revenue Service dismantle a $20 billion UBS program to help wealthy U.S. residents evade taxes and forced Switzerland to accept a new, somewhat more transparent tax treaty with the United States. Birkenfeld described in court how UBS bankers would frequent events like the UBS Trophy yacht race off Rhode Island, the Art Basel contemporary art fair, classic car shows and concerts, and—his personal favorite—a ten-thousand-dollar-a-head evening with Elton John at the Waldorf Astoria in 2005, illegally soliciting client business. "I'd say, 'Do you want to go to Wimbledon, have lunch and see the match?" Birkenfeld recalled.[2] "'Do you want to come to Oktoberfest and drink some beer and look at hot girls? Whatever you want to do.' I would go to the Cannes Film Festival, the Venice Film Festival, the Bangkok Film Festival." On one occasion, he smuggled diamonds into the United States in a toothpaste tube. His star client, Oleg Olenicoff, explained how impressive the Swiss bankers' performance was while courting his tax-evading business. "It's all very proper and precise," Olenicoff recalled. "You feel you're in the German Reichstag with all the generals there!"[3]

While visiting the Caymans in 2009, I was chatting with a former senior Caymanian politician at his house when a thickset, dark-skinned Caymanian, probably in his forties, wearing a blue polo shirt, khaki shorts, and sunglasses, walked in and introduced himself as "The Devil."

I still do not know his name, though my sober and well-connected host vouched firmly for him. The mystery stranger said he had serious credentials in international law enforcement so—this was all I could think of—I tested him by showing a photo on my phone that I'd recently taken of Robert Morgenthau, the Manhattan district attorney, a legend in the business. Not a sophisticated test, for sure, but my stranger passed it without hesitation.

He said he had spent years probing some of the global sins that freewheel through the Cayman Islands and chatted about several cases, many of which I'd never heard of. One concerned Imad Mugniyah, whom I later discovered to be a senior Hezbollah official killed in Syria in 2008; another was about a Cayman company fingered in the transfer of missile technology to Iran (later I checked with the U.S. Office of Foreign Assets Control and discovered this was still a very live investigation). He touched on some Cayman operations of the international arms dealer Victor Bout that never reached the media. He spoke of Cayman hedge funds, mutual funds, and special purpose vehicles, and he described these sectors as being riddled with crime, though he declined to go into any real details. At this point, he supplied me with a health warning.

"If we discuss this with you, you will end up like Salman Rushdie. There are things here not to be discussed. I mean it," he said. "This is a wicked, vicious place."

He said he had become too interested in certain stones that would normally, and deliberately, have been left unturned—and this had made him an enemy of the establishment. This, he said, was why he called himself "The Devil"—for that was how they treated him now.

"You have to have a deep soul," he continued. "They carry out economic isolation—they destroy your credibility and your integrity. They will strip you of your dignity. We operate here under a code of silence—*omertà*. They will tell you this is not so."

"There is a cabal here. . . . These people in [the] firms get together—it is an informal thing—and say this guy is causing trouble. You will get hints: Be careful! from your boss. I got this." Powerful Masonic and other networks are at play; the cabal does not include Caymanian politicians, he said, but added, "They will give the politicians a call and tell them what to do." My host—the only dissident I encountered on the island—interjected, adding that this cabal was "spoken of in terms you'd speak of a ghost."

"The very difficult part of this," The Devil continued, "is that a few people here—those people who have committed what the international community would consider unlawful acts—they get the CBEs, the OBEs [British royal decorations] . . . they sit on boards, they have high status, and they are looked on as statesmen."

He described another avenue around the legislation. Cayman boasts of its intrusive Know-Your-Customer laws, which are fairly strong—on paper. Yet it was just as Krall had found it in the Bahamas: The rules fall away if you are a trusted part of the network. "If I do not have a relationship [with an institution] they will want to know even my underwear size," The Devil said. "But if you have an established relationship with a bank over time, the rules don't apply to you. If you are established as a well-to-do person, your credibility isn't questioned." His words remind me of an internal memo at the Riggs Bank brought to light in 2004 by the U.S. Permanent Committee on Investigation. "Client is a private investment company domiciled in the Bahamas," it said, "used as a vehicle to manage the investment needs of beneficial owner, now a retired professional who achieved much success in his career and accumulated wealth during his lifetime for retirement in an orderly way." The "retired professional" was the Chilean torturer-in-chief and former dictator Augusto Pinochet.

Beneath the Caymans' standard official line that it is a "transparent, well-regulated and co-operative jurisdiction" lies a more fiendish reality.

Later I recounted my "Devil" story and Krall's tale to an accountant who had worked in the Caymans, who nodded fiercely when I mentioned the reference to Salman Rushdie. "Yes, yes, it's serious," he said. "It's not naive to take these threats seriously. You will be the first to go to prison if something goes wrong." He told me about several mysterious offshore deaths, including that of a Swiss banker, Frederick Bise, who was found dead in 2008 in the hatchback of a burning car in Grand Bay, on the Caymans, with blunt force injuries to his head.

My interlocutor, a former hedge fund administrator, compliance officer, and chief accountant, described how he slowly grew to see what was going on.

"I started feeling bad three or four years after I arrived," he said. "We ran business through the accounts, which was kind of dubious: you'd get information here and there and put it together—but you could not ask questions. Even if you had indications, you could not speak up. I did speak up, and the result was that I got less information at meetings. Information was sort of prediscussed: I felt that a kind of show was going on."

He came under suspicion and was overloaded with work: twelve hundred hours of overtime in a year, with no compensation. "The CEO said, 'This is part of your job.'"

"We replaced 40 to 50 percent of our staff within two years: people who do not fit into the system for any reason are pushed out. Ask questions, and you can get fired, or given so much work [that] you [eventually] resign. It is not done obviously: they won't call you into meetings and say, 'Stop asking questions.' These are highly intellectual, well-educated people: they have their own way of communicating. You learn to read between the lines. They will not say, 'I am threatening you.' They will say, 'This person does not fit into the picture.' I have been in the business for years, and I know what they mean."

Most people working offshore only see fragments of the big picture, so cannot understand what is going on. "For example, if there is a trust set up in the Caymans, and the securities portfolio is in Switzerland, you will get very little information in the Caymans: you won't know the reason why things happen. The ones who commit the crimes—those people who set up the trust or the Special Purpose Vehicle—will often sit in New York or London. The employees in many cases are honest people, trying to do their best: it will be the lawyer, or the CEO, or the chief operating officer, who knows the truth." Once you become part of senior management, then "you are part of the inner circle and things become much clearer. You are part of the plot. You know what the real products and services are, and why they are so expensive."

An old offshore saying encapsulates it: "Those who know don't talk, and those who talk don't know."

Other subtle checks on troublemakers abound. To stay in the Caymans, for example, you need a work permit. Any expatriate who causes trouble—whether a seconded police official, lawyer, regulator, or auditor—can have his or her work permit revoked by the "Cayman Protection Board," which grants permits. Foreigners in the Caymans are made painfully aware of their vulnerability on this.

"If you blow the whistle and stay on the island—and this is general in offshore centers—you don't have whistle-blower protections at all. If you speak up in one place, the network works in a way that you will never get work again. It is suicide, physically and economically. There is *no way* you would find protection." My interlocutor chopped the palm of one hand with the other for emphasis.

"Have you seen the John Grisham film *The Firm?* It's worse. It's not only the lawyers—it's the whole political environment."

––––––––––––––

Before visiting the Caymans in 2009, I had contacted island authorities to request interviews and told them I had done work for the Tax Justice Network (TJN), the expert-led organization that criticizes secrecy jurisdictions like Cayman. On arrival, the government spokesman Ted Bravakis said because of this there was "no willingness to engage." A decision to shun me, he said, had been taken "at the highest levels of government."

Earlier, I had emailed a top official in the Cayman Islands regulatory apparatus, requesting an interview. He copied me into an email to local practitioners, criticizing efforts by his predecessor, Tim Ridley, to help me get interviews during my trip. "I do wish Tim would stop hawking this chap around as if to say he is doing us a favor," the official wrote. "We are going to prepare a factual anodyne piece in writing but will decline any on the record interview." I told him he may not have meant to copy me in on the mail. "Quite so," he replied, then put his finger squarely on an important truth about such places. "I have no problem with you understanding how the world at large regards the comments of TJN," he said. "I say so directly at every opportunity and meet with uniform agreement."

In the official's "world at large"—the offshore environment—there is no opposition to the establishment consensus, it seems.

There is, in fact, something generic about island life that encourages the groupthink that the official describes. In his novel *Snow Falling on Cedars,* the writer David Guterson captures an essence of it. "An enemy on an island is an enemy forever. There is no blending into an anonymous background, no neighboring society to shift toward. Islanders were required, by the very nature of their landscape, to watch their step moment by moment." The social and political inhibitions islanders feel, he continued, "are excellent and poor at the same time—excellent because it means most people take care, poor because it means an inbreeding of the spirit, too much held in, regret and silent brooding, a world whose inhabitants walk in trepidation, in fear of opening up."

In the island goldfish bowl, you cannot hide. This ease of sustaining an establishment consensus and suppressing troublemakers makes islands especially hospitable to offshore finance, reassuring international finance that they can be trusted not to allow democratic politics to interfere in the business of making money. In the British tax haven of Jersey, three local sayings encapsulate the constant social pressure: "Don't hang your dirty linen out in public," "Don't rock the boat," and "If you don't like it, there's always a boat in the morning."

This groupthink does not originate with the island havens, which are just fortified nodes in bigger global power networks led by Britain and other large powers. But they have, with their intolerant environments, come to host and protect cultural concentrations of antigovernment, kick-the-poor attitudes that originate elsewhere. In the absence of reliable dissent, these attitudes have flourished, unchecked.

John Christensen, Jersey's former economic adviser who turned dissident, describes encountering extremist right-wing offshore attitudes when he returned to his native island in 1986 after working overseas as a development economist.

In this year of the City of London's "Big Bang" of financial deregulation, he found a tax haven amid a spectacular boom. Old town houses, tourist gift shops, and merchant stores in Jersey's beautiful capital St. Helier were being knocked down and replaced by banks, office blocks, car parks, and wine bars. An employment agency told him he could have any job he wanted; he had three offers the next day. He began employment with an accounting company, working with over 150 private clients.

The firm practiced reinvoicing: the practice I described earlier, where trading partners agree on a price for a trade but record it officially at a different price to shift money secretly across borders. Global Financial Integrity, in Washington, D.C., estimates that about $100 billion is drained from developing countries each year just from reinvoicing—about as much as all foreign aid from the rich world to the poor. It is just one part of a much larger picture of outflows of capital. "This was about capital flight . . . shifting capital out, and evading tax: the really nasty stuff," Christensen said. "I saw this stuff coming in daily." The accountancy firm provided a fax number, headed notepaper, a bank account, and a veneer of exceedingly British solidity and respectability.

Christensen worked there for 20 months, mostly handling clients based in South Africa (where much of the work involved evading antiapartheid sanctions), Nigeria, Kenya, Uganda, and Iran. Working undercover, he systematically combed through hundreds of client files and gradually put pieces together. He learned that a very senior right-wing French politician was using his political influence to secure planning permission on behalf of developers with whom he was involved, in a series of property deals. The Jersey link meant nobody in France could find out what he was up to. "You don't get that information from a cursory look at the file," he said. "I got hold of this guy's name by talking to an office in France: they told me 'I'll have to speak to the Senator about that.' If you work there long enough, they get to know you, and get comfortable telling you things. The market rigging, the insider trading: I was sitting there thinking, 'Holy shit—this is dynamite.' These were very prominent families; this would be on the front pages if it got out."

But even today Christensen, like Krall, won't tell tales about the particular secrets he encountered, having signed oaths and contracts for life. "If I transgressed those I could be thrown into a pit forever."

Reinvoicing is just one more workaday business sector in the world of offshore finance, and his firm and colleagues saw it as good business practice. "They rationalized it in all sorts of ways: foreigners were protecting their money from political risk or unstable currencies. People in Africa are poor because they don't work hard enough or they are corrupt; countries are poor so we send them aid money. That kind of thing. They didn't want to think about economic systems."

He moved through various jobs, and each time he expressed unease about the origins of some of the money, much of it from Africa, he was brushed aside. One Friday, ahead of the habitual office binge-drinking session, his section supervisor told him she didn't want to discuss these things and didn't "give a shit about Africa anyway." Her attitude, Christensen said, was typical. "Profitability was sky-high, and nobody made the connection between their actions and criminality and injustice elsewhere. None of the financial intermediaries involved—banks, law firms, accountants, and auditors—bothered to report or even question illicit transfers."

He met an old childhood acquaintance, now a chartered accountant, drunk in a pub, and told him all about his recent experiences in India and Malaysia. "No interest. He was in a bubble: last night's party, which car I was driving, who's screwing whom—that was it. I can't tell you how much of a shock it was to come back. There were really extreme views I was picking up on in Jersey: deep racism; sexism; the repressive feel; the awful in-your-face and aggressive consumerism I'd never seen before—and an almost fanatical hatred of any progressive ideas."

Progressive legislation takes years to seep to Jersey from outside. Britain abolished its antisodomy laws in 1967, but Jersey only repealed its law, under subtle pressure from an embarrassed Britain, in 1990. "There was this 'don't speak out' mentality," Christensen said. "In London, all my mates had taken antiracism, and stuff like that, as normal. Back in Jersey, I got, 'You *don't* do that here, sonny.'"

He turned up at a cocktail party on a motorcycle and was assailed by a guest, a senior Jersey business figure, who said his crash helmet was an infringement on his liberty. "He was anti-seatbelts, anti-tax, and anti-government. He would say apartheid was good for black South Africans; that we should reestablish colonialism; that 'these people' had been much better off under white governments." Christensen clashed with Sir Julian Hodge, a pillar of the Jersey banking establishment: "a mega-apologist for apartheid; a mega-pusher for empire; a libertarian beyond anything I've met." He remembers a stand-up row at a public meeting with the Reverend Peter Manton, a Jersey senator and Anglican minister who had also said publicly that "the blacks" in South Africa were better off under apartheid than anywhere else (Manton was subsequently prosecuted for sex offenses and later died).

Offshore can feel like an adolescent fantasy of the world, where white men sort things out over Scotch whisky and see the rest of the world as a consumable resource. At a government committee meeting exploring sexual discrimination and equal opportunities for women, Christensen remembers a senior politician made a show of falling asleep and snoring. Another politician, who ran his own business, went further. "He said, 'If any of my girls got pregnant I would sack them immediately: nobody wants to see a pregnant girl behind the desk.' That is how he referred to all women—girls."

"The ruling classes realize they don't need to worry about the Democrats coming to power in the U.S., or Social Democrats coming to power in Germany, or Labour coming to power in Britain," Christensen continued. "They realized they didn't need to fight the fight at home: they already had this flotsam and jetsam of the empire strewn across the globe, with their red post boxes and British ways of life, and incredible subservience to the English ruling class. In Jersey I was amazed by how fawning the local politicians were to outsiders with money. There was this idea, 'We can take over our own little places, and the locals will be grateful to us. The checks and balances aren't there; the press isn't there; and they resent interference from outsiders.' Happy Days: Wall Street and the City gentlemen had found a way around the threat of democracy."

Offshore attitudes are characterized by amazing similarities of argument, of approach, and of method, and some striking psychological affinities, in a geographically diverse but like-minded global cultural community of offshore. A peculiar mixture of characters populates this world: castle-owning members of old continental European aristocracies, fanatical supporters of the American libertarian writer Ayn Rand, members of the world's intelligence services, global criminal networks, assorted lords and ladies, and bankers galore. The bugbears for this zone are government, laws, and taxes, and its slogan is "freedom"—at least for wealthy elites.

And these attitudes fit seamlessly with another characteristic of small jurisdictions: collective inferiority complexes where residents see themselves as plucky defenders of local interests against the predations of big, bullying neighbors. From this worldview of mistrustful self-regard, it is but a short step to a libertarian, leave-us-alone worldview that sees any self-advancement at the expense of outsiders as valiant resistance against tyranny. This worldview, of course, dovetails closely with offshore's ethical framework, which holds the rights of citizens and governments elsewhere to be inconsequential, which sees democracy as a "tyranny of the masses," and holds the very idea of society with disregard, even contempt. Providing facilities for foreign tax evasion clearly fits this framework, as does a general hatred of tax.

This concentration of extremist attitudes in Jersey was self-reinforcing, as Christensen explains. "Most liberal people like myself left," he said. My socially liberal friends from school, almost all of them left Jersey to go to university, and almost all of them didn't go back. I can't tell you how dark it felt. I have never been a depressed person but I went into a big one there. Everything I valued seemed of no significance. There was no one I felt I could turn to."

He almost left but was persuaded to stay by an academic researcher who was putting together a new framework for understanding tax havens, and who persuaded him how important it was to understand the system from the inside. "I went undercover not to dish the dirt on individuals and companies, but because I couldn't understand it—and none of the academics I spoke to could either. There was no useful literature." He did not even tell his brother what he was doing and kept this cover for 12 years. He grew roots: He became president of the Jersey Film Society, raced high-speed catamarans, and started a family. He never made a secret of his distaste for the system, but his lighthearted capers, such as founding the island's first and only Jean-Claude Van Damme Appreciation Society, helped politicians to see him as a lightweight and therefore not a threat.

When he was appointed economic adviser in 1987, he began to feel the full force of what it means to stand out against an accepted, all-embracing consensus. Occasionally, he said, the pressure was so severe that he physically lost his voice. "Tension gets me around my neck. At times, in meetings . . . there were moments when I was literally choking with anger. It took real strength to stand up and say 'I'm sorry, I don't agree with this.' I felt like the little boy farting in church: I felt so lonely during those committee meetings; nobody ever supported me."

Many people who came to see him as economic adviser wanted him to join their Masonic lodge, and he frequently received the secret signal. "It was a finger twisted back on itself in a handshake," he said. "These were mainly people I knew vaguely, who would come into my office: 'Blah blah,' general talk, then quite openly: 'Are you interested in joining this lodge?' I always said I would consider it, and I never did. The type of people doing this were bankers, senior merchants, and senior politicians. You don't look at people's hands: you feel a lump there when you shake. For me it felt slightly dirty—covert, as if we were all part of some dirty deal; a schoolboy thing."

"Their thinking is very much of the Old Boy network—you are either one of us, or you are against us," he continued. "It means they can trust you to do the right thing without having to be told—an insidious meaning of the word *trust*." He was labeled untrustworthy and was frequently called "Not One of Us." The media was captured. The dominant newspaper in Jersey was owned for many years until 2005 by a company chaired by Senator Frank Walker, head of the powerful Jersey Finance and Eco-nomics Committee and one of the most vociferous cheerleaders for Jersey's finance industry. As a *Financial Times* editorial said in 1998, "That is akin to [UK Chancellor] Gordon Brown or [Germany's finance minister] Oskar Lafontaine owning all their country's national newspapers. Few on Jersey see it as odd."[4] Walker left the newspa-per in 2005, and it does carry dissenting views and plenty of decent reporting. Yet its overall editorial tone and content staunchly favor the tax haven industry.

Patrick Muirhead, an experienced former BBC radio journalist who spent time as the anchorman of Jersey's nightly ITV news until 2004, described the atmosphere.

"In an island of 90,000 souls, one is only removed from another by the smallest step of separation," he said. "My co-host's home became a popular salon for politicians and decision-makers. In such an atmosphere of closeness, any meaningful challenge becomes impossible. 'You rub people up the wrong way,' she said, primly dismissing my methods. After I left, my integrity, professional ability and popularity were trashed by a hostile and defensive Jersey media and island population."[5]

Unaccountable elites are always irresponsible, and I got my own taste of Jersey's moldy governance on the very first day of a visit in March 2009, when I bought the *Jersey Evening Post* and read its front-page story, entitled "States in Shambles."

"The States resembled a school playground yesterday as foul language and per-sonal insults flew across the chamber," read the text. Senator Stuart Syvret, a popular but controversial local politician, had complained publicly in the States assembly, Jer-sey's parliament, that the health minister was whispering in his ear. Syvret, the news-paper reported, "stood up and said: 'On a point of order, I am sorry to interrupt the minister. But the minister to my right, Senator Perchard, is saying in my ear "you are full of f*****g s**t, why don't you go and top yourself, you bastard." Senator Perchard immediately responded by saying: 'I absolutely refute that. I am just fed up with this man making allegations.' The BBC, which was broadcasting the sitting live, had to apologise for the language."

Syvret has been a regular victim of efforts to suppress dissent. "Any anti-estab-lishment figure here is bugged," said Syvret.[6] "There is a climate of fear. Anyone who dares disagree is anti-Jersey, an enemy of Jersey. You are a traitor, disloyal. There is all this Stalinist propaganda." A few weeks after my visit, eight police officers arrested him and jailed him for seven hours while they ransacked his home and personal files, including his computer files. The next day Syvret's blog administrator told him someone had clumsily been trying to hack his passwords. His blog describing his incarceration summed up the atmosphere. "Come to Sunny Jersey. The North Korea of the English Channel!"

In October 2009, having been accused of leaking a police report about the conduct of a nurse, Syvret fled to London and claimed asylum in Britain. He returned in May 2010 to fight an election and was arrested at the airport. Not long afterward, he outlined his views about Jersey plainly.

"It is an utterly lawless jurisdiction. Jersey is an environment under the grip of a wholly criminal regime. So absolute—and absolutely corrupted—is all meaningful power in Jersey that the island possesses less scrutiny and fewer checks and balances than a Balkan state."[7]

Corruption could tarnish Jersey's international reputation. Skittish financiers dislike places that are chaotically corrupt, as do onshore regulators elsewhere. Secrecy jurisdictions steeped in sleaze confront this by putting on a strenuous theater of rectitude that involves repeatedly projecting the essential message that they are clean, well-regulated, transparent, and cooperative jurisdictions—burnished by carefully selected comments and praise from toothless offshore watchdogs like the IMF's Financial Action Task Force or the OECD.

It is hard to construct coherent intellectual justifications for hosting secretive offshore finance, so the usual technique is to engage the messenger, not the message. Attacks on dissidents mostly consist of mean-spirited little slurs and innuendoes: "This person is ignorant, motivated by envy, economically illiterate, unreliable, or mentally unbalanced; this person cannot be trusted." Geoff Southern, a dissident deputy, said he now tries to avoid pointing in public: Last time he did he appeared in the *Jersey Evening Post* in a stunningly Hitler-like pose. He and his friend, Senator Trevor Pitman, wearily describe being tarred with terms like "Destroyers of Jersey" or "The Enemy Within": They are accused in public of being driven by personal bitterness; hints are dropped about darker motives. When we spoke, both Southern and Pitman's wife, Shona, another deputy, were being prosecuted for helping elderly and disabled residents fill in requests to opt for postal votes, albeit in breach of an arcane electoral law. They were later found guilty and fined. The amorphous finance industry is, locals say, ultimately behind the attacks. "The finance industry is like an amoeba," said another Jersey politician, who declined to be identified. "You attack it, and it absorbs that, and attacks back. It is the parasite in the island. It has taken it over; it controls us and decides on everything that happens here."

John Heys, a tour guide at Jersey's world-famous Durrell Zoo, and his friend Maurice Merhet, a former printer and pig farmer, now retired, tell a similar story. "We live in a dictatorship," Heys said, jabbing his finger at the table. "This is not a democratic country. John Christensen is public enemy number one. We call them the Junta, and people are afraid to stand up against them." Heys showed me an email sent by a government minister to a dissident friend who had, in a cheeky Christmas message, pointed out the large sums stashed in secrecy in Jersey, amid global poverty. The minister responded—mistakes included:

> *Hi Traitor*
>
> *Please refrain from sending me your unsolicited garbage . . . I am surprised you still decide to live in this "tax haven" island.ifs its so bad why do you not leave to live somewhere else . . . good riddance I would say. . . . but perhaps NOT because you get a damm good living here no doubt perhaps funded by banks and your morgage lende r . . . in fact my family have lived in Jersey for several generations and I am so very proud of it but to listen to traiterous idiots like you makes me furious. .*
>
> *I would not have the nerve to wish you a happy christmas in fact I hope you continue to to live a miserable existence in your traiterous world*
>
> *Do not respond*

In tiny states everyone knows everyone else, and conflicts of interest and corruption are inevitable. There are no independent think tanks or universities; a small and vulnerable civil service; no clear division among the legislature, the judiciary, and the executive; and no second chamber to scrutinize the States Assembly's deliberations. When Christensen was Economic Advisor, the public could not attend committee meetings and there was no written record of parliamentary debates on major laws. These problems extend to the governance of the finance industry. In Jersey there are no credible and truly independent processes for internally scrutinizing or regulating offshore finance. A 2002 publication from the Association of Accountancy & Business Affairs, one of the most detailed academic analyses of Jersey's politics, puts it concisely. "Most Jersey politicians are in business," it said. "They lobby for business and promote business interests. They draft, refine and pass legislation. They have also sat on regulatory bodies, effectively acting as 'gatekeepers' adjudicating on complaints and malpractices. Politicians sit on the boards of the companies that they are supposed to regulate."[8]

Close relationships are inevitable in a small island, but it is precisely because of this that Jersey needs extra checks and more transparency, to weigh against the inbuilt tendency toward conflicts of interest. This is *especially* important when Jersey plays such a major role in international finance. This affects you and me.

Extreme economic inequalities are tolerated offshore—and often welcomed as incentives for the poor to work harder. It is an ethos memorably summarized by the economist J. K. Galbraith as "the 'horse and sparrow' theory of income distribution and tax: if you feed a horse enough oats, some will pass through to the road for the sparrows."[9]

This soak-the-poor attitude is a constant theme as Jersey seeks to stay ahead of other jurisdictions in its race to attract capital. In 2004 Jersey cut the corporation tax rate from 20 percent to zero, except for finance, which pays 10 percent. This tax cut blew a hole in the budget big enough to finance Jersey's entire benefits system, so they made hundreds of redundancies and introduced a tax on consumption, hitting the poor especially hard. Shona Pitman, a States deputy, calls this the "tax the poor to save the rich" approach.

Super-wealthy people and corporations can *actually negotiate* the tax rates they will pay. For most of the 1990s, wealthy people wanting to take residence sent their lawyers directly to Christensen's office to negotiate their rates. Jersey would insist on a minimum annual tax payment, and the millionaire or billionaire would then simply remit to Jersey the amount of money that, when calculated at Jersey's flat 20 percent tax rate, would reach this sum. Christensen's predecessors had settled on a £25–30,000 tax payment each time; Christensen raised this to £150,000—which meant remitting income of £750,000 each year to Jersey. If you had worldwide income of £10m, say, your effective tax rate would really be 1.5 percent. A similar principle applies to corporations. For a Jersey International Business Company, the top rate starts at 2 percent and falls from there depending on how much profit they plan to book in Jersey.[10]

"Jersey has the social structure of a Hilton hotel," explained Jerry Dorey, a Jersey senator. It contains "a collection of alienated individuals who are just here to make money."

At the time of writing, six of Jersey's ten ministers are multimillionaires. "This is a parliament of wealthy people," said the dissident Jersey deputy Geoff Southern. "I think there is still a resentment that peasants have got into power."

———————————

One winter night in 1996, toward the end of his time in Jersey, Christensen opened the books for a reporter from the *Wall Street Journal* who was investigating a fraud ring involving a Swiss bank operating out of Jersey that had been ripping off American investors and who posed some very precise questions. The story, entitled "Offshore Hazard: Isle of Jersey Proves Less Than a Haven to Currency Investors," ran on the *Journal*'s front page several months later.

Jersey's finance industry and politicians went into spasm: This was one of the first times Jersey's supposedly clean and well-regulated finance sector had been challenged in a serious global newspaper. The end of the article quoted a senior civil servant who, everyone in Jersey knew, was Christensen. He knew that in talking to the reporter, he was effectively resigning.

"From then on, they would have done anything to get rid of me. But I had tenure: The only way they could do it was to find me guilty of professional misconduct or in bed with a choirboy. The tension was incredible." He did not leave immediately: His second son was born the following month, and it took him some time to serve out a long notice period.

Now that he is a dissident, the barbs continue to fly across the English Channel. "Grapes come no sourer than those trodden by Mr. Christensen, who once worked in Jersey and was passed over for promotion," the *Jersey Evening Post* thundered later. "Ever since, he has worked unceasingly to undermine the Island that foolishly slighted him." A quote from Jersey, published in France's *Le Monde* newspaper in April 2009, called him a "traitor to the nation." He attacks Jersey, the whisper goes, because he was not promoted as chief adviser. Insiders in the Jersey establishment have confirmed that it is *semi-official policy* to attack him in exactly these terms.

Offshore thrives on narrow self-interest combined with a culture of collusion. Its defenders are neurotically quick to impute mean motives and a hidden agenda to their critics. But men angling for promotion do not usually speak freely with the *Wall Street Journal* as they raise their voices in dissent.

The offshore intolerance is not confined to small jurisdictions. Rudolf Elmer, a Swiss banker who worked for several banks in several offshore centers before becoming a whistle-blower on some of the corruption he had seen, felt the pressure in Switzerland, a country of 8 million people.

Not long after speaking out and returning to Switzerland, he began to notice two men following him to work. He saw them in the parking lot of his daughter's kindergarten, then outside his kitchen window. Then his wife was followed, and the men offered his daughter chocolates in the street. In 2005 he was imprisoned for thirty days, accused of violating Swiss bank secrecy. There has been no determination as to who might have been following him.

"I was bloody naive to think that Swiss justice was different," Elmer said. "I can see how they might control a population of eighty thousand people in the Isle of Man," he said. "But 8 million people? How can a minority in the banking world manipulate the opinion of an entire country? What is this? The Mafia? This is how it works. Jersey, the Cayman Islands, Switzerland: this whole bloody system is corrupt."[11]

Ruling class ideologies that for years were beyond the pale in the larger democracies have been allowed to grow offshore, without restraint. As offshore finance has grown increasingly influential in the global economy, rebounding back and reengineering the onshore economies in ever more significant ways, so its attitudes have flourished, gaining the strength and confidence to capture the perceptions and attitudes of public life. This offshore consensus is evident in the intransigent arrogance of bankers who, having nearly brought the world economy to its knees, ask for still more and continue to threaten to relocate elsewhere if they are regulated or taxed too much. It is visible in the demands of the super-rich, who have come to expect and demand tax rates below those of their office cleaners. It is visible in the actions of the Irish musician Bono, perhaps the world's most prominent poverty campaigner, who legally shifts his financial affairs offshore to the Netherlands to avoid tax and is still warmly welcomed in high society. The United States, the greatest democracy the world has known, is now in thrall to the worldviews of unaccountable, abusive, and often criminalized elites.

To a very substantial degree, indeed, we have offshore finance to thank for that.

10

RATCHET

How Secrecy Jurisdictions Helped
Cause the Latest Financial Crisis

THE PRACTICE OF *USURY*, OR THE LENDING OF MONEY at excessive interest rates, has a nasty historical taint. The prophet Ezekiel included it with rape, murder, and robbery in a list of "abominable things." Plato and Aristotle called it immoral and unjust, and the books of Exodus, Deuteronomy, and Leviticus forbid it. In Dante's *Inferno*, "lewd usurers" sit in the seventh circle of hell, and the Koran states that "whoever goes back to usury will be an inhabitant of the Fire." When the ancient Greeks deregulated interest rates, indebted Athenians ended up being sold into slavery.

One can argue about the merits and evils of usury, but in a deregulated market the poor and vulnerable inevitably pay the most. Annualized rates of 400 percent or more are not uncommon.

Historically, the United States regulated lending rates carefully. In 1978, however, a new era began when the First National Bank of Omaha started enrolling Minnesota residents in its BankAmericard Plan. At the time, Nebraska let banks charge interest up to 18 percent a year, while Minnesota's usury limits were 12 percent. Minnesota's solicitor general wanted to stop the bank from charging higher interest rates. Could the Nebraska bank "export" the 18 percent rate to charge Minnesota residents?

The Supreme Court ruled that it could—and Wall Street noticed. If one state removed interest rate caps entirely, Wall Street could export this deregulation across the United States. Then in March 1980, South Dakota passed a statute eliminating its anti-usury interest rate caps entirely. The statute was, according to Nathan Hayward, a central player in this drama, "basically written by Citibank." A new opportunity for U.S. banks had opened up: By incorporating in South Dakota, they could roll out credit card operations across the country and charge interest rates as high as they liked.

Then came Delaware. The tale of its Financial Center Development Act of 1981 is a story about 10–15 powerful people who came together to pass an enormously significant piece of legislation, from which many of them, along with friends and colleagues, reaped huge wealth.[1]

David Swayze, a grizzled and affable lawyer who was chief of staff to Delaware's then governor, Pierre S. "Pete" du Pont, picks up the story.

"What Citibank did [in South Dakota] was not lost on the other money center banks," Swayze said. "They wanted some—but they didn't want to be in South Dakota. It's cold out there."

Hayward, who is du Pont's second cousin and was a du Pont cabinet member at the time, picks up the story. "Pete [du Pont] inherited a state that was in bad financial shape," he said. "There had been a continuous stream of red ink and the deficits were hidden with tricks and budget games." After being elected governor in 1976, du Pont had overseen an improvement in state finances, and he was a shoo-in for re-election. "We weren't on a cocaine high," said Hayward, "but we were beginning to feel pretty good."

In early June 1980, a group from Chase National Bank came to the venerable University & Whist Club in the state's commercial capital, Wilmington, to meet Delaware officials.[2] The link man was Henry Beckler, an ex-Chase banker at the Bank of Delaware, and he had already persuaded Chase to manage some of its foreign operations out of Delaware. "Henry Beckler's son and my son went together to school," said du Pont. "When you put a statute like this together you have to talk to the banks. He was very important, he asked them what things we should be putting in there."

Du Pont, who is reminiscent of an aging, if less handsome, Mitt Romney, comes from a family that has dominated Delaware politics for over a century, and he seems to have been a surprisingly passive player given his position. His memory of the episode was not so fresh, and he is clearly not a detail guy: Three or four times when asked to explain the episode he replied vaguely, ending by saying something like, "It was good. It was very good." When challenged about certain Delaware corporate forms offering ironclad secrecy, he offered no detailed rebuttal, just: "I don't think that's right. It all works nicely." But he did put his finger on one important element of the process: the small-town groupthink that let it happen. "One of the nice things about Delaware is that it's a small state," du Pont said. "We all have the same ideas."

Hayward says the aim of the June meeting was "to listen to New York bankers who were friends of the Delaware bankers who had helped us. They said, 'We'd love it if Delaware allowed market rate banking.'"

The Chase team wanted this rushed through in a few weeks, well ahead of the November 1980 gubernatorial elections. That was too tight. But what happened next was remarkable. Confirmed by several interviewees, by a 1981 *New York Times* investigation,[3] and by du Pont's official biography, it is a testament to the ability of elites in small offshore jurisdictions to create and sustain a consensus in their favor.

Frank Biondi, a powerful Democrat lawyer,[4] and Chuck Welch, du Pont's general counsel, went to see Hayward. "[They] said that the locker room on this was very small," Hayward remembers. "If the idea got out in public, the Democratic candidate for governor, a downstate farmer named Bill Gordy, is going to grab onto this and the Democrats in the House and Senate will make this a big campaign issue. We'll lose the battle before we even get suited up in our armor."

Du Pont was popular, and Republicans weren't that worried about the state election, but they did fret that if this story got out, it might affect the campaigns of other Republican candidates, including U.S. presidential nominee Ronald Reagan.

"Gordy was one of the unsung heroes of the whole story," Hayward continued, "a good old pig farmer. Frank [Biondi] and Chuck Welch got into a helicopter in Wilmington and went to see him and said, 'Bill, we want you to know what we're working on. We're here to ask you to keep your mouth shut and not make it an issue in the campaign.' Bill Gordy, God bless him, said yes."

The entire Democrat establishment in Delaware seems to have bought into the silence. And not just them. "If you go back and read the *News Journal*," said Hayward, "you will not find one mention of it in the press in the campaign season."[5] This proposal was circulating among Delaware's entire top business and political elite, including a couple of "populist" legislators who saw this—usury—as a threat to the basic consumer. "We had all these major bankers in Delaware through the whole summer," said Glenn Kenton, another key player, reeling off names like Citicorp's CEO Walter Wriston and Chase's president Tom LaBreque. "Nobody found out about it. It's just an amazing thing."

Still, inside this rarefied secret circle, a pushback did materialize. "The most significant counterforce, though not overt, was the local banks," said Swayze. "In the cold citadels of privilege there was a fear the big banks would run rings around them."

Wall Street began to apply pressure. Chase stiffened Delaware spines at a meeting at the Wilmington Club in June, threatening to pull up stakes for South Dakota.[6] "The banks would come down and say, 'Now if we come [and build these institutions], are you guys, meaning the government, you're not going to cut us off at the knees here?'" du Pont explained. He agreed to form an informal task force to look into Chase's plan and promised to reply by September.

In the end, Wall Street and Delaware's bankers settled on a compromise. To protect the local banks, they promised clauses to prohibit the outsiders from touting for local retail business. By mid-August the local banks were on board, and the task force turned to the legislative process. A special session of the legislative assembly was called outside of normal procedures to insulate this from the democratic process. As the *Delaware Lawyer* explained it, the special session's purpose "was to prevent the proposal from becoming encumbered in the 'horse trading' that typically occurs in the regular session."

While bigger states saw laws regulating economic activity as complex moral, political, and economic issues, Delaware was seeing them instead through an offshore lens: as pieces of sovereignty that could be sold to make locals rich.

Chase had opted for Delaware, not South Dakota, partly because it did not want to be following in Citicorp's slipstream. "Chase said, 'We're not going to the same place Citicorp is going,'" Kenton remembered. Citicorp, he added, had said we're "only out in South Dakota because we had to go someplace. But if you are going to open up, count us in too."

As Wall Street interest grew, Delaware kept brainstorming for still more business. Biondi suggested talking to JP Morgan, where he had some connections: It did not issue credit cards, but Delaware hoped to find other business. "We went up to see Morgan and we said, 'What do you want?'" Kenton explained. "And they said, 'We're just getting the heck taxed out of us up here and we need to have a low-tax environment.'" So Delaware served up the offshore classic of a regressive state tax structure: the richer you are, the lower your tax rate. They set the bank franchise tax at about 8 percent on income under $20 million, then 6 percent on $20–25 million, and so on, until the really big incomes got away with just 1.7 percent. The goal, as Swayze put it, was "sheltering the indigenous banking community against competitive threats on the one hand, and attracting and growing the business of newly created Delaware bank subsidiaries of non-Delaware bank holding companies on the other."[7] As for the lost tax dollars from the banking behemoths—well, American taxpayers elsewhere could pick up the tab for *that*.

Biondi's firm Morris, Nicholas, Arsht & Tunnell represented both Chase and JP Morgan, and both he and his firm are frank about their role in the local bonanza. "The Chase Manhattan and J. P. Morgan banks hired Morris, Nicholas's Frank Biondi to draft the law," the firm's official history notes, "and help convince the state legislature to adopt it."[8]

Biondi himself adds, "Did I lobby the state legislature? You're damn right I did."

So Chase and JP Morgan, in effect, wrote the law through their local representatives. The *New York Times* noted later that it was drafted without any written analysis by a Delaware official, and that Biondi's drafts got their primary reviews from other bank attorneys.[9] Biondi denies any conflict of interest, saying he disclosed his connections to all parties.

On November 4, 1980, du Pont was reelected as governor of Delaware, and the draft legislation was unveiled in public two months later, on January 14. Du Pont's administration gave the state general assembly the deadline the banks demanded: pass the bill by February 4 or the deal was off.[10]

The bill sailed through on February 3, and du Pont signed the Delaware Financial Center Development Act two weeks later.

Delaware was to remove interest rate ceilings on credit cards, personal loans, car loans, and more. Banks would have powers to foreclose on people's homes if they defaulted on credit card debts; they could establish places of business overseas or offshore, and they got a regressive state tax structure to boot. And crucially, because Delaware law could now be "exported" to other states, this was to be rolled out across America.

Two hundred years of legislation capping interest rates in the United States had now lost all force.[11]

Despite the timing—the bill was passed less than a week before Ronald Reagan took office as U.S. president—all interviewees stressed that this came purely from

Delaware and the New York bankers, not from Washington. "Lawmakers quickly realized," wrote du Pont's biographer, "that the Financial Center Development Act was favored by almost everybody in the state's power structure—and by the powers most likely to contribute significantly to their future election campaigns."[12]

Out-of-state banks flooded into Delaware, and the credit card industry took off. Within months the credit card giant MBNA had opened its first office in a vacant supermarket; within a decade it had over $80 billion in outstanding credit card debt. "Every night helicopters took off from here carrying receipts and paperwork from all the credit card business," said du Pont. "It gave us 25 years of growth and revenues growing every year." Before 1980, Delaware's revenue just from the bank franchise tax had trickled in at just $3 million–odd per year. By 2007 it was taking $175 million.[13]

Just as Ronald Reagan prepared his assault on America's unions, American workers began to trade their union cards for credit cards.

Two months after the bill's passage, the New York Times summed up.[14] "To bankers and their supporters the law is modern and comprehensive, drafted in a thoughtful manner. To some state officials, legislators and consumer advocates, both in Delaware and elsewhere, the bill was stampeded through the Delaware Legislature, is one-sided and, as one critic put it, a banker's 'dream.'"

"Bankers say the possibility that the Delaware plan could be enacted in other states is a sign of healthy competition among the states and a reflection of the current emphasis on states' rights," continued the article. "Their critics say it illustrates the ability of powerful private interests to pass laws with national ramifications by singling out and exploiting the weakest and most malleable states."

The same Times article noticed something else. "Many legislators say they did not read the 61-page bill before agreeing to sponsor it and did not understand the complicated measure before voting on it." Harris B. McDowell, the majority whip for the Democrat-controlled Senate, said he was told at the last minute. "I confess I have no expertise in the banking area," he said. "I am mystified by the bill." He voted for it on a promise that it would create jobs. Others said the only hearing for the bill, which lasted just three hours, was handled and timed in ways that prevented many legislators from attending and inhibited rebuttal. Delaware's Consumer Affairs Department never saw the bill before its passage, a deliberate exclusion that Kenton defended by saying that he and du Pont shared the "bias" that "banks should charge what they want in fees."

"I didn't see any sense in running that fundamental principle by anybody who doesn't agree with it," he added.

This pattern will be familiar to offshore legislators worldwide. In Delaware, bankers had found a small and malleable legislature, used special legislative tricks to stymie bothersome objectors from other stakeholders, worked hard to keep objectors in the dark, reassured bamboozled legislators that all would be well, and created "ring-fences" giving special exemptions to outsiders that were not available to locals.

Most important was this typically offshore feature that made all these things possible. "It's small, you can get the leadership together because of that," Biondi said. "The leadership was accessible at the governor's office but also in the legislature and in the business community." Du Pont made exactly the same point. "I used to say to them, if you've got a problem, you come on in and around this one table, we can put together all the people we need to solve your problem, whatever it may turn out to be. And we'll talk about it. We're small enough. We can move fast. We can get things done."[15] Swayze agreed and added a detail. "There were significant forces in the New York legislature opposed to this," he said. "Delaware took advantage of the fact that New York couldn't turn the dreadnought around in the harbor. We're small, we take advantage of opportunities, and we can fill that void."[16]

In other words, we can give the bankers what they need, faster than anyone else. Delaware is a legislature for hire.

Once Delaware fell, the banks then wielded it as a crowbar against other states. Thomas Shriver of the Pennsylvania Bankers Association warned that Delaware is "a very viable option if the Pennsylvania Legislature doesn't enact a bill we have proposed." Robert Erwin, head of Maryland's consumer protection division, warned that if other states gave in to the "pressure" from Delaware, "then it becomes a game of Russian roulette among the 50 states, trying to outdo themselves."

With interest rates caps removed, the credit card industry took off, and Americans splurged on debt. By mid-2007, as the global financial crisis emerged, U.S. consumers owed nearly $1 trillion on their credit cards[17]—and that is not to mention loans people took out against their homes to pay the credit card bills. Not a single one of those interviewed for this book who were involved in the passage of the Financial Center Development Act showed any signs of doubt that it was a very good thing.

The respected liberal lawyer Thomas Geoghegan points to the significance of this episode.[18] "Some people still think our financial collapse was the result of a technical glitch—a failure, say, to regulate derivatives or hedge funds," he wrote. "No, the deregulation that led to our Time of Troubles was of a deeper, darker kind. The problem was not that we 'deregulated the New Deal' but that we deregulated a much older, even ancient, set of laws . . . the laws against usury, which had existed in some form in every civilization from the time of the Babylonian Empire to the end of Jimmy Carter's term, and which had been so taken for granted that no one ever even mentioned it to us in law school. That's when we found out what happens when an advanced industrial economy tries to function with no cap at all on interest rates."

This probably overstates the case: There is no single explanation for the latest crisis. Still, Geoghegan has identified an important contributing factor. The elimination of usury caps spilled out into a wide variety of financial fields.

Credit card debt, money market funds, and numerous other instruments that fueled the borrowing binge and the crisis—the removal of interest rate caps—had effects that are incalculable.

Having helped deregulate and boost the supply of debt, Delaware also set about getting a share of the demand side. It did this by setting itself up as a major player in the securitization industry—the business of parceling up mortgages and other loans, including on credit cards, and repackaging the debt and selling it on. Once again, Delaware did this simply by establishing the exact legal framework that corporations demanded.

The Delaware Financial Center Development Act of 1981 itself contained a section eliminating "affiliated finance companies" from all state taxes. These act like banks but aren't formally banks, so they fall outside banking regulations. Along with structured investment vehicles and their like, these are a core part of the global "shadow banking system"[19] that dragged the world into economic crisis from 2007. These companies were especially prominent in the United States, notably in Delaware. In 1983 a new International Banking Development Act got Delaware into the new offshore game of international banking facilities. When that was enacted, Chase and several other banks promptly moved foreign offshore activities to Delaware.

Biondi outlines several other statutes that followed and his role in them. "I wrote those bills with my boys here," he said. The 1986 Foreign Act Development built on the 1983 legislation designed to let foreign banks take advantage of Delaware's regressive bank franchise taxes. New tax legislation in 1987 enticed banks that wanted to get into dealing securities. "My staff and I wrote it," Biondi explained. "We represented Morgan, Chase, Citicorp, Bank of New York, and Bankers Trust." Biondi's team also wrote the Bank and Trust Company Insurance Powers Act of 1989, authorizing banks to sell and underwrite insurance.[20] The Delaware Statutory Trust Act of 1988, giving huge flexibility to people setting up such trusts, and "the protection of trust assets from creditors," made Delaware the top jurisdiction for setting up so-called Balance Sheet CDOs, which allowed banks to offload their assets onto other investors and were another important contributor to the crisis.[21] A new act in January 2000 allowed Limited Liability Partnerships: a major contributor to the degradation of corporate governance, which I will soon explore in detail. There was also the Asset-Backed Securities Facilitation Act of 2002, which further opened the securitization spigots.

All these helped Delaware become, as one expert put it, "The Jurisdiction of Choice in Securitisation."[22]

Even more broadly, Delaware has played a central role in transforming global banking from its traditional fare of funneling savings into productive investments toward more speculative, risky, fee-based banking models. "Delaware recognized the quantum shift in the financial services industry toward fee based activities," said Swayze, "and it provided the legislative and regulatory framework to accommodate that shift."[23]

Now here is the big point. I do not claim that this story constitutes an explosive new revelation about the ultimate causes of the latest mortgage and financial disasters. This was just one among the many tangled roots of the crisis—though an important one. My point is to show just what a tax haven is: a state captured by financial interests from elsewhere. Mark Twain said that history does not repeat itself—but it rhymes. My next story, from thousands of miles across the Atlantic Ocean in the British tax haven of Jersey, rhymes almost perfectly with this tale from Delaware.

In June 1995 the director of Jersey's Financial Services Department met with a partner in Mourant du Feu & Jeune, a member of the so-called "Offshore Magic Circle," made up of the ten or so law firms most active offshore. They discussed a corporate form known as the Limited Liability Partnership (LLP).

A letter then began to circulate in Jersey political circles, dated October 9, 1995.

"My firm has been working with the UK partnership of Price Waterhouse (PW) and English solicitors, Slaughter and May, to find a method of obtaining some limited liability protection for the partners' personal assets without completely restructuring PW's business and losing the cultural benefits of a partnership," the letter said. After surveying several jurisdictions, it continued, Jersey was deemed the most suitable. "We are therefore seeking support of your Committee for the introduction of a Special Limited Partnership Law in Jersey during 1996."

In short, the private firms wanted to write a new law for Jersey. In fact, a draft law had already been prepared in London.

The letter urged Jersey's powerful Finance and Economics Committee to consider the law by December, then have it debated in the States Assembly the following January or February. "We would also propose that we would prepare any necessary subordinate legislation required in connection with the Special Limited Partnership Law. We appreciate that this is a very short time scale."

"It would be very important for PW and I believe, Jersey's finance industry, that the correct messages are sent to the media," the letter continued, proposing that Jersey's PR firm Shandwicks and Price Waterhouse's media team get straight to work.

The Big Four accounting firms—PricewaterhouseCoopers (PWC), Ernst & Young, KPMG, and Deloitte Touche—are giants: PWC employed over 146,000 people and generated $28 billion in revenues in 2008, making it the world's largest professional services firm. Auditors also occupy a very special place in the global economy. Their audits are the main tools by which societies know about, and regulate, the world's biggest corporations: In a sense, they are the private police forces of capitalism.[24] Audit failures lie behind most great corporate scandals: Enron, WorldCom, and most of the collapses related to the latest financial crisis. Because of the extreme dangers bad audits pose to corporate capitalism in general, and to you and me in particular, governments try to regulate this profession with extra care.

Since the middle of the nineteenth century, limited liability has been part of a grand bargain at the heart of corporate governance. If a limited liability company goes bust, owners and shareholders may lose the money they invested, but their losses (or liabilities) are limited to that: They are not liable for additional debts the corporation has racked up. This concept was controversial when it was first introduced: It was feared that it would erode standards of accountability, but it was justified on the grounds that these investor protections would encourage people to invest and boost economic activity. But there was a caveat: In exchange for the gift of limited liability, corporations must agree to have their accounts properly audited, and have these audits published, to open a true and fair window into what they were up to. It was an early-warning system to keep the risks manageable.

By contrast, a general *partnership* is very different from a limited liability company. Investors in a partnership are experienced professionals who should know what they are doing, and they have *un*limited liability. When things go wrong they are personally liable for all losses: Creditors can theoretically take even the shirts off the partners' backs. Since they have given up the right to shift losses onto the rest of society, partners are held to less stringent standards of disclosure. Partners were also subjected to "joint and several" liability, in which a partner is liable not only for his or her own mistakes but also for the mistakes of others in the partnership.[25] All this helps focus auditors' minds on doing their job properly—and to police their colleagues too.

Konrad Hummler, the managing partner of an unlimited liability company, Wegelin Private Bank, in Switzerland, explains what it is like to operate under such rules.[26]

"Partners who have [joint and several] unlimited liability have a solidarity; the dynamic within the group is totally different," Hummler said. "On so many boards— and I have quite some experience of this—one doesn't dare to ask the right questions. This [unlimited liability] is the only way of doing business where you dare to ask the really difficult questions—mostly the simplest questions. I will say, 'Listen, Mr. Chairman, I still don't understand the case.' The chairman will say, 'You obviously haven't read your papers properly.' At this point I don't stop the discussion, but I say again, 'Mr Chairman I still don't understand this bloody thing.' That's the difference. Because of your unlimited liability, you think twice."

Joint and several unlimited liability for partners in audit firms is clearly, given their special role in policing modern capitalism, a very good idea.

What was being proposed in Jersey, however, was different again: a law allowing *limited liability partnerships* (or LLPs.) An LLP for accountancy firms is an example of having your cake and eating it: An LLP partner not only gets the benefits of being in a partnership—less disclosure, lower taxes, and weaker regulation—but it gets the limited liability protection too. And if a partner commits wrongdoing or is negligent, other partners who are not involved aren't accountable for the consequences. This law was the product of what Professor Prem Sikka, of Essex University, calls auditors' ultimate aim "to use the state to shield it from the consequences of its own failures."[27] For those involved, it is the best of all worlds. For the rest of society, it is the worst of all worlds.

The draft Jersey LLP Act was worse still. LLPs would not need to have their own accounts audited or even to say on their invoices or letterheads that they were registered in Jersey. It had no provisions for regulating audit firms or investigating misdemeanors, and it offered other audit stakeholders—that is, the public—almost no rights. To get these astonishingly generous concessions from the public at large, these multibillion-dollar global corporations would have to pay a one-time fee of just ten thousand pounds at first, then five thousand pounds a year afterward.

As with the liberalization of usury provisions in Delaware, the Jersey proposal was a delayed reaction to the ideological revolution associated with Ronald Reagan and Margaret Thatcher: a shift away from the view that competitive markets need robust regulation to a childlike faith in self-regulation by market actors.

Big accountancy firms had already gotten LLPs in the United States after first influencing the Texas legislature in 1991; within four years nearly half of U.S. states had it. These limited liability provisions "took away the most powerful incentive for self-policing by the corporate professions of law and accounting," wrote the tax expert David Cay Johnston, and "help explain the wave of corporate cheating that swept the country."[28] Already there was evidence from the United States that whenever these provisions are introduced, less time is allocated to each audit, and quality suffers. It is nearly impossible to provide a smoking gun in such cases, but these kinds of concessions were undoubtedly important factors in the Enron and WorldCom disasters and in the destruction of Enron's auditor, Arthur Andersen LLP.

In Britain, following high-profile audit failures such as BCCI, Polly Peck, and many others, auditors had already squeezed major concessions out of the government, having won the right in 1989 to be limited liability companies[29]—though few audit companies converted, since many did not want to have to publish their accounts. A British House of Lords decision in 1990 worsened matters, ruling that auditors owe no "duty of care" to any individual stakeholder injured by audit failures.

Still, the UK had been holding out against an LLP law and for once was doing the right thing. "The UK . . . wanted to tell the world, 'You can trust London,'" said Sikka, who researched the Jersey LLP affair. "If it is impossible to sue the auditors, that makes it harder to look clean." The accountants had other ideas. "I think the calculation was that if the UK fell, the rest of Europe would fall, and the former British Colonies would also fall into place. They thought: 'If the UK gets going, everything else is won.'"

The accountants' strategy was simple: find an easy-to-influence legislature off-shore, win LLP concessions there, then threaten to relocate there if the UK refused to create its own LLP law. First they approached the Isle of Man, then Guernsey, for an LLP law, but they were turned down. Then they came to Jersey, which is, as Jersey senator Stuart Syvret put it, "a legislature for hire."

A month after that initial letter, Price Waterhouse and Ernst & Young publicly announced the proposed Jersey LLP legislation. Senior Jersey politicians had assured them that the bill would be "nodded through," as one insider notes.

Not everybody was happy. Jersey's senior law draftsman complained that the new law was like "getting a completed crossword and being asked to write the clues." Syvret remembers first coming across the proposed law. "I knew bugger-all about accountancy, and suddenly it was on our desks and we had to debate it in two weeks," he remembers. He and Gary Matthews, one of the only other dissidents in the legislature to smell a rat, set about educating themselves about LLP laws. Matthews contacted a British parliamentarian, Austin Mitchell, who in turn called Sikka. They soon began to understand what this law meant. Matthews put it bluntly. "This law is poison."

Sikka remembers Matthews and Syvret first contacting him as they scrambled to get up to speed. "Gary Matthews said, 'They want to rush this through parliament and I don't understand a word—and other people I've spoken to don't understand it either.'" "I'd been there on holiday but had taken no interest in this funny little island, until that fateful call from Gary Matthews. The more we looked into it, the more rotten the place looked."

Matthews and Syvret were up against a well-resourced and motivated establishment on an island whose very political structure makes dissent extremely hard. Jersey has no political parties. The 53 members of the States (or government) are directly elected, but in three separate groups: 12 senators, 29 deputies, and 12 parish constables (known as connétables). Elections are staggered over time, so there has never been a general election or a change of government. There is no tradition of "government" versus "opposition" but instead a permanent regime that evolves over time.

This dramatically weakens opponents of an establishment consensus. "When bad men combine," the conservative thinker Edmund Burke wrote, "the good must associate; else they will fall, one by one, an unpitied sacrifice in a contemptible struggle." Without political parties, good men and women are isolated, then picked off.

"Democracy doesn't work here," said Geoff Southern, one of few dissident deputies in the Jersey assembly. "There are 53 Members, but nobody can stand up and say, 'Vote for us and we will do this as a bloc.' Instead, it's 'I am a good bloke— vote for me.' Manifestos are just candy floss."[30] Jersey politics is about personalities, not issues; without shared platforms States Assembly members tend to look after themselves rather than embrace common agendas more likely to reflect the public interest. "For the last two hundred years the establishment has cultivated the notion that party politics is wicked, divisive, and harmful," Southern said. "The media spreads it. If you did a survey, I expect two-thirds would say they think party politics is a bad idea. Propaganda is everywhere. The media here is like in Soviet Russia."

Voter turnout reflects the absence of local democracy. The 33 percent turnout in the November 2005 election would have put Jersey in 165th position of 173 countries in a world ranking: marginally better than Sudan and far below the 77 percent European average since 1945.[31] Poorer voters are especially disenfranchised, facing endless little hurdles that deter them from voting. Much of the Portuguese-origin working class subgroup that makes up nearly 10 percent of the population is unaware they even can vote, Southern said; voters must reregister every three years, and he has found dead people on his voters' rolls.

The connétables, by virtue of the parochial system through which they emerge, are intrinsically conservative and inexperienced, and make a powerful voting bloc— voting with the establishment every time. They tend to be small shopkeepers, farmers, guest house owners, and plumbers, and they get into major positions of power, and into the finance sector. When it comes to decisions on whether Jersey should adopt a global standard of banking regulation, they are unable to judge responsibly. A *Wall Street Journal* article in 1996 noticed, "Jersey is an island that until two decades ago lived off boat building, cod fishing, agriculture and tourism. It is run by a group who, although they form a social and political elite on Jersey, are mostly small-business owners and farmers who now find themselves overseeing an industry of global scope involving billions of dollars."[32] The article goes on to report the judgment of John Christensen, who was Jersey's economic adviser at the time: "By and large they are totally out of their depth."

Christensen remembers a legislature made up largely of small-town politicians with no understanding of the complex currents of international finance and who simply pass legislation through on the nod. "When I talked to the politicians on the Finance and Economics Committee," he said, "time and time again I talked about proposals coming forward. They said, 'I'm being honest John: I don't understand the detail, but I trust the lawyers and the bankers when they say it is necessary.'" The similarities with what members of the Delaware legislature were saying in 1980–81 are striking.

It is as if a vast global financial center had been tacked onto a couple of small-town parish councils in England or a smaller U.S. county. "They can argue at enormous length about the budget for the local pony club," said Christensen, "but a new limited liability law or a new trust law will go unchallenged. It's the captured state."

Syvret also noticed that Senator Reg Jeune, one of the most powerful politicians on the island and a major supporter of the LLP legislation, was simultaneously a consultant to Mourant du Feu & Jeune, the lawyers who had brought in the legislation in the first place: He had a direct financial interest in supporting it. "I thought, 'Whoa!' This is extraordinarily brazen," said Syvret. "When the States Assembly convened I stood up and said that Jeune has a conflict of interest—a financial interest. Jeune looked as though somebody had shot him. He staggered out of the chamber."[33]

Syvret came under ferocious pressure from the Jersey establishment to apologize. He declined, was pressed again, and refused again. Another top politician threatened him with "serious implications" if he did not recant, adding, "which is a pity, since you had such a lot to offer." The politician emphasized the word *had*, which Syvret took as a threat.

He stood his ground. "I just wasn't going to take that crap," he said. He was suspended from parliament, and in States Assembly deliberations in his absence he and Matthews were referred to as "The Enemy Within." Sikka, for his part, was called "Enemy of the State."

Senator John Rothwell, responding to Matthews's concerns, pointed to the Jersey establishment's approach to ethics. "The Island has done extremely well in projecting an image of low-profile respectability," he said, "but people in the finance industry, having heard speeches in the House about ethics of government, are getting rather twitchy about what members might embrace."[34] Rothwell, a public relations adviser by trade, knew exactly what he was saying. Oppose the LLP law and the financial services industries will see Jersey as unreliable—and the money will go elsewhere.

Matthews's and Syvret's robust challenges slowed the fast-track passage of the legislation but did not stop it: It was finally enacted in November.

In elections that year, well-financed candidates stood against Matthews under the banner "Don't Rock the Boat," and Matthews was vilified in public. He lost his seat and was unable to get a job afterward. He fled to England and his marriage fell apart. As Sikka put it, "They put that man through the mincer."

On the surface Jersey feels terribly British, and the island's rulers always say it is a well-regulated, transparent, and cooperative jurisdiction. The reality is shockingly different. It is a state whose leadership has essentially been captured by global finance and whose members will threaten and intimidate anyone who expresses dissenting views.

———————————

After the LLP law passed, the accounting firms next opened a new front in London. They publicly threatened to relocate to Jersey if the UK did not create its own LLP law.

Sikka fought to stop it. "We told the politicians, 'You can't concede this—these firms have held you to ransom,'" he said. He wrote in *The Times* of how harmful this legislation would be, and that the Jersey card was clearly a bluff. He noted that the big firms would never close up in London, sack their clients and staff, renegotiate contracts, and reopen in Jersey. "If the Government were to concede a liability cap to auditors, it would hardly be able to deny the same to producers of food, drink, medicine and cars. None of this would be welcomed by consumers."

The *Financial Times* saw the real agenda too. The accountants "want to keep the threat of moving 'off-shore' as a cosh with which to threaten the [UK] government if it fails to come up with a workable LLP law," it said.

But the accountants got most of the British financial press behind them, roundly criticized Sikka, and wielded the old favorite that Britain's government was "anti-business."

The campaign worked. Britain passed its LLP law in 2001. The accountants never did relocate to Jersey: They had simply used it as a crowbar. "It was the work that Ernst & Young and Price Waterhouse undertook with the Jersey government," an Ernst & Young partner crowed, "that first concentrated the mind of UK ministers. . . . I've no doubt whatsoever ourselves and Price Waterhouse drove it on to government's agenda because of the Jersey idea."[35]

As Sikka put it: "The Jersey sprat had served its purpose, now that the UK mackerel had been landed."[36]

The UK law was not quite as bad as the Jersey one—it involves more disclosure, for example—and perhaps Sikka's campaigning helped. Yet it still drastically diluted auditors' incentives to take care over their accounting. Ernst & Young became an LLP in 2001; KPMG went in May 2002; PricewaterhouseCoopers made the move in January 2003; Deloitte & Touche followed that August. A host of lawyers, architects, and others joined in, getting the tax perks and limited disclosure available to partnerships but with limited liability. Canada took on the LLP law in 1998; it has been followed by New Zealand, Australia, South Africa, Singapore, Japan, and India—to name a few. These different countries' LLP laws can only have contributed to the latest financial crisis. Had auditors faced getting personally into big trouble when they or their partners screwed up, they might not have been so hasty to sign off on all this off-balance-sheet financing.

The Jersey and Delaware episodes are stunningly similar despite happening fifteen years and an ocean apart and concerning entirely different subject matter. Deep truths about global finance are at work here. Robert Kirkby, technical director for Jersey Finance, described the generic process. "Someone comes up with a new idea but onshore regulation blocks it," he said. "You can lobby onshore but there are lots of stakeholders: you have to get past them all, and it takes a long time. In Jersey, you can bash this thing through fast. We got the leading edge years ago. We can change our company laws and our regulations so much faster than you can in, say, the UK, France or Germany." Talking in March 2009, in the depths of the financial crisis provoked by reckless deregulation, Kirkby lauded Jersey's new unregulated funds regime specializing in securitization—the pooling and repackaging of mortgages and other assets into securities to sell on to investors that has caused such mayhem.

Here in these deregulated offshore zones our democratic controls on finance and business are being hollowed out, year after year, around the world, out of sight.

I have no objection to deregulation in principle, as long as it is a process of genuine—and I mean genuine—democratic bargaining that considers the needs of all affected stakeholders, at home and overseas. What we have in Jersey and Delaware, by contrast, is rampant, *uncontrolled* deregulation, harnessed to the interests of a few insiders and large corporate players.

Just as European nobles used to consolidate their unaccountable powers in fortified castles, to better subjugate and extract tribute from the surrounding peasantry, so financial capital has coalesced in offshore's fortified nodes of unaccountable political and economic power, capturing local politics in these jurisdictions and turning them into fast and flexible private law-making machines, defended against outside interference and protected by establishment consensus and the suppression of dissent.

Offshore is not just a place, an idea, a way of doing things, or even a weapon for the finance industries. It is also a *process:* a race to the bottom where regulations—laws and trappings of democracy—are steadily degraded, as one arrangement ricochets from these fortified redoubts of finance to the next jurisdiction, and the offshore system pushes steadily, further, deeper, onshore. The tax havens have become the battering rams of financial deregulation.

Most people have not yet understood these deep truths about offshore, because of two related confusions.

The first stems from efforts to use technical criteria to define secrecy jurisdictions: tax rates, forms of secrecy, and so on. But these are just outcomes of the deeper truths. Our maps of offshore need to identify, first of all, these strongholds of financial power. A definition like my loose one—that secrecy jurisdictions are *places that seek to attract money by offering politically stable facilities to help people or entities get around the rules, laws, and regulations of jurisdictions elsewhere*—helps us see what we are looking for.

A second confusion is to think that this is about physical geography, when it is really about political jurisdiction and trust-based networks. The future that the offshore system promises has a distinctly medieval quality: In a world still nominally run by democratic nation-states, the offshore system is more like a network of guilds in the service of unaccountable and often criminal elites.

These stories of Delaware and Jersey should serve as a warning to larger economies about what happens when the offshore ethic isn't challenged.

––––––––––––

The Delaware story is one part of an explanation of how offshore contributed to the latest financial crisis, and the Jersey example helps explain why nobody saw it coming. Both of these jurisdictions got rich by eroding standards in the service of financial capital. The consequences are not just insidious but devastating.

In considering how the offshore system contributed to the financial and economic crisis, it's useful to look at the issue of debt. Why has so much debt built up in the world's richest economies? An article in the *Financial Times* in June 2009 ("Debt Is Capitalism's Dirty Little Secret") provides one answer. "The benefits of economic growth have gone into the pockets of plutocrats rather than the bulk of the population," the article reads. "So why has there been no revolution? Because there was a solution: debt. If you couldn't earn it, you could borrow it." As we have seen, the infrastructure was put in place to make this change happen. The tax havens were a big part of it.

As the 1990s progressed, occasional expert warnings about systemic, debt-related threats from offshore *did* emerge.

The IMF pointed squarely at the problem in 1999 when discussing the interbank market, where banks lend to each other. "A large part of the growth in OTC trading of derivative instruments may have involved offshore banks," the IMF said.[37] "The interbank nature of the offshore market implies that, in the event of financial distress, contagion is likely. . . . Offshore banks are likely to be highly leveraged, that is less solvent, than onshore banks." The report, which contains plenty more along these lines, frets especially about lax offshore regulation. It was a direct warning, long before the crisis struck.

That report followed soon after the implosion of the hedge fund Long Term Capital Management (LTCM), a classic slice-and-dice offshore structure that nearly destroyed the U.S. banking system in 1998 after the fund took on massive risks, covered by near-paranoid secrecy. LTCM's managers were in Greenwich, Connecticut; the hedge fund was incorporated in Delaware; and the fund it managed was in the Cayman Islands. Yet none of the agonized analyses that followed took any serious interest in the offshore angle.[38] And the pattern just keeps being repeated.

The latest financial crisis was incubated in the so-called "shadow banking system"—a vast, unregulated economic terrain containing all manner of Special Purpose Entities (SPEs, also known as shadow banks) that borrowed money to lend out again at a profit but fall outside normal bank regulation, partly by separating themselves legally from the regulated institutions that sponsor them, off their balance sheets.

The shadow banking system is not traditionally described as either an "offshore" or "onshore" phenomenon, but an in-depth 2008 study on SPEs by the Swiss-based Bank for International Settlements is very clear about where the dangerous shadow banks were mainly located.[39] "The most common jurisdictions for US securitisations are the Cayman Islands and the state of Delaware," the BIS said. "The most common SPE jurisdictions for European securitisations are Ireland, Luxembourg, Jersey, and the UK." Every last one is a major secrecy jurisdiction that used a simple business model: ask the financial institutions exactly what they need, then shape the laws accordingly and without democratic debate.

The BIS report calls Cayman "offshore" and Delaware "onshore."[40] It is exactly this misunderstanding—confusing physical geography with political geography—that has led to widespread claims that the secrecy jurisdictions had nothing to do with this gigantic mess. The Bank for International Settlements, along with every other major international financial institution, needs to understand what offshore is and how it works.

Among the only academic experts to have seriously examined offshore's role in the financial crisis is Jim Stewart, senior lecturer in finance at Trinity College, Dublin.

In reports in July 2008 Stewart investigated the Dublin International Financial Services Centre (IFSC), a secrecy jurisdiction set up in 1987 under the corrupt Irish politician Charles Haughey with help primarily from City of London interests.[41] A showcase for high-risk, Wild West financial capitalism, the Dublin IFSC emerged the year after London's giant deregulatory Big Bang and now hosts over half the world's top 50 financial institutions. It became a big player in the shadow banking system and now hosts eight thousand funds with $1.5 trillion in assets. Perhaps most alluring of all Dublin's lures, Stewart said, is its "light touch regulation."[42]

In June 2007 two Bear Stearns hedge funds incorporated in the Cayman Islands announced huge losses, presaging its collapse. Bear Stearns had two investment funds and six debt securities listed on the Irish Stock Exchange and operated three subsidiaries in the Dublin IFSC through a holding company, Bear Stearns Ireland Ltd., for which every dollar of equity financed $119 of gross assets—an exceedingly high and dangerous ratio.

The accounts of Bear Stearns Ireland Ltd. state that it was regulated by the Irish Financial Services Regulatory Authority, and EU directives state that the host country—Ireland, in this case—is responsible for regulation. Yet in an interview, the Irish regulator said he considered his remit to extend to "Irish banks": It was effectively regulated nowhere. The Irish regulator did not feature in any media analysis of Bear Stearns's insolvency; Stewart cited nineteen funds in difficulties in the crisis and added that "almost always, the IFSC link is not discussed."

Several German banks that got into trouble also had funds quoted in Dublin. These included IKB, which got €7.8 billion in German state aid; and Sachsen, which got €17.8 billion of emergency funding and €2.8 billion in state aid. "And yet none of the accounts or prospectus for any of the years examined mentioned regulation or the Irish regulator," Stewart reported. "Within Ireland the Financial Regulator has been quoted as saying that they have no responsibility for entities whose main business is raising and investing in funds based on subprime lending." The *Financial Times* analysis of the episode laid the blame almost entirely on the structure of the German banking system.

In Ireland, Stewart noted, if the relevant documents are provided to the regulator by 3 P.M., the fund will be authorized the next day. Yet a prospectus for a quoted instrument is a complex legal and financial document; a debt instrument issued by Sachsen Bank ran to 245 pages. The regulator could not have assessed it in the two hours between 3 P.M. and the normal close of business. In Luxembourg, Stewart noted, a new law stated that a fund can enjoy preauthorization approval if the fund manager "notifies" the regulator within a month of launch. It is the captured state, over again.

In April 2010 the U.S. Securities and Exchange Commission (SEC) opened a fraud probe into Goldman Sachs, alleging that it misled investors by misrepresenting the role of a CDO in a deal known as Abacus 2007-AC1. In July 2010 Goldman agreed to pay $550 million to settle the charge without admitting or denying the SEC's allegation. The deal's structure is notable[43]:

Issuer: ABACUS 2007-AC1, Ltd., Incorporated with limited liability in the
Cayman Islands.

Co-Issuer: ABACUS 2007-AC1, Inc., a corporation organized under the
laws of the state of Delaware.

McClatchy's, the only mainstream media organization to investigate the deal's offshore nature, found 148 such deals by Goldman Sachs in the Cayman Islands over a seven-year period.[44] In fact, every big Wall Street player used the Caymans for this business. These deals "became key links in a chain of exotic insurance-like bets called credit-default swaps that worsened the global economic collapse by enabling major financial institutions to take bigger and bigger risks without counting them on their balance sheets . . . sheltered by the Caymans' opaque regulatory apparatus."

It was not so much the Caymans' opacity that attracted these large players— though that helped—as its "flexibility." When tax haven supporters say they promote "efficiency" in global markets, this is the kind of thing they are talking about. At the heart of this efficiency is these jurisdictions' flexibility, which, as we have seen, is really about their political capture by financial capital. Whatever the banks want, they get. And from this flows power.

Rudolf Elmer, a senior accountant in a Swiss bank's Caymans office until 2003, takes the story further.[45]

Supervision in the Caymans was especially lax, he said. "Even if you have the right regulatory framework," he said, "you need the brainpower to audit the banks and companies. There is a general lack of this in the offshore world. You get a lot of high-risk issues running through the islands, being covered by junior auditors in CIMA [the Cayman Islands Monetary Authority]."

One of his office's functions was to take out cheap short-term loans and invest the proceeds in longer-term assets with higher rates of return. This is an easy way to make tax-free money—but it is dangerous too: You must "roll over" short-term loans every few days, replacing one loan with another. This is easy in the good times, but when lending dries up, as it did in 2007, you must still repay the short-term loans fast—but suddenly nobody will provide new loans to replace them. You can fall into default very quickly. This is exactly what brought down the British bank Northern

Rock in 2007. Yet the Caymans regulator, Elmer said, took an extremist laissez-faire approach to these so-called maturity mismatches. "This is a short-term and long-term problem," said Elmer. "From a regulatory point of view we couldn't have done that in the UK or Switzerland. The Cayman Islands Monetary Authority (CIMA) should have picked that up."

Elmer was involved in two CIMA audits. In the first one, he and his local CEO talked for an hour or so with a CIMA official. "The CIMA person said, 'Is it the same as it used to be?' The CEO said, 'Yes, it is the same.' The CIMA guy said, 'No problem.' The Cayman regulator knew our CEO well, and he knew he would tell him the truth. Personal relationships were key." A subsequent, later audit was more extensive and lasted about a week. "You have to be very experienced in that sort of thing," said Elmer. "Two junior auditors came in and made a lengthy report, which had little content. I went through those audits, and from a regulatory point of view, they were not sufficient at all." No further action was taken.

"It was quite crucial for [our] group to use Cayman and BVI vehicles," he said. "It boils down to three things: tax, regulatory, and legal advantages. You have a lot of freedom."

This extreme freedom, turning the secrecy jurisdictions into hothouses for risky new banking products, contributed massively to the crisis of the world's major economies.

————————————

The rise of debt in our economies has yet more offshore fathers. There is only space here briefly to sketch a few important ones.

In 2009 the IMF published a detailed report explaining how tax havens, combined with distortions in onshore tax systems, cranked up the global debt engine by encouraging firms to borrow rather than finance themselves out of equity.[46] These effects, it said, "are pervasive, often large—and hard to justify given the potential impact on financial stability." Amid all the noise from G20 leaders about tax havens in 2008 and 2009, the IMF concluded, this dangerous offshore aspect went entirely unnoticed.

The core principles the IMF outlined are simple. A corporation borrows money from offshore, then pays interest on that loan back to the offshore financing company. It then uses the old transfer pricing trick: the profits are offshore, where they avoid tax, and the costs (the interest payments) are onshore, where they are deducted against tax.

This simple trick is central to the business model of private equity companies. They will buy a company that someone has sweated for years to create, then load it up with debt, cutting the tax bill and magnifying the returns.

Leveraged buyouts—always involving offshore leverage—accelerated fast ahead of the crisis: The amount raised by private equity funds rose more than sixfold from 2003 to over $300 billion in 2007, by which time their share of all U.S. merger and ac-quisition activity had risen to 30 percent.[47] Reports praise private equity companies for excellent "value creation." Sometimes private equity companies do create real value. But this core feature of their business model is not value creation but value skimming. A big tax bill is slashed, the company's shares or value rise, managers' re-munerations become engorged, and wealth is shifted away from taxpayers to wealthy managers and stockholders. Nowhere in any of this did anyone produce a better or cheaper widget. And in the process, extra debt is injected into the financial system. Plenty of good firms have gone bust as a result of this offshore debt-loading, which the *New York Times* in 2009 described as "a Wall Street version of 'Flip This House.'"[48] More than half of the companies that defaulted on their debt that year were either pre-viously or currently owned by private equity firms.

A lot of innovation that corporations do—I'm talking about *useful* innova-tions to make better and cheaper goods and services, not the financial innovations that simply shift wealth upward and risks downward along the social scale— happen in small and medium enterprises. But the offshore system works directly against this.

First, it subsidizes multinationals by helping them cut their taxes and grow faster, making it harder for the innovative minnows to compete. And when small innovative firms do emerge they becomes targets for predators who seek to "unlock value" from "synergies" created by bringing the small firm into the bigger, more diversified one. Some synergies may be useful—economies of scale, for instance—but too often the predator can "unlock value" simply by being better at squeezing out these abusive, unproductive offshore tax privileges. Some make their best profits by seeking out and harvesting those small, genuinely innovative companies that haven't yet been abusive enough on offshore tax avoidance to "unlock" those abuses for themselves.

This harvesting then removes nimble, competitive, and innovative firms from the marketplace and relocates them inside large corporate bureaucracies, curbing competition and potentially raising prices. Debt rises, and ordinary people pay more tax, or see their schools and hospitals fall into disrepair. And if the predators leave their earnings offshore they can "defer" tax on them indefinitely. Deferred taxation is, as the accountant Richard Murphy puts it, "an interest-free loan from the government, with no repayment date." In other words, more debt.

Consider what happens when this multinational corporation is a bank. Like multinationals on steroids, banks have been particularly adept at going offshore to grow fast: by using it to escape tax, to dodge reserves requirements and other financial regulation, and to gear up their borrowings.

Banks achieved a staggering 16 percent annual return on equity between 1986 and 2006, according to Bank of England data,[49] and this offshore-enhanced growth means the banks are now big enough to hold us all ransom. Unless taxpayers give them what they want, financial calamity ensues. This is the "too big to fail" problem—courtesy of offshore.

But even that is *still* not all.

This one takes a little bit of explanation. Many blame the latest crisis not just on deregulation but also on global macroeconomic imbalances, as funds have flowed from countries with export surpluses, like China, India, Russia, and Saudi Arabia, and into deficit countries like the United States and Britain. This has led to overconsumption and borrowing in the deficit countries.

Now look at Global Financial Integrity's estimate that illicit financial flows out of developing countries has been running at up to a trillion dollars each year. Most has flowed out of large developing countries like China and Russia and Saudi Arabia and into large OECD countries like Britain and the United States. Illicit flows in the other direction are much smaller, so the net result is a flow worth hundreds of billions of dollars each year into rich economies and secrecy jurisdictions.[50] The illicit flows, which are unrecorded and hardly noticed, *add to* those recorded imbalances.

Let's look quickly at what happens on the ground. Imagine a Mexican company orders construction equipment from the United States and agrees to a price of $10 million. But the Mexican company asks for the commercial invoice to be drawn to read $12 million. The buyer does this because when he pays his $12 million, $2 million of that is secretly deposited into his Miami bank account. The missing $2 million is invisible to the numbers crunchers who compile the trade statistics—though it represents a very real illicit financial flow from Mexico to the United States—and it has tangible effects: It will push up U.S. house prices, distort the U.S. housing market, and boosts bank profits from their mortgage operations. First-time buyers find it harder to get on the property ladder, a housing bubble inflates further, and debt builds up in the economy.

As if all this were not enough, there is yet more.

Trust is a central ingredient in any economy. Where participants in a market don't trust each other, expensive litigation substitutes for honest behavior. And there is nothing—*nothing*—like the offshore system to generate opacity and erode trust and the behavioral constraint. When nobody can find out what a company's true financial position is until after the money has evaporated, trickery and bamboozlement abound. Financial markets seized up in 2007 because nobody knew, or trusted, what the other players in the market were doing, or what they were worth, or what or where their risks were. It is no coincidence that so many of those involved in great financial trickery, like Enron, or the empire of the fraudster Bernie Madoff, or Sir Allen Stanford's Stanford Bank, or Long Term Capital Management, or Lehman Brothers, or AIG, were so thoroughly entrenched offshore.

The secrecy jurisdictions specialize in bamboozlement. Along with the secrecy, and a curmudgeonly reluctance to co-operate with foreign jurisdictions, the offshore system provides endless incentives for corporations—especially financial ones—to festoon their affairs across jurisdictions, usually a complex mix of onshore and offshore, to fox the regulators. These giant impenetrable offshore trails, sliced, diced, and trailed around the world, increased the distance between the lenders and their borrowers until bankers no longer knew who their ultimate clients were. It is hardly a surprise that the Royal Bank of Scotland in 2003 offered a gold credit card with a ten-thousand-pound spending limit to a Monty Slater in Manchester, England. Monty Slater was a Shih Tzu dog.[51]

John Maynard Keynes summed up the problem well. "Remoteness between ownership and operation is an evil in the relations among men, likely or certain in the long run to set up strains and enmities which will bring to nought the financial calculation."

With this observation, Keynes exposed the flaw in the grand bargain at the heart of the globalization project. In giving freedom to finance, people in democratic nation-states lost their freedom to choose and implement the laws and rules that they wanted. But they handed these freedoms to the world's financiers in exchange for a promise: that the efficiency gains from those free financial flows will be so great as to make that loss of freedom worthwhile.

The tax havens helped bring this calculation to naught.

CONCLUSION
Reclaiming Our Culture

JOHN MAYNARD KEYNES'S OBSERVATION IN THE AFTERMATH of the Wall Street Crash, which I cited in chapter 3, is as apt today as it was when first articulated: "We have involved ourselves in a colossal muddle, having blundered in the control of a delicate machine, the working of which we do not understand." But the financial system is vastly more dangerous and pervasive now. Changes to domestic banking regulations matter but will never suffice. Reform must be based on a thorough grasp of the new, globalized reality—and anyone who wants to understand the modern financial machine must understand what tax havens are and how they work.

We must tackle the offshore system. I will point to ten major areas for change, in no particular order and as briefly as I can. All overlap with each other—and the last ties them all together.

First, we can **pursue transparency.** Many and varied changes are needed; here are two.

About 60 percent of world trade happens *inside* multinational corporations, which cut taxes by shuffling money between jurisdictions to create artificial paper trails that shift their profits into zero-tax havens and their costs into high-tax countries. The complexity and cost of this system cause great harm.

But these maneuverings are invisible in corporations' annual reports. Under current accounting rules corporations can scoop up all their results—profits, borrowings, tax payments, and so on—from several countries and consolidate each into one figure, perhaps broken down by region. So a corporation may publish its profits from, say, Africa, but nobody can unpick those numbers to work out the profits in each country. You can't find the information anywhere. *Trillions* of dollars' worth of cross-border flows simply disappear from view. So a citizen in a country where a multinational operates cannot tell from these reports even *whether* that corporation operates there, let alone what it does, its level of activity, its profits, its local employment, or its tax payments. As multinationals become ever more complex, this problem just gets worse.

One might think that the main global rule-setter for international accounting standards would be a public international body accountable to democratic governments. It is not. The International Accounting Standards Board (IASB) is a private company financed by the Big Four accountancy firms and global multinationals, headquartered in the City of London, and registered in Delaware.[1]

Richard Murphy, an accountant arguing for reform of international accounting standards, summarizes the problem as it stands. "A company gets its license to operate in any territory from the government that represents those people. It has a corporate duty to account in return. This is the essence of stewardship and accountability. Instead we have companies pretending they float above all these countries. They don't."

If multinationals had to break their financial information down by country and disclose what they do in each place, global markets would immediately become more transparent. A secret trove of information vital to citizens, investors, economists, and governments would come onshore and into view. *Country-by-country reporting,* as it is known, is already making progress in policymaking circles, particularly for the extractive industries.[2] It now needs major support and must be expanded to include *all* businesses—especially the banks.

Another essential step concerns how governments share information about the local incomes and assets of each others' citizens. If a person in one country owns an income-generating asset in another country, his or her tax authorities need to know about it. So governments need to share relevant information, subject to appropriate safeguards.

But the dominant standard for exchanging information is the OECD's "on request" standard: a cheats' charter whereby a country already has to know what it is looking for before it requests the information from another on a bilateral basis. Developing countries are particularly vulnerable here. The OECD's standard can be replaced by the far better alternative: *automatic* information exchange on a multilateral basis, where countries automatically tell each other what their respective taxpayers own and earn. Such a system exists in Europe: It works well and does not leak information (though major loopholes need plugging to defend against the Caymans trusts, Nevada corporations, Liechtenstein foundations, Austrian hidden Treuhands, and various other secrecy facilities that infest the offshore system). Momentum is just starting to build for change here[3]—and this can now be rolled out worldwide and vigorously supported. Sanctions and blacklists can spur the shift.

As a second major area for reform, we can prioritize the needs of **developing countries**.

The pattern always seems to be the same. A secrecy jurisdiction comes up with a new abusive offshore structure, and wealthy countries construct defenses against it as best they can. But poor countries, without the relevant expertise, are left wide open to the new drain. In February 2010 Misereor, a German development organization, researched the new information exchange agreements that had been signed between countries after world leaders promised to crack down on tax havens at a G20 meeting in Washington in 2008. Misereor found that just 6 percent of the tax treaties, and *zero* percent of the tax information exchange agreements, were signed with low-income countries. "While G20 and OECD are promoting DTTs and TIEAs as centre-pieces of a global standard on transparency and cooperation," Misereor concluded, "statistics show that poor developing countries are simply left out."[4]

Tax is the Cinderella in the debates about financing for development. Overshadowed for decades by its domineering sisters—aid and debt relief—tax is now, at last, starting to emerge from the shadows. Tax is the most sustainable, the most important, and the most beneficial form of finance for development. It makes rulers accountable to their citizens, not to donors, and the right kinds of taxes stimulate governments to create the strong institutions they need for getting their citizens and corporations to pay tax.

Three things can now happen. First, developing and middle-income countries can find a voice to articulate their concerns about this global system for transferring wealth from poor to rich and work together. A few countries like Brazil and India are beginning to construct serious offshore defenses, and the time is ripe for this to become a mass movement. Second, official development assistance in this area can rise dramatically: Less than one-thousandth of development aid is currently spent on helping countries improve their tax systems[5]—and much of that is spent on ideas that may make poverty worse, not better. Third, if citizens and civil society organizations were to stop focusing so exclusively on aid, in order to help revitalize the debates about tax and its role in fostering accountability, things can change. Aid can help—but with ten dollars being drained out of the developing world for every dollar going in, we need new approaches. If there were ever a movement that could unite the citizens of developing *and* wealthy countries in one cause, this is it.

––––––––––––––

The third big change to make is to **confront the British spiderweb,** the most important and most aggressive single element in the global offshore system.

The City of London Corporation—the offshore island floating partly free from Britain's people and its democratic system—must be abolished and submerged into a unified and fully democratic London. The City's international offshore spiderweb, the mechanism for harvesting and profiting from financial capital from around the globe, however dirty it may be, must be dismantled. It harms the people of Britain, and it harms the world at large. Britain is too thoroughly captured by the City and its offshore sector to do this alone: Pressure from outside is essential. Developing countries in particular need to appreciate how offshore is a somewhat imperial economic system, in which their own elites are deeply implicated. Alongside this new focus we need a greater understanding of the role of the United States as an offshore jurisdiction in its own right and the harm this causes, inside and outside the United States.

––––––––––––––

Onshore tax reform presents another arena where changes can be made. Endless possibilities exist, and I will focus on just two big, promising solutions that have been almost entirely overlooked.

The first is land value taxation.[6] This needs a very brief detour. A street musician who sets up his stall in the middle of the main street will earn far more than if he plays on the outskirts of town. The additional earnings on the best sites, over and above what he would earn on a just-worthwhile site, owe nothing at all to his skill or efforts[7]—they are pure, unearned "rental value." If a government builds a major new railway line, property owners near the new stations will see their properties rise in value through no efforts of their own. It is pure windfall: unearned rental value. The correct approach to unearned natural rents like these is to tax them at high rates (and use the proceeds to either cut taxes elsewhere or spend more). This is not a tax on property ownership, but a tax on *land:* whether or not that piece of prime real estate is owned by a Russian oligarch hidden behind a Liechtenstein *anstalt,* the bricks of the building sited there are rooted firmly into the soil, and the tax can be levied. Because land cannot move, this tax is insulated against offshore escape. It encourages and rewards the best use of land and keeps rents lower than they would otherwise be.

Not only that, but a huge share of the profits of the financial sector derive ultimately from real estate business and land value. Tax land's rental value, and you capture a big slice of this financial business, however much it is reengineered offshore. When Pittsburgh became one of the few places in the world to adopt the tax in 1911, in the teeth of massive resistance from wealthy landowners, it had dramatic and positive effects: While the rest of America went on an orgy of land speculation ahead of the Crash of 1929, prices in Pittsburgh only rose 20 percent. Harrisburg's adoption of the tax in 1975 led to a dramatic inner-city regeneration. The tax is simple to administer and progressive (that is, the poor pay less)—and can be especially useful for promoting growth in developing countries.

Another promising, much-overlooked scheme concerns mineral-rich countries. Tides of looted or tainted oil money sluice constantly into the offshore system, distorting the global economy in the process. A radical and controversial proposal would upend this phenomenon by distributing a large share of a country's mineral windfalls directly, and without discrimination, to every inhabitant. This has only been implemented in a few places like Alaska, but in many other mineral-rich countries, even poor ones, it is feasible. Doing so could prevent hundreds of billions of dollars of stolen mineral-sourced loot from draining to offshore centers and deliver tremendous benefits for the populations concerned.

A corollary of onshore tax reform is **leadership and unilateral action.**

After the September 11, 2001, attacks, U.S. legislators tried to insert stronger anti-money-laundering provisions into the PATRIOT Act. In the halls of Congress, civility collapsed, and shouting matches erupted between bank officials and congressional staffers.[8] Among other things, the bankers were defending offshore shell banks, which hide behind nominees and trustees so no one can know who their real owners and managers are. Senator Carl Levin who led the charge—after having had eleven transparency bills shot down by Senator Phil Gramm—stuck to his guns, and in the post-9/11 environment he at last got his way: remarkable provisions saying that no U.S. bank may receive a transfer from a foreign shell bank, and no foreign bank may transfer money to the United States that it has received from a foreign shell bank. The result, as Raymond Baker explains, is that "the thousands of shell banks that used to run loose have been reduced to perhaps a few dozen. . . . With a stroke of the legislative pen, a major threat to economic integrity has been almost completely removed from the global financial system." International agreement is generally a good thing, in cases like this. But leadership can work wonders too.

Too often, when corporations or individuals threaten to relocate offshore if they are taxed or regulated too highly, or asked to be too transparent, or to submit to criminal laws, government officials quail and give the wealthy owners of capital what they want. Not only that, but efforts to stop people from using abusive offshore loopholes are *also* greeted with the same cries of "Don't crack down on that loophole or we will go elsewhere!"

The latest crisis has made clear that much financial services activity is actually harmful. So if certain parts of the financial industry leave town—so much the better. Good projects will always find financing, whether or not your country is stuffed with foreign financiers, and local bankers are better placed to supply it because they know their customers. Tax and regulate the financial industries according to an economy's real needs, ignore the screams that capital and bankers will flit offshore, and you will tend to drive out the harmful parts, leaving the useful bits behind. The key is leadership. Unilateral action can work.

Another major task is to **tackle the intermediaries and the private users of offshore**.

Rudolf Strahm, a Swiss parliamentarian, studied every historical episode where Swiss bank secrecy has been loosened in response to foreign pressure and concluded that pressure only works when applied to Swiss banks. Every attempt to pressure the Swiss *government* was seen as an attack on national pride—and failed.

When a kleptocrat loots his country and shifts the looted wealth offshore, the banks, accountants, and law firms that assist him are just as guilty as the kleptocrat. When a client gets caught and goes to jail, so should his or her relationship manager, accountant, trustee, lawyer, and corporate nominee. A few organizations like London-based Global Witness have sought to call these intermediaries to account—but we now need a sea change in the world's approach. Get serious with these people at last.

As regards the end users of offshore services, many strategies are needed. I will mention just one. Its awful-sounding name—Combined Reporting with Formula Apportionment and Unitary Taxation—masks a simple, powerful, and straightforward approach to tax, which California already uses successfully to confront transfer pricing abuses.

Instead of the current approach of trying to tax each separate bit of a multinational as if it were a free-floating entity, tax authorities could treat the multinational group as a single unit, then "apportion" its taxable income out to the different jurisdictions where it operates, under an agreed formula based on real things like sales, payrolls, and assets in each place. Each jurisdiction can tax its portion at whatever rate it wants. So consider a U.S. multinational with a one-man booking office in Bermuda, with no local sales. Current rules let it shift billions of dollars in profits there to skip tax. But under the alternative system based on sales and payroll, the formula would allocate only a minuscule portion of the income to Bermuda—so only a minuscule portion of its overall income would be subject to Bermuda's zero tax rate. The rest would get taxed properly based on the substance of what it does in the real world, rather than on the gymnastic legal form its accountants have created for it. Several U.S. states already use it quite successfully. Countries can do this unilaterally—and if this happened widely a vast part of the tax havens' business model would disappear. Again, developing countries could be particularly helped by this.

In this context, the **financial sector** needs special mention as a vast area to reform. Severe pundit fatigue has already set in on this topic, so I will just make two short recommendations that have not been a part of the general clamor.

First, policymakers, journalists, and many others can start to understand and accept how tax havens have become the fortified refuges of financial capital, protecting it from tax and regulation and in the process contributing to the latest crisis in many and varied ways. The veil of silence and ignorance can be lifted and the message spread.

Second, countries worried about the safety of their financial systems could compile blacklists of financial regulatory havens based on the Jersey-Delaware notion of the captured state: *a place that seeks to attract money by offering politically stable facilities to help people or entities get around the rules, laws, and regulations of jurisdictions elsewhere.* This blacklisting will be easy enough, technically speaking, once we understand what we are looking for. With these blacklists, appropriate prohibitions and regulations—many of them very simple—can be put in place to help countries reclaim their sovereignty and respect voters' wishes once more. Along with this another benefit would flow: Once these berserkers in the international regulatory system are out of the picture, international cooperation on financial reform will become much easier. This proposal will also help us guard not only against repeating the errors that led to the latest crisis but also against those of the next one, whose causes we may not even be able to imagine yet.

Next, we should rethink **corporate responsibility.**

Societies grant corporations immense privileges, such as limited liability, which lets investors cap their losses and shift outstanding debts onto the rest of society when all goes wrong. They have also been granted the right to be treated as artificial legal entities that can relocate to different jurisdictions almost at will, irrespective of where they really do business. In exchange for these remarkable privileges, corporations were originally held to a set of obligations to the societies in which they are embedded: notably to be transparent about their affairs and to pay tax.

The offshore system has undermined all this. The privileges have been preserved and enhanced, but the obligations have withered. Tax must now be brought squarely into corporate responsibility debates. Corporate managers are taught to think that they are accountable only to shareholders. From this perspective, escaping tax seems to be their duty. But we have forgotten the fundamental truth that corporations get their license to operate, and the tools and confidence to do so effectively, from society. Seen this way, tax is not a cost to shareholders, to be minimized, but a distribution to the stakeholders in the enterprise: a return on the investment societies and their governments make in infrastructure, education, law and order, and the other basic prerequisites for all corporate activity. The shareholders must get their due, but the societies they depend on must too. When we start to make corporations feel they are accountable not only to shareholders but to societies too, a whole new arena will have been created in which the offshore system can be questioned and challenged.

We can also reevaluate **corruption**. I have already indicated how predominant corruption rankings of countries rate many of the world's top tax havens—the repositories of trillions of dollars of corrupt, stolen loot—as the world's "cleanest" jurisdictions, and how a new Financial Secrecy Index, which I mentioned in chapter 6, has started the process of setting the record straight.

But we can move beyond rearranging the geography of corruption and reassess what corruption *is*. At heart, corruption involves insiders abusing the common good, in secrecy and with impunity, undermining the rules and systems that promote the public interest, and undermining our faith in those rules and systems. In the process it worsens poverty and inequality and entrenches vested interests and unaccountable power.

Bribery does all these things. But many of the services tax havens provide also do these things. This close analogy between bribe-paying and the business of secret offshore escape is no coincidence: We are talking about similar underlying processes. Some people have praised bribery as a way of getting around bureaucratic obstacles: Without that bribe, that company won't get its container through the port. They are wrong, of course: Bribery may benefit the bribe-payer, but it damages the system as a whole. Similarly, the defenders of secrecy jurisdictions argue that their services help private actors get around "inefficiencies" in mainstream economies, smoothing the way for business to proceed. And they do. But what are those "inefficiencies"? They are, most importantly, tax, financial regulations, criminal laws, and transparency—all of which are there for good reason. To help someone get around the obstacle is to corrode the system and trust in the system. Bribery rots and corrupts governments, and tax havens rot and corrupt the global financial system.

Once we start seeing this we will no longer limit ourselves to pointing fingers at developing country kleptocrats and rogue officials but will begin to examine a much broader array of actors and their facilitating activities. And we will have found a rubric for the citizens of rich and poor countries to find common cause in fighting a global scourge.[9]

The final and most important thing is to **change the culture**. When pundits, journalists, and politicians fawn over people who get rich by abusing the system—getting around tax and regulation and forcing everyone else to shoulder the associated risks and taxes—then we have lost our way.

Language can change. When someone claims that tax havens make global finance more efficient, we can ask, "Efficient for whom?" When someone says countries should compete with each other on tax or financial regulation, or that policymakers should aim for a more competitive tax or regulatory system—one may ask: "What kind of competition are you talking about? A race to the bottom on tax, secrecy, or financial regulation? Or a race to the top, such as when corporations operate in competitive markets on a level playing field?" When we hear "privacy" or "asset protection" or "tax efficient" in the context of private banking, companies can be asked *exactly* what they mean. When a private equity company shows record profits, we can be told how much of that comes from genuine productive improvement, and how much comes from gaming the offshore system. When hearing a pillar of society say that they are a well-regulated, cooperative, and transparent jurisdiction, the investigator can assume the opposite and probe further. When magazines carry alluring advertisements from seedy offshore promoters who may be inciting clients to criminal behavior, we can complain. When corporations talk about social responsibility, we can ask if they mean tax. When journalists need expert commentators to advise them about that tax story they are writing, they must understand that their interviewee from the big accountancy firm works for a business that makes a living out of helping wealthy corporations and individuals get around paying tax, and that their opinions will reflect that corrupted worldview. They must find alternative opinions to balance those views.

The world's international institutions and responsible governments could create and promote new guidelines and codes of conduct outlining responsible and irresponsible behavior in the fields of international tax and regulation, with special focus on offshore abuse. They could introduce general antiavoidance principles into their tax laws so that complex and abusive trickery, while technically not breaking the details of legislation, can be disallowed. Tax evasion can become a predicate crime for money laundering, and tax offenses, among others, could be included in international conventions such as the United Nations Convention Against Corruption. Professional associations of lawyers, accountants, and bankers could create codes of conduct stressing, among other things, that it is unacceptable for a member to help a client commit a financial crime, whether the crime occurs at home *or* overseas. The economics profession needs to reappraise its approach to understand the effects of things such as secrecy and regulatory arbitrage. It could start to measure illicit, secret things, difficult though that may be.

We can recapture our culture from the forces of unaccountable privilege that have taken it away from us.

––––––––––––––––

At the time of writing, heavy government spending around the world has staved off outright economic collapse following the meltdown in global finance, but at huge costs to taxpayers. "Never in the field of financial endeavor has so much money been owed by so few to so many," said Mervyn King, the governor of the Bank of England. "And, one might add, so far with little real reform."

It is time for the great global debate about tax havens to begin in earnest. Whoever you are, wherever you live, and whatever you do, offshore is at work nearby. It affects you. It is undermining the government you elect, hollowing out its tax base and corrupting your elected politicians. It is sustaining a vast criminal economy and creating a new, unaccountable aristocracy of corporate and financial power. If we do not act together to contain, control, and eradicate financial secrecy, then the world I found in West Africa more than a decade ago, a world of suave insiders, criminal complicity, and desperate poverty, will become the world we leave to our children. A tiny few will have their boots washed in champagne, while the rest of us struggle to make our lives in conditions of steepening inequality. We must avert this future.

NOTES

PROLOGUE

1. US Energy Information Administration (EIA), "U.S. Imports by Country of Origin," http://tonto.eia.doe.gov/dnav/pet/pet_move_impcus_a2_nus_ep00_im0_mbbl_m.htm.
2. The episode is covered in detail in the author's book *Poisoned Wells: The Dirty Politics of African Oil* (New York: Palgrave, 2007), chapters 4 and 5.
3. Valerie Lecasble and Airy Routier, *Forages en eau profonde* (Paris: Grasset, 1998).
4. Ibid., p. 252.
5. Eva Joly, *Est-ce dans de monde-là que nous voulons vivre?* (Paris: Les Arènes, 2003).
6. "Scandale!: How Roland Dumas Got France Gossiping," *The Independent*, January 30, 2001.
7. See Jean-Marie Bockel, "Je veux signer l'acte de décès de la Françafrique," *Le Monde*, January 16, 2008. Omar Bongo is now dead; the palace is now inhabited by his son, President Ali Bongo.
8. "Rupert Laid Bare," *The Economist*, March 18, 1999.
9. John Lanchester, "Bravo l'artiste," review of *Rupert Murdoch: The Untold Story of the World's Greatest Media Wizard*, by Neil Chenoweth, *London Review of Books*, February 5, 2004.
10. Eva Joly, *Notre affaire à tous* (Paris: Les Arènes, 2000).
11. Eva Joly, in Norway's official aid newsletter, *Development Today*, March 7, 2007.
12. See Martin Woods, "Banks Financing Mexico Gangs Admitted in Wells Fargo Deal," *Bloomberg*, June 29, 2010.

CHAPTER 1   WELCOME TO NOWHERE

1. These figures should be taken as very rough estimates, not least because there is no agreement as to what a tax haven is, and estimates can vary widely. Once we understand that the United States and United Kingdom are major tax havens, the eye-catch figure is quite reasonable, if vague. This particular statistic is from French finance minister Dominique Strauss-Kahn in a speech to the Paris Group of Experts in March 1999; quoted in J. Christensen and M. Hampton, "All Good Things Come to an End," *The World Today* (Royal Institute of International Affairs) 55, nos. 8–9 (1999). The share has grown substantially since then, because offshore financial services have been growing at substantially faster rates than the growth in trade.
2. See Ronen Palan, Richard Murphy, and Christian Chavagneux, *Tax Havens: How Globalization Really Works* (Ithaca, NY: Cornell University Press, 2010), p. 51. This work uses BIS data to show offshore's share of banking assets and liabilities rising to around 65 percent in 1990, before falling to 51 percent in 2007. Other measures of offshore, in various

tables in the book, show explosive recent growth (interrupted by the financial crisis). Also see Luca Errico and Alberto Musalem, "Offshore Banking: An Analysis of Micro- and Macro-Prudential Issues," IMF, January 1999, pp. 17–19. This study cites a figure of 54 percent in 1999, which is based on a relatively restrictive definition of offshore; subsequent measurements are affected, according to the IMF, because "the distinction between onshore and offshore banking has become progressively blurred."

3. Data from Palan et al., *Tax Havens;* from "IMF Finds 'Trillions' in Undeclared Wealth," *Wealth Bulletin,* March 15, 2010; and from M. K. Lewis, "International Banking and Offshore Finance: London and the Major Centres," in Mark P. Hampton and Jason P. Abbott, eds., *Offshore Finance Centres and Tax Havens: The Rise of Global Capital* (London: Macmillan Business, 1999).

4. The U.S. Government Accountability Office (GAO) reported in 2008 that 83 of the nation's hundred biggest corporations had subsidiaries in tax havens; the following year the Tax Justice Network, an advocacy organization that criticizes tax havens, used a broader definition of a tax haven and found that 99 of Europe's 100 largest companies used offshore subsidiaries.

5. This loose definition is the result of collegiate discussions among members of the Tax Justice Network and other contacts primarily in the United States. It is similar to a definition offered by Richard Murphy, of the tax consultancy and advocacy company Tax Research UK, who defines secrecy jurisdictions as "places that intentionally create regulation for the primary benefit and use of those not resident in their geographical domain. That regulation is designed to undermine the legislation or regulation of another jurisdiction. To facilitate its use secrecy jurisdictions also create a deliberate, legally backed veil of secrecy that ensures that those from outside the jurisdiction making use of its regulation cannot be identified to be doing so."

6. See "The Cayman Islands as an Offshore Tax Haven," http://www.cayman-information .com/cayman-islands_offshore_tax_haven.php.

7. See Jesse Drucker, "Google 2.4 percent Rate Shows How $60 Billion Lost to Tax Loopholes," *Bloomberg,* October 21, 2010.

8. See Martin A. Sullivan, "Microsoft Moving Profits, Not Jobs, Out of the U.S.," Tax Notes, October 18, 2010; and Martin A. Sullivan, "Cisco CEO Seeks Relief for Profits Shifted Overseas," Tax Analysts, November 29, 2010.

9. John W. Diamond, "International Tax Avoidance and Evasion," *National Tax Journal,* December 1, 2009.

10. Form 10-Q for Chiquita Brands International Inc., Quarterly Report, May 5, 2009, http://biz.yahoo.com/e/090505/cqb10-q.html.

11. See Senator Carl Levin news release, "Dorgan and Levin Release Study Showing Majority of Corporations Pay No Federal Income Tax," August 12, 2008.

12. The problem is getting worse—it is estimated that by 2007 the United States was losing an *additional* $28 billion in annual revenue, over and above what it was already losing before 1999, due to the worsening offshore shenanigans by nonfinancial U.S. corporations. If you include financial corporations, the sum is far bigger. See Testimony of Martin A. Sullivan, contributing editor, *Tax Analysts,* Before the Committee on Ways and Means U.S. House of Representatives, July 22, 2010. As Sullivan reported, in 2007 a quarter of all foreign profits of U.S.-based multinationals outside the financial sector were realized in just five tax havens: Bermuda, Singapore, Ireland, Switzerland, and the Cayman Islands.

13. Media reports have claimed that Switzerland's banking secrecy laws were the product of efforts to protect German Jews from the Nazis. This story originated from a November 1966 bulletin from the Schweizerische Kreditanstalt (today's Credit Suisse), and it is false.

See Bruno Gurtner, "Swiss Secrecy Had Nothing to Do with the Nazis," *Financial Times* letters, March 26, 2009; and Sebastién Guex, "The Origins of the Swiss Banking Secrecy Law and Its Repercussions for Swiss Federal Policy," *Business History Review* 74 (summer 2000): 237–266, http://www.jstor.org/pss/3116693. Note also that tiny Liechtenstein next door emerged as a kind of Swiss appendage after the First World War.

14.   Luxembourg specializes in holding companies exempt from income taxes, introduced in 1929.

15.   IMF data records Luxembourg's investment liabilities at $2.5 trillion and its assets at only $1.5 trillion, a discrepancy of a trillion dollars. And these are just portfolio investments: add cash deposits, and the sums are bigger still. See "IMF Finds 'Trillions' in Undeclared Wealth," *Wealth Bulletin*, March 15, 2010.

16.   "Kim Jong-il Keeps $4bn 'Emergency Fund' in European Banks," *Daily Telegraph*, March 14, 2010.

17.   See, for example, Akin Gump Strauss Hauer & Feld LLP news release, "Halliburton Co., KBR, Inc. and KBR LLC Agree to Largest Combined Settlement of FCPA Charges by U.S. Companies," February 13, 2009. Halliburton and KBR settled with the Department of Justice for $579 million in 2009.

18.   It is no coincidence that London, the former capital of the greatest empire the world has known, is also the center of the most important part of the global offshore system. Until the early 1990s, economic historians had viewed the British empire in large part as a corollary of the industrial revolution, which had made the empire both necessary and possible; empire was, to a large degree, a story about industrial capitalism and trade. But in 1993 the economic historians P. J. Cain and A. G. Hopkins transformed this view with a two-volume book, *British Imperialism: Innovation and Expansion 1688–1914* (London: Longman, 1993) and *British Imperialism, Crisis and Deconstruction 1914–1990* (London: Longman, 1993), which recast the empire as something that was most fundamentally a story about financial capital, international credit, and the City of London, the governor of the imperial engine. This imperial connection, which will become clear as the book progresses, is of paramount importance to any understanding of the offshore system and of the City of London, the governor of a large part of the offshore engine.

19.   Martin A. Sullivan, "Offshore Explorations: Jersey," *Tax Notes*, October 23, 2007; "Offshore Explorations: Isle of Man," *Tax Notes*, November 5, 2007; "Offshore Explorations: Guernsey," *Tax Notes*, October 10, 2007. These are considered conservative estimates: Offshore bank deposits in Jersey alone were worth $800 billion in mid-2009; Colin Powell, chairman of the Jersey Financial Services Commission, estimated in 2009 that trusts in Jersey alone might involve another $300 to 400 billion.

20.   Seven, including the Falkland Islands and the British Antarctic Territory, are not havens. Ascension Island, which houses highly secretive U.S. and British military bases, serves a quasi-imperial purpose as a base to help project British power overseas.

21.   For example, 2003 saw the collapse of major money-laundering trials in which a key witness was forced to admit that he had been serving as an MI6 agent.

22.   The Cayman Islands reported to the IMF $750 billion in portfolio assets (that is, loans, securities, and other profitable things) in 2008. This quantity of assets ought to be matched, more or less, by similarly sized liabilities (deposits and other obligations) on the other side of the balance sheet—yet these added up to $2.2 trillion for the Cayman Islands, three times as much as the assets. See David Bain, "IMF Finds 'Trillions' in Undeclared Wealth," *Wealth Bulletin*, March 15, 2010. The IMF report is Philip R. Lane and Gian Maria Milesi-Ferretti, "Cross-Border Investment in Small International Financial Centers," IMF Working Paper 10/38, February 2010.

23. See Palan et al., *Tax Havens*, p. 11. The authors estimate that the Crown Dependencies and Overseas Territories, plus the former empire, account for 37 percent of all banking liabilities and 35 percent of all banking assets; the City of London accounts for 11 percent. Even back in 1996, the U.S. lawyer John Moscow estimated that apart from Switzerland and Liechtenstein, nearly every offshore dirty-money center was British run or controlled. See Chris Blackhurst and Clare Garner, "A Trillion Dollars in Dirty Money Keeps Island Tax Havens Afloat," *The Independent*, September 11, 1996.

24. The term "British Spiderweb" was coined, I believe, by Jim Henry, author of *Blood Bankers*.

25. See, for example, "Britain Imposes Direct Rule on Turks and Caicos," Associated Press, August 14, 2009. Plans are now afoot to prepare new elections for 2011.

26. Although Ireland lies in the Eurozone, its emergence as a secrecy jurisdiction in the late 1980s was substantially linked to interests in the City of London, and its Wild West spirit of laissez-faire financial market regulation—the turning of a blind eye to nefarious activities and potential risks—was inspired by British, not continental European, models. It is also part of a British sphere of influence.

27. "Users of 'Tax Havens' Abroad Batten Down for Political Gale," *New York Times*, February 26, 1961.

28. Next came Bank of America, Lehman Brothers, and Wachovia Corp., with 115, 59, and 57 tax haven subsidiaries, respectively. See "Large U.S. Corporations and Federal Contractors with Subsidiaries in Jurisdictions Listed as Tax Havens or Financial Privacy Jurisdictions," U.S. Government Accountability Office, December 2008.

29. A conference in the City of London in 1995 was told that the industry objective was to shift offshore the majority of financial assets owned by the world's high-net-worth individuals by the end of the decade. See Steven Hiatt, ed., *A Game as Old as Empire: The Secret World of Economic Hit Men and the Web of Global Corruption* (San Francisco: Berrett Koehler, 2007), p. 55.

30. See Senator Levin, news release, "Senate, House Members Introduce Stop Tax Haven Abuse Act: Bill Targets $100 Billion in Lost Tax Each Year from Offshore Tax Dodges," March 2, 2009. This $100 billion has several components and is in the middle of a range of estimates: The U.S. Treasury in 2007 cited estimates ranging between $40 and $123 billion annually. See Treasury Inspector General for Tax Administration, Office of Inspections and Evaluations, "A Combination of Legislative Actions and Increased IRS Capability and Capacity Are Required to Reduce the Multi-Billion Dollar U.S. International Tax Gap," January 27, 2009.

    Levin also states that "abusive domestic tax shelters cost tens of billions of dollars more." The United States has unusually sophisticated systems in place to stem offshore leakage; developing countries suffer far more in relation to the size of their economies. Education budget details from Office of Management and Budget, www.whitehouse.gov.

31. From the 2008 GAO report. A number of companies, including Delphi, Dow Chemical, MetLife, Pfizer, and Washington Mutual, referred to the "Virgin Islands" but did not differentiate between the British Virgin Islands and the U.S. Virgin Islands.

32. The *Deepwater Horizon* switched from Panama to the Marshall Islands in 2004. Transocean, the owner of the *Deepwater Horizon*, has 35 vessels registered in the Marshall Islands. Transocean moved from the Cayman Islands to the Swiss canton of Zug in 2008. For Zeder and the Marshall Islands, see U.S. Office of Insular Affairs, "Fred Monroe Zeder: In Memoriam," http://www.doi.gov/oia/press/2004/fred_zeder.htm. While Bush's ambassador to the region, Zeder's private company, Island Development, became incorporated on October 14, 1986, four days before Zeder signed a treaty providing for $6 million in aid for the Marshall Islands, of which $1.2m was used to help set up the ship registry. Zeder died in 2008. See "Bush Friend, Former Ambassador: Company Wasn't

Disclosed," Associated Press, reproduced in *The Victoria Advocate,* April 30, 1990. The United States is responsible for foreign affairs and defense, just as the UK is responsible for the foreign affairs and defense of its Overseas Territories. Khadija Sharife in the *London Review of Books* blog ("Offshore Exploitation," June 9, 2010) established that "During a joint hearing to investigate the explosion and sinking of the Deepwater Horizon, Hung Nguyen, a captain in the Coast Guard, was surprised to learn from the US Interior Department's Mineral Management Service—the unit responsible for overseeing offshore exploitation—that 'there is no enforcement.' Each operator 'self-certifies and establishes what they think is adequate,' . . . This system of self-regulation was formulated by Dick Cheney's Energy Task Force."

33. Khadija Sharife, "Offshore Exploitation," *London Review of Books* blog, June 9, 2010.

34. About the Liberian Registry, see Liberian International Ship & Corporate Registry (LISCR, LLC), www.liscr.com, accessed September 30, 2010. For the Standard Oil link, see Andrew Leonard, "Big Oil's Slick Trick," *Business Spectator,* May 15, 2010.

35. Jeffrey Robinson, *The Sink: How Banks, Lawyers and Accountants Finance Terrorism and Crime—and Why Governments Can't Stop Them* (London: Constable & Robinson Ltd., 2003), p. 63.

36. Widely cited. See, for example, Simon Raftopolous, "Tax Havens: The Red Herring of the Global Financial Crisis," Appleby Global press release, May 2009, www.appleby-global.com.

37. *The Economist,* however, has called tax havens "good for the financial system" and routinely carries advertisements for offshore corporations on its back pages.

38. See "World Governments Chip Away at Bank Secrecy," German Press Agency, April 12, 2010.

39. Nicolas Sarkozy, "Just Ahead of the G20 Pittsburgh Summit," from "Paradis fiscaux: bilan du G20 en 12 questions," CCFD-Terre Solidaire, April 2010.

40. For a list of uncooperative tax havens, see OECD Center for Tax Policy and Administration, http://www.oecd.org/document/57/0,3343,en_2649_33745_30578809_1_1_1_1,00 .html, accessed 2010. At the time of writing, countries could get off the blacklist by signing 12 "tax information exchange agreements" (TIEAs) with other jurisdictions—relying on extremely weak standards of information exchange. Many havens got off the blacklist by signing TIEAs with such global heavyweights as Greenland and San Marino.

41. E. G. Richard Salsman, "Treasury Secretary Paul O'Neil Confuses Tax Avoidance versus Tax Evasion," *Capitalism Magazine,* September 13, 2002.

42. That is a gross figure. See "The Dutch Trust Industry: Facts and Figures," International Management Services Association (VIMS) & Dutch Fiduciary Organization (DFA), April 2008.

43. Author's interview with Morgenthau, New York, May 4, 2009.

44. Oliver Arlow, "Kim Jong-il Keeps 4bn Emergency Fund in European Banks," *The Telegraph,* March 14 2010.

45. Dev Kar and Devon Cartwright Smith, *Illicit Financial Flows from Developing Countries, 2002–2006* (Washington, D.C.: Global Financial Integrity, 2008). The authors define illicit money as that which is "illegally earned, transferred or utilized." Economists from the Oxford Centre for Business Taxation have called these figures "drastically overstated." Dev Kar, the GFI economist (formerly an IMF Senior Economist), has in turn effectively countered their arguments, noting the blind spot in traditional estimates. Traditional models will estimate the magnitude of illicit outflows from a country, then estimate the magnitude of illicit inflows, and then subtract one from the other to achieve a net result. Kar explains, however, that the estimates should not be subtracted, but added. For further details, see "Time to Bury the Oxford Report," Tax Justice Network blog, July 16, 2009, plus associated links; and Dev Kar, "The Alpha, but Whither the Omega, of the

Greek Crisis?" Task Force on Financial Integrity & Economic Development blog, May 11, 2010.

46. Raymond Baker, *Capitalism's Achilles Heel: Dirty Money and How to Renew the Free Market System* (Hoboken, N.J.: Wiley, 2005). That book's headline $1–1.6 trillion figure was subsequently endorsed in "Stolen Asset Recovery (StAR) Initiative: Challenges, Opportunities, and Action Plan," World Bank / UN Office on Drugs and Crime, June 2007.

47. A picture of the book may be found at "Illicit Flows: We Finally Reveal the Official Data," Tax Justice Network blog, July 23, 2009.

48. Josh Rogin, "Clinton Presses Pakistan to Raise Taxes on Wealthy," *Foreign Policy,* September 28, 2010.

49. Author's interviews with Blum, and "A Conversation with Jack Blum," *The American Interest,* November/December 2009.

50. Office of Management and Budget, "Budget of the U.S Government, Fiscal Year 2011, Historical Tables," February 2010 (calculations by Citizens for Tax Justice [CTJ], emailed to author by Bob Mcintyre, CTJ director). Also see Ben Bagdikian, "The 50-Year Swindle," *The Progressive,* April 31, 2002.

51. For instance, the share of total income going to the top 1 percent of earners rose from 8.9 percent in 1976 to 23.5 percent by 2007, while the average inflation-adjusted hourly wage declined by over 7 percent. See Robert H. Frank, "Income Inequality: Too Big to Ignore," *New York Times,* October 16, 2010.

52. Chuck Collins, Alison Goldberg, and Sam Pizzigati, "Shifting Responsibility: How 50 Years of Tax Cuts Benefited the Wealthiest Americans," report for *Wealth for the Common Good,* April 12, 2010.

53. KPMG press release, "Cyprus, Ireland and Switzerland Have Most Attractive Corporate Tax Regimes in Europe, Finds KPMG International Poll," December 17, 2007, http://www.kpmg.co.uk/news/detail.cfm?pr=3008. Cyprus achieved a score of 90 percent.

54. A notable exception is "Business Unprepared as Fair Tax Follows Fair Trade into the Spotlight," *SustainAbility,* March 14, 2006, which examined the role of paying tax in the corporate responsibility debate.

55. See Hogan speaking on video, embedded in "Hogan Loses High Court Battle to Keep Financial Records Secret," *Sydney Morning Herald,* June 16, 2010.

CHAPTER 2   TECHNICALLY ABROAD

1. Philip Knightley, *The Rise and Fall of the House of Vestey* (London: Warner Books, 1993), p. 8.

2. Cain and Hopkins, pp. 150 and 157; statements in June 1929 and October 1929 by ambassador Robertson. The Argentine beef industry relied almost exclusively on the British market for its exports; by 1929 Argentina generated about 12 percent of Britain's income from overseas investments.

3. Charles Edward Russell, *The Greatest Trust in the World* (1905; reprint New York: Arno Press, 1975).

4. Rodolfo Roquel, *Nosotros, los Peronistas* (Buenos Aires: Dunken, 2005), p. 34.

5. Vestey Group History, Vestey Group website, http://www.vesteyfoods.com/en/vestey-group/vestey-group-history.html.

6. Knightley, *The Rise and Fall of the House of Vestey,* p. 63.

7. Ibid., p. 27.

8. Leslie Bethell, ed., *Cambridge History of Latin America,* vol. 8 (Cambridge: Cambridge University Press, 1991).

9.   "A: The Secretary of the Treasury," Washington, D.C., May 29, 1937, from Henry Mor-
      genthau to FDR, from Franklin D. Roosevelt Presidential Library; given to author in 2008
      by Morgenthau's son Robert Morgenthau, then Manhattan district attorney.

10.   For instance, in 1899 the state allowed corporations to own equity in other corporations,
      setting the scene for the emergence of large, interlinked networks of companies, the
      multinational corporation, and transfer pricing activities.

11.   Some of this analysis is derived from Ronen Palan, Richard Murphy, and Christian Chav-
      agneux, *Tax Havens: How Globalization Really Works* (Ithaca, NY: Cornell University
      Press, 2010).

12.   Most accounts say it was Bedford Gunning Jr. who made that statement at the constitu-
      tional convention.

13.   When Britain decided to tax the worldwide profits of any person resident in the UK, the
      judges decided that in the case of corporations they should be treated as resident where
      the company's most important decisions were taken, at meetings of their boards of di-
      rectors. This suited Britain, since thousands of firms with activities all over the world
      were financed through the City of London, and their boards were normally located there.
      Germany, by contrast, placed more emphasis on the "seat of management"—that is,
      where the company's actual operations were managed—a subtly different definition. For
      more on this history, see Sol Picciotto, *International Business Taxation* (London: George
      Weidenfeld and Nicholson Ltd, 1992), pp. 4–13.

14.   Until then, tax had not been a big issue for the Vesteys because Britain did not tax
      British-based companies on profits they made overseas—that is, unless they repatri-
      ated these profits. This had suited the brothers, who argued that most of their profits
      arose overseas.

15.   Picciotto, *International Business Taxation*, pp. 1–37.

16.   Knightley, *The Rise and Fall of the House of Vestey*, p. 34.

17.   Some tax havens claim that trustees are required by law to know the identity of all ben-
      eficiaries. Contacts indicate, however, that generally offshore jurisdictions do not ade-
      quately police these laws, and trustees often do not know the real beneficiaries.

18.   The U.S. Internal Revenue Service sums it up quite simply: "Although these schemes give
      the appearance of separating responsibility and control from the benefits of ownership,
      as would be the case with legitimate trusts, the taxpayer in fact controls them." See In-
      ternal Revenue Service, "Abusive Trust Tax Evasion Schemes—Facts (Section I)," June
      12, 2008, http://www.irs.gov/businesses/small/article/0,id=106537,00.html.

19.   *Vestey's (Lord) Executors and another v. Inland Revenue Commissioners. Same v. Colquhoun
      (Inspector of Taxes.) Same v. Inland Revenue Commissioners*, All England Law Reports,
      May 28, 1949, p. 1108.

20.   Sol Picciotto also describes this in his "Offshore: The State as Legal Fiction," in Mark P.
      Hampton and Jason P. Abbott, eds., *Offshore Finance Centres and Tax Havens: The Rise
      of Global Capital* (New York: Macmillan, 1999), pp. 43–79.

21.   Obituary: Edmund Hoyle Vestey, 1932–2007, Blue Star Line, http://www.bluestarline.org/
      edmund_vestey2.htm, accessed Sept 12, 2010.

22.   See "Heirs and Disgraces," *The Guardian*, August 11, 1999.

CHAPTER 3   THE OPPOSITE OF OFFSHORE

1.   Robert Skidelsky, *John Maynard Keynes: Fighting for Freedom, 1937–1946* (New York:
      Penguin, 2000), p. xiv.

2.   Ibid., p. xv.

3.   Ibid., preface and p. 98.

4. See Thomas Friedman, "Foreign Affairs Big Mac I," *New York Times,* December 8, 1996. The claim ended in March 1999 when NATO forces bombed Belgrade.

5. John Maynard Keynes, "National Self-Sufficiency," *The Yale Review* 22, no. 4 (June 1933): 755–769.

6. Robert Skidelsky, *John Maynard Keynes: Hopes Betrayed 1883–1920* (London: Macmillan, 1983), p. 220.

7. Robert Heilbroner, *The Worldly Philosophers: The Lives, Times and Ideas of the Great Economic Thinkers* (Austin, TX: Touchstone, 1999), p. 251.

8. Skidelsky, *Fighting for Britain,* p. 92.

9. Ibid., p. 112.

10. Ibid., p. 432.

11. Robert Skidelsky, *John Maynard Keynes: Fighting for Freedom, 1937–1946* (New York: Penguin, 2000), p. xxii.

12. J. Bradford DeLong, review of Skidelsky, *John Maynard Keynes: Fighting for Britain 1937–1946,* July 2001, http://www.j-bradford-delong.net/Econ_Articles/Reviews/skidelsky_jel .html.

13. Helleiner, *States and the Reemergence of Global Finance,* p. 4.

14. Skidelsky, *Fighting for Britain,* pp. 340, 348.

15. Barry Eichengreen, ed., *Europe's Post-War Recovery* (Cambridge: Cambridge University Press, 1995), p. 99.

16. Geoff Tily, the author of a book on Keynes, believes that the main reason Keynes supported capital controls was his belief that interest rates should be set and held low. This would place Keynes firmly on the side of the industrialist (for whom interest payments were a cost) against the financier (for whom interest payments were income). See Geoff Tily, "The Policy Implications of the General Theory," *Real-World Economics Review,* no. 50 (2009): 16–33, http://www.paecon.net/PAEReview/issue50/Tily50.pdf.

17. Capital controls had emerged during the First World War as countries had sought to stop capital fleeing their countries in order to be able to tax capital income and keep interest rates low in order to finance their war efforts. Controls evaporated after the war, following lobbying by bankers, but then returned partially during the Great Depression and finally swept the world after the Second World War and the Bretton Woods arrangements. They slowly became leaky and then were progressively dismantled around the world from around the 1970s. The United States got rid of its most important controls in 1974.

18. Eric Helleiner, "Regulating Capital Flight," in Gerald A. Epstein, ed., *Capital Flight and Capital Controls in Developing Countries* (Cheltenham: Edward Elgar, 2005), pp. 290–91.

19. Helleiner, *States and the Reemergence of Global Finance,* p. 58.

20. Ibid., p. 59.

21. Ha-Joon Chang, *Bad Samaritans: The Guilty Secrets of Rich Nations and the Threat to Global Prosperity* (London: Random House, 2007), p. 27.

22. Dani Rodrik and Arvind Subramanian, "Why Did Financial Globalization Disappoint?" IMF Staff Papers (2009), pp. 56, 112–138. They seek other explanations, especially exchange-rate factors, for the disappointing performance of liberalized economies, but they do note the close correlation. Also see Monique Morrissey and Dean Baker, "When Rivers Flow Upstream: International Capital Movements in the Era of Globalization," Center for Economic Policy Research Briefing Paper, March 2003. "A striking feature of the distribution of current account surpluses and deficits among developing countries is that most of the countries that are experiencing high GDP growth have surpluses, and often large surpluses. . . . The fact that most of these nations continue to experience rapid GDP growth, in spite of this large outflow of capital, suggests that the availability of capital has not been a major impediment to economic growth."

23. Martin Wolf, "This Time Will Never Be Different," *Financial Times*, September 28, 2009.

24. "Capital Inflows: The Role of Controls," IMF Staff Position Note, February 19, 2010.

CHAPTER 4   THE GREAT ESCAPE

1. Catherine R. Schenk, "The Origins of the Eurodollar Market in London: 1955–1963," *Explorations in Economic History* 35, no. 2 (1998): 221–238.

2. Ibid., p. 225.

3. Ibid., p. 227.

4. Anthony Sampson, *Who Runs This Place?: The Anatomy of Britain in the 21st Century* (London: John Murray, 2005), p. 246.

5. David Kynaston, *The City of London Volume IV: A Club No More 1945–2000* (London: Pimlico, 2002), p. 54.

6. Ibid.

7. U.S. banks had started expanding overseas after the First World War but mostly in Latin America and Asia, and in the 1950s their presence was still hardly discernible in London.

8. E. A. McCreary, *The Americanization of Europe: The Impact of Americans and American Business on the Uncommon Market* (1964), quoted in Stefano Battilosi and Youssef Cassis, *European Banks and the American Challenge: Competition and Cooperation in International Banking under Bretton Woods* (Oxford: OUP, 2002).

9. Until then, London's role as a financial center had been based primarily on the British Imperial currency zone, whose member countries banked in London and whose nations used the pound sterling as their currency or pegged their currencies to the pound. Inside the zone trade and capital could flow quite freely, but flows in and out of the area were closely controlled. The pound sterling still financed about 40 percent of world trade, and the Bank of England wanted it to stay that way. See Gary Burn, *The Reemergence of Global Finance* (New York: Palgrave, 2006), p. 26.

10. These terms are a bit of a misnomer today: They are neither named after today's euro currency nor are they a creature only of American dollars. All the world's main currencies are traded in this stateless unregulated space today.

11. "With the creation of the Euromarket," wrote Helleiner, "bankers in both countries stumbled on a solution to the problem of how to reconstruct the London-New York financial axis that had been prominent in the 1920s." Helleiner, *States and the Reemergence of Global Finance*, p. 89.

12. P. J. Cain and A. G. Hopkins, *British Imperialism: Crisis and Deconstruction 1914–1990* (London: Longman, 1993), p. 293.

13. Quoted in Kynaston, *The City of London Volume IV*, pp. 696–97.

14. Ibid., p. 697.

15. See "Linklaters Sees Fallout from Repo 105," *Financial Times*, March 13, 2010; and "Report of Anton R. Valukas, Examiner," Southern District Court, Jenner & Block LLP, vol. 3 of 9, March 11, 2010. The loophole was neither purely a UK matter nor a U.S. matter but derived from arbitrage between the two jurisdictions. See "FSA on Defensive over Lehman Failings," *Financial Times*, March 18, 2010.

16. In this process an investment bank, say, lends money to a hedge fund, and the hedge fund posts collateral against that loan, but then the investment bank is allowed to reuse this collateral for its own business, as if it were its own collateral.

17. See Manmohan Singh and James Aitken, "The (Sizable) Role of Rehypothecation in the Shadow Banking System," IMF Working Paper WP/10/172, IMF, July 2010. See also Gillian Tett, "Web of Shadow Banking Must Be Unravelled," *Financial Times*, August 12, 2010. If you take this practice into account, the IMF reckoned, then the shadow

banking system in the United States—the giant, unregulated financial marketplace that lay at the heart of the global financial catastrophes that erupted from 2007—was in fact a full 50 percent bigger than had previously been thought. The IMF concluded that "the United Kingdom provides a platform for higher leveraging not available in the United States."

18. "Energy Market Manipulation and Federal Enforcement Regimes," Michael Greenberger Testimony to U.S. Senate Committee, June 3, 2008, http://commerce.senate.gov/public/_files/IMGJune3Testimony0.pdf.

19. Michael Foot, "Final Report of the Independent Review of British Offshore Financial Centres," HM Treasury (UK), October 2009.

20. "Reaction to the Tax Gap Series," *The Guardian,* February 14, 2009.

21. Prem Sikka, "UK Company Law Is Terrorism's Friend," *The Guardian,* January 20, 2010.

22. Will Stewart, "Londongrad . . . Russia's Money Laundry," *The Express* (UK), February 27, 2010; and "Britain Called Crooks' Haven," *Sydney Morning Herald,* February 28, 2010.

23. See "Lloyds Forfeits $350m for Disguising Origin of Funds from Iran and Sudan," *The Guardian,* January 20, 2009; and "Lloyds TSB to Pay $350 Million to Settle Probe," *Bloomberg,* January 10, 2009.

24. Megan Murphy, "Banking: City Limits," *Financial Times,* December 13, 2009; and Richard Roberts, *The City: A Guide to London's Global Financial Centre,* 2nd ed. (London: The Economist/Profile Books, 2008), pp. 261–73.

25. The voting is supposed to reflect the "composition" of the workforce but not the "wishes" of the workforce. It is done through voting appointments: Business managers appoint voters from the workforce, who must be UK or Commonwealth or European Union residents. Source: Corporation of London website.

26. City of London, City Livery Companies, www.cityoflondon.gov.uk, accessed August 2010.

27. The Corporation itself hints at this: "The right of the City to run its own affairs was gradually won as concessions were gained from the Crown. London's importance as a centre of trade, population and wealth secured it rights and liberties earlier than other towns and cities. From medieval to Stuart times the City was the major source of financial loans to monarchs, who sought funds to support their policies at home and abroad." Source: City of London, "Development of local government," www.cityoflondon.gov.uk, November 19, 2009, http://www.cityoflondon.gov.uk/Corporation/LGNL_Services/Leisure_and_culture/Local_history_and_heritage/development.htm.

28. Clement Attlee, *The Labour Party in Perspective,* first published in 1937.

29. John David, *Reforming London: The London Government Problem, 1855–1900* (Oxford: OUP, 1988), p. 51.

30. Reginald R. Sharpe, *London and the Kingdom,* Volume 1 (Bibliobazaar LLC, 2008).

31. Ibid., p. 42. Winchester was left out of the original survey too, but was later surveyed; the City never was.

32. Which King James I had granted to the City of London.

33. While the 6,000 human residents would still get a vote each, the corporate vote was widened, increasing their votes from about 23,000 to 32,000. Voting rights would reflect the number of employees, but not the "wishes" of the workforce.

34. His role is, as the Remembrancer's Office puts it, to have "day to day contact with officials in Government departments responsible for developing government policy, the drafting and promotion of legislation and responsibility for relations with both Houses of Parliament and their Committees." City of London, City Remembrancer's Office, www.cityoflondon.gov.uk, accessed August 2009.

35. A previous Remembrancer boasted that his operating principle was to "oppose every bill which would interfere with the rights and privileges enjoyed by the Corporation."

36. "House of Lords European Union Sub-committee A (Economic and Financial Affairs and International Trade): Inquiry into Directive on Alternative Investment Fund Managers," memorandum from the City of London Corporation, submitted by the Office of the City Remembrancer, September 2009.

37. "House of Lords European Union Sub-committee A: Inquiry into the Commission's Communications on Ensuring Efficient, Safe and Sound Derivatives Markets," memorandum from the City of London Corporation, submitted by the Office of the City Remembrancer, January 2010.

38. City of London, "City of London funds," www.cityoflondon.gov.uk, accessed August 2010.

39. Developments are described in the blog "Mammon. From Superhero to Subzero," Open Shoreditch, February 8, 2009.

40. City Cash funds offices in Brussels, Mumbai, Beijing, and Shanghai.

41. David Hencke and Rob Evans, "Medieval Powers in City Trial of Strength," *The Guardian*, October 5, 2002.

42. Jason Beattie, an experienced British political reporter, tried to dig into City Cash using Freedom of Information (FOI) requests—standard journalistic tools that force reluctant British government departments to yield information. He had no success, and the Corporation's website, in fact, reveals why. The FOI Act of 2000, it admits, "applies to the City of London as a local authority, police authority and port health authority only," and the last word is emphasized with boldface type. In other words, everything is open to examination, except the money, which is the part that matters. City of London, "Access to Information," www.cityoflondon.gov.uk, accessed August 2010.

43. Some of this sentence was drawn directly from Burn, *The Reemergence of Global Finance*, pp. 151 and 158.

44. Ibid., p. 160.

45. Schenk, "The Origins of the Eurodollar Market in London," p. 235.

46. "The Earl of Cromer Is Dead at Seventy-Two: Former Head of Bank of England," *New York Times*, March 19, 1991.

47. See Eddie George, "The Bank of England: How the Pieces Fit Together," Bank of England Lectures, 1996, p. 91, http://www.bankofengland.co.uk/publications/quarterlybulletin/qb960110.pdf.

48. Burn, *The Reemergence of Global Finance*, p. 142.

49. Ibid., p. 124.

50. Jeffrey Robinson, *The Sink: How Banks, Lawyers and Accountants Finance Terrorism and Crime—and Why Governments Can't Stop Them* (Robinson Publishing, 2004), p. 57.

51. Burn, *The Reemergence of Global Finance*, p. 161.

52. Ibid., p. 164.

53. Richard Sylla, "United States Banks and Europe: Strategy and Attitudes," in Stefano Battilossi and Youssef Cassis, eds., *European Banks and the American Challenge* (Oxford: OUP, 2002), p. 62.

54. Cited in Martin Mayer, *The Bankers* (London: W. H. Allen, 1976), quoted in Burn, *The Reemergence of Global Finance*, p. 165.

55. Burn, *The Reemergence of Global Finance*, p. 125.

56. Thomas A. Bass, "The Future of Money," *Wired*, October 1996, http://www.wired.com/wired/archive/4.10/wriston_pr.html.

57. Kynaston, *The City of London Volume IV*, p. 569.

58. Ibid., p. 442, quoting Janet Kelly, *Bankers and Borders* (Cambridge, MA: HarperBusiness, 1977).

59. Mostly this involved borrowing from the Euromarkets in London and its fast-growing tax haven satellites, then lending out to other parts of the world; and through investment

banking activities that they were not allowed to do at home. See Ulrich Ramm, "German Banks and the American Challenge," in Battilossi and Cassis, eds., *European Banks and the American Challenge*, p. 182. According to Ramm, the share of U.S. banks' foreign balance sheet business handled via London fell from 50.6 percent to 37.5 percent from 1973–76, while the Bahamas and Caymans increased their shares from 19.5 to 30.6 percent.

60. Anthony Sampson, *Who Runs This Place? The Anatomy of Britain in the 21st Century* (New York: John Murray, 2005), p. 255.

61. See "The Economic Effects of Capital Controls," Congressional Budget Office, August 1985, http://www.cbo.gov/doc.cfm?index=5981&type=0.

62. Burn, *The Reemergence of Global Finance*, p. 146.

63. Bass, "The Future of Money."

64. Kynaston, *The City of London Volume IV*, p. 396; and Mark P. Hampton and Jason P. Abbott, *Offshore Finance Centres and Tax Havens* (London: Macmillan, 1999), p. 91.

65. Letter from HB Mynors of the Bank of England to Sir Charles J. Hambro of Hambro Bank, January 29, 1963. Cited in Schenk, "The Origins of the Eurodollar Market in London."

66. In 1962 *Time* magazine concluded that "the Eurodollar, most experts agree, will gradually disappear if U.S. interest rates rise to European levels, or the U.S. payments deficit ends." "Western Europe: Those Eurodollars," *Time*, July 27, 1962.

67. Burn, *The Reemergence of Global Finance*, pp. 36, 140.

68. These concerns would be echoed a generation later when the Bank for International Settlements asked in June 2008, as financial panic spread around the globe, "How could a huge shadow banking system emerge without provoking clear statements of official concern?"

69. But add "In private meetings and speeches," the Corporation notes, "the Lord Mayor expounds the values of liberalisation." See City of London, the Lord Mayor's International World, www.cityoflondon.gov.uk, accessed August 2010.

70. See, for example, "Ordinance 10 and Its Impacts on Chinese Companies London IPOs," Fasken Martineau Corporate e-bulletin, July 2009, http://www.fasken.com/china_equity/. The Lord Mayor was told that Ordinance 10 was designed to "prevent the illegal transfer of assets overseas."

71. "Report by the Rt Hon. the Lord Mayor (Alderman John Stuttard) on His Visit to China, Hong Kong and South Korea," City of London Corporation, November 8, 2007.

72. For example, David Kynaston's magnum opus of the modern City of London, subtitled "A Club No More," regarded by some as the definitive work on the City, hardly mentions the Corporation of London, and even then it hardly strays beyond discussing the Corporation's role in City construction projects.

73. All Glasman quotes are from the author's interviews with Glasman, 2009 and 2010.

CHAPTER 5   CONSTRUCTION OF A SPIDERWEB

1. See Tom Naylor, *Hot Money and the Politics of Debt*, 3rd ed. (McGill-Queen's University Press, 2004), pp. 20–22.

2. Jeffrey Robinson, *The Sink: How Banks, Lawyers and Accountants Finance Terrorism and Crime—and Why Governments Can't Stop Them* (Robinson Publishing, 2004), pp. 29–37.

3. E.g., Baron Grey of Naunton, 1964–1968; Francis Edward Hovell-Thurlow-Cumming-Bruce, 8th Baron Thurlow KCMG, 1968–1972; Sir John Warburton Paul, GCMG, OBE, MC.

4. The Bahamas became internally self-governing in 1964 and fully independent in 1973, though remaining a member of the British Commonwealth.

5. Memo V 122/2 to Rickett from M. H. Parsons, June 5, 1963.

6. See, for example, Lisa S. King, "Sir Stafford Sands' Legacy Reviewed," *Freeport News*, Nassau, August 31, 2005.

7. See Marvin Miller, compiler, "The Breaking of a President 1974—The Nixon Connection," http://www.mail-archive.com/ctrl@listserv.aol.com/msg11727.html.

8. See Tom Naylor, *Hot Money and the Politics of Debt*, 3rd ed., p. 40; also see Oswald Brown, "Restore Sir Stafford's Portrait to the $10 Bill," *Freeport News* (Bahamas), Feb. 13, 2009, http://freeport.nassauguardian.net/editorial/293789643182596.php; "The Bahamas: Bad News for the Boys," *Time*, Jan. 20, 1967, http://www.time.com/time/magazine/article/0,9171,843308,00.html.

9. Anthony Sampson, "Treasure Island," published in YellowBlackRed, 1999, www.reocities.com/blackyellowred/#top.

10. Report on a team visit to the Cayman Island, British Development Division in the Caribbean, April 14–17, 1969. From the British National Archives.

11. Paul Sagar, the primary researcher for this material, provides the essence of this summary.

12. DSC 203940.

13. Research conducted in British national archives by Paul Sagar on behalf of this book.

14. Thanks to Paul Sagar for this concise summary.

15. William Brittain-Catlin, *Offshore: The Dark Side of the Global* Economy (New York: Picador, 2005), p. 33.

16. In the interview, and J. A. Roy Bodden, *The Cayman Islands in Transition* (Kingston/Miami: Ian Randle Publishers, 2007), p. 105.

17. Robinson, *The Sink*, p. 48.

18. Widely cited. See, for example, "Bernard Cornfeld," www.includipedia.com, accessed August 2010.

19. Author's interview with Gill, George Town, Grand Cayman, May 2009.

20. Field refused to testify, pleading Fifth Amendment protection, but the U.S. Court of Appeals rejected this plea.

21. The Confidential Relationships (Preservation) law was amended in 2009, making the law somewhat less hard-line, but the essential elements providing criminal sanctions against breaking secrecy remain in place.

22. *Norman's Cay: Playground for Drug Smugglers*, PBS Frontline, www.pbs.org.

23. Seamus Andrew and Niall Goodsir-Cullen, "Accountability of Cayman Islands Directors," published by SC Andrew LLP, London, 2008.

24. See "Companies and Partnerships," published by Cayman Islands Financial Services, Cayman Islands government, http://www.scandrew.com/publications/Accountability%20of%20Cayman%20Islands%20Directors.pdf, accessed August 27, 2010.

25. Letter to Benn from Michael Dun, one of Benn's constituents, "Ref. Tax Havens and the Bank of England," May 30, 1975. The letter was forwarded to the UK Chancellor, Dennis Healey.

26. Author's interview with Scriven, March 2009.

27. Michael Foot, "Final Report of the Independent Review of British Offshore Financial Centres," HM Treasury, October 2009, http://www.hm-treasury.gov.uk/d/foot_review_main.pdf.

28. "Jersey Banking: The International Finance Centre," Jersey Finance Ltd., Fact Sheet, August 2009, http://www.jerseyfinance.je/_bluebox/download.cfm?attachment=18FCF7CA.

29. Some illustrative comparative data is provided at Ann Hollingshead, "Bamboozled!," Task Force on Financial Integrity blog, October 16, 2009.

30. When Lee Kwan Yew approached the Bank of England for support in setting up an offshore market, it was less encouraging, saying that it supported Hong Kong as a financial

center instead. See Lee Kwan Yew, *From Third World to First: The Singapore Story, 1965–2000* (Singapore: Singapore Press Holdings, 2000), p. 90.

31.   This was widely reported. E.g., Netty Ismail, "Morgan Stanley Fallout from Andy Xie Costs More Jobs," *Bloomberg*, October 12, 2006; and Netty Ismail, "Morgan Stanley Fallout From Andy Xie Costs More Jobs (Update1)," *Bloomberg*, October 12, 2006.

CHAPTER 6   THE FALL OF AMERICA

1.   From author's interview with Hudson, New York, 2008.
2.   These days, it is intangibles like patents or brands that are most often abused: Transfer mispricing on oil is much harder because the market price of oil is widely known.
3.   As told to author by Hudson in New York in 2008; the memo is reproduced on p. 33 of the 2004 paperback edition of Tom Naylor's *Hot Money and the Politics of Debt*, 3rd ed. (McGill-Queen's University Press).
4.   Raymond Baker, *Capitalism's Achilles Heel: Dirty Money and How to Renew the Free Market System* (Hoboken, NJ: John Wiley & Sons, 2005). Baker is a world authority on illicit cross-border financial flows. The chapter 4 table entitled "Specified Unlawful Activities under U.S. Anti-Money Laundering Laws" lists 65 crimes—aircraft piracy, human trafficking, alien smuggling, bank fraud, bribery, ocean dumping, and so on—that can be used as a basis for money-laundering charges under U.S. law. The table then cross-checks each crime against two columns: first, if the crime underlying the money flow is committed in the United States; and second, if the crime is committed overseas. The table shows all 65 crimes triggering U.S. money-laundering laws if the crime is committed in United States. But if the crime is committed overseas, three-quarters of them—including alien smuggling, racketeering, peonage, and slavery, and nearly all forms of tax evasion—are excluded from the "prohibited" list.
5.   See, for example, "US Bankers Attack IRS Deposit Interest Reporting Requirement," *Tax News*, December 3, 2002.
6.   "Miami: The Capital of Latin America," *Time*, December 2, 1993.
7.   See Naylor, *Hot Money and the Politics of Debt*, p. 292.
8.   Author's interviews with Blum.
9.   Blum, by correspondence, and Naylor, *Hot Money and the Politics of Debt*, p. 293.
10.   This was the Interest Equalization Tax. The Kennedy speech on this subject is available at the American Presidency Project, http://www.presidency.ucsb.edu/ws/index.php?pid=9349.
11.   The tax did not cover loans, so many corporations simply switched from bond financing to lending. To check bank loans to foreign countries, the U.S. Congress enacted the Voluntary Foreign Credit Restraint Program (VFCRP) in February 1965, broadening it in 1966. U.S. corporations were asked to voluntarily limit their direct foreign investment. The program was made mandatory in 1968. Capital controls were relaxed in 1969 and phased out in 1974, after the United States left the Bretton-Woods system of fixed-exchange rates. See, for example, "Introduction to Capital Controls," *St. Louis Fed. Review*, November/December 1999, p. 24.
12.   This "deferral," as it is known, was not uniformly available. The Kennedy administration had enacted Subpart F of the Code in 1962, which defended against tax havens by curbing deferral of U.S. corporate taxes in certain situations, deeming the income of foreign subsidiaries and affiliates of U.S. corporations to have been distributed to the U.S. parent and taxed in the U.S. even though this income is not actually distributed.
13.   Some countries have limited defenses against deferral; so-called "Subpart F" legislation in the United States (disallowing deferral on passive income) is an example. Even this de-

fense is patchy, however, and developing nations usually find it impossible to construct meaningful defenses using this strategy.

14. David Cay Johnston, *Perfectly Legal: The Covert Campaign to Rig Our Tax System to Benefit the Super Rich—and Cheat Everybody Else* (New York: Penguin, 2003).

15. Eric Helleiner, *States and the Reemergence of Global Finance: From Bretton Woods to the 1990s* (Ithaca, NY: Cornell University Press, 1996), pp. 135–6. "Ironically the triumph of 'monetarism' seemed to be occurring at just the time that international linkages were reducing the Fed's ability to control the monetary base."

16. Ibid., p. 137.

17. Ronen Palan, *The Offshore World: Sovereign Markets, Virtual Places, and Nomad Millionaires* (Ithaca, NY: Cornell University Press, 2003), p. 134.

18. The Federal Reserve Bank of St. Louis, which studied the new offshore IBFs, noted that the decline in Caribbean business "suggests that the growth of business in this area was almost entirely intended to bypass U.S. monetary regulations." See K. Alec Chrystal, "International Banking Facilities," *St. Louis Fed. Review,* April 1984, https://research.stlouis fed.org/publications/review/84/04/International_Apr1984.pdf.

19. Mark Hampton, *The Offshore Interface: Tax Havens in the Global Economy* (London: Macmillan, 1996), p. 63.

20. Palan, *The Offshore World,* p. 135.

21. Author's interview with Rosenbloom, December 1, 2009.

22. The Portfolio Interest Exemption.

23. Author's interview; also see Testimony of Michael J. McIntyre and Robert S. McIntyre on Banking Secrecy Practices and Wealthy American Taxpayers before the U.S. House Committee on Ways and Means, Subcommittee on Select Revenue Measures, March 31, 2009.

24. Testimony of Michael J. McIntyre and Robert S. McIntyre on Banking Secrecy Practices and Wealthy American Taxpayers Before the U.S. House Committee on Ways and Means Subcommittee on Select Revenue Measures, March 31, 2009, http://www.ctj.org/pdf/mcintyresw&mtestimony20090331.pdf.

25. The U.S. Foreign Account Tax Compliance Act (FATCA) of 2010 tightens up some aspects of the QI rules, making it harder for U.S. tax cheats, but it leaves the secrecy for foreigners in place. See "FATCA: New Automatic Info Exchange Tool," Tax Justice Network, May 18, 2010.

26. See Michael J. McIntyre, "How to End the Charade of Information Exchange," *Tax Notes International,* October 26, 2009, p. 194.

27. Much of the information comes from "Failure to Identify Company Owners Impedes Law Enforcement," Hearing Senate Permanent Subcommittee, November 14, 2006. Also "U.S. Corporations Associated with Viktor Bout," Prepared by Senate Permanent Subcommittee on Investigations, November 2009, on Senator Carl Levin's webpage, levin.senate.gov.

28. "Failure to Identify Company Owners Impedes Law Enforcement," Hearing Senate Permanent Subcommittee, November 14, 2006, p. 3.

29. L.J. Davis, "Delaware Inc.," *New York Times,* June 5, 1988.

30. Corp 95, http://www.corp95.com/, accessed June 10, 2010.

31. The forms of secrecy are different: lack of corporate transparency in Delaware and lack of financial transparency in Switzerland.

32. "Failure to Identify Company Owners Impedes Law Enforcement," Hearing Senate Permanent Subcommittee, November 14, 2006. A new act was introduced in 2008, the Incorporation Transparency and Law Enforcement Assistance Act, aiming to beef up transparency in this area. At the time of writing, the bill was on the sidelines.

33. Jeff Gerth, "New York Banks Urged Delaware To Lure Bankers," *New York Times*, March 17, 1981.

34. Chancery courts emerged out of English ecclesiastical courts and trust laws, where concepts of legal guardianship and fiduciary duty were paramount, and this makes them useful for what Delaware's Court of Chancery does most of all: rule on the nitty-gritty of how corporations organize themselves internally, and what happens when things go awry: whether internal rules have been followed, whether management insiders are illegally abusing shareholders, and whether corporate statutes were applied fairly. The Chancery court has no close competitor in this arena.

35. Bernard S. Black, "Shareholder Activism and Corporate Governance in the United States," *New Palgrave Dictionary of Economics and the Law* 3 (1998): 459–465, http://papers.ssrn.com/sol3/papers.cfm?abstract_id=45100.

36. Senate Bill No. 58, An Act to Amend Title 10 of the Delaware Code Relating to the Court of Chancery, State of Delaware Division of Corporations, http://corp.delaware.gov/sb58.shtml.

37. Matthew Goldstein, "Special Report: For Some People, CDOs Aren't a Four-Letter Word," Reuters, May 17, 2010.

38. Madhav Mehra, "Are We Making a Mockery of Independent Directors?" World Council for Corporate Governance, http://www.wcfcg.net/ht130304.htm, accessed August 15, 2010. Dr. Madhav Mehra is president of the council.

39. There are salient differences with the Cayman Islands. For example, most Cayman companies (the "exempt" companies) are by Cayman law not permitted to do business in Cayman. Such is not the case in Delaware. Also: typically, in Delaware, federal but no state taxes are paid; in Cayman, no taxes are paid.

40. Twelve thousand was the figure cited; the true figure is closer to eighteen thousand.

41. List of Delaware Registered Agents, Delaware Department of State division of corporations, corp.delaware.gov, http://corp.delaware.gov/agents/agts.shtml, accessed August 15, 2010.

42. The 2008 and 2007 reports are available at the state of Delaware's official website, http://sos.delaware.gov/2008AnnualReport.pdf.

43. Transcript of interview with Mrs. Ngozi Okonjo-Iweala, Nigerian finance minister, interview by Paul Vallely, *The Independent,* May 16, 2006, http://www.independent.co.uk/news/world/africa/transcript-of-interview-with-mrs-ngozi-okonjoiweala-nigerian-finance-minister–478337.html.

44. Transparency International has started to embrace this issue and called in November 2008 for a "second wave" of corruption campaigning to tackle these and other matters. As I write this, it is in the process of reevaluating its stance.

CHAPTER 7   THE DRAIN

1. "Interview: John Moscow," *Money Laundering Bulletin,* April 1997.

2. A range of estimates for the size of the narcotics trade exists. This one comes from "The Global Narcotics Industry," Center for Strategic and International Studies, Washington, D.C., http://csis.org/programs/transnational-threats-project/past-task-forces/-global-narcotics-industry.

3. Based on the current price of $75 per barrel.

4. This section on BCCI is drawn mostly from Peter Truell and Larry Gurwin, *False Profits: The Inside Story of BCCI, the World's Most Corrupt Financial Empire* (New York: Houghton Mifflin, 1992); from Jeffrey Robinson, *The Sink: How Banks, Lawyers and Accountants Finance Terrorism and Crime—and Why Governments Can't Stop Them*

(London: Robinson Publishing, 2004); as well as various newspaper and academic reports, plus author's interviews with Robert Morgenthau and Jack Blum in 2008 and 2009.

5. For most of its life, Ernst & Whinney (now Ernst & Young) audited BCCI Luxembourg, while Price Waterhouse (now PWC) audited BCCI Cayman.

6. See Peter Truell and Larry Gurwin, *False Profits: The Inside Story of BCCI, the World's Most Corrupt Financial Empire* (New York: Houghton Mifflin, 1992), p. 87.

7. Ibid., p. 189.

8. Ibid., pp. 193–97 and pp. 290–91; and Robinson, *The Sink*, pp. 79–81. Some of the capital was real money, but much of it was not.

9. Author's interview with Morgenthau, May 4, 2009. Morgenthau didn't name Scott, but he was the attorney general at the time.

10. Ibid.

11. Robinson, *The Sink*, pp. 318 and 357.

12. Ibid., p. 84.

13. In 2009, Britain's Information Commissioners refused a Freedom of Information request by Prem Sikka finally to publish PriceWaterhouse's 1991 "Sandstorm" report on BCCI, in an extraordinary and long-winded reply arguing that "it is very clearly in the public interest that the UK maintains strong and effective relations with its international partners"—a clear defense of tax haven London. See Freedom of Information Act 2000 (Section 50), Decision Notice, December 14, 2009, Information Commissioners (UK), http://www.ico.gov.uk/upload/documents/decisionnotices/2009/fs_50202116.pdf. In an email to the author on June 15, 2010, Sikka said he remained committed to securing publication of the report. Sikka also provides a useful in-depth examination of the BCCI affair in Austin Mitchell, Prem Sikka, Patricia Arnold, Christine Cooper, and Hugh Willmott, "The BCCI Cover-Up," Association for Accountancy & Business Affairs, 2001, http://visar.csustan.edu/aaba/BCCICOVERUP.pdf.

14. Author's interview with Morgenthau, May 4, 2009; and "More Offshore Tax Probes in Works: NY's Morgenthau," Reuters, April 27, 2009.

15. See the author's *Poisoned Wells: The Dirty Politics of African Oil* (New York: Palgrave, 2007).

16. French magistrates issued an international arrest warrant for Gaydamak in January 2001, and he moved to Moscow; in October 2009 he was convicted in absentia for arms trafficking, fraud, and tax offenses. Gaydamak says the magistrates used forged documents and said he owed no French taxes because he had been resident in London at the time in question. Author's interview with Gaydamak, and *Le Monde*, December 8, 2000, cited in Global Witness, *All the President's Men*, 2002, p. 26.

17. The arms he helped finance did, it is true, hasten victory over UNITA, though not everyone would agree that helping supply arms constitutes "bringing peace." Gaydamak had recently bought the Israeli football team Hapoel and a basketball team, Betar Jerusalem, with, he said, political aims.

18. Russia agreed, with Gaydamak's help, to cut the debt down to just $1.5 billion, sliced into 31 promissory notes with a face value of $48.3 million each. Angola would pay these off at face value in six monthly installments, after a five-year grace period, from 2001 to 2016. Gaydamak and his partner Pierre Falcone then set up a private company, Abalone Investments, with an account at UBS in Geneva. Abalone bought the 31 notes from Russia for $750 million—at a 50 percent discount—though Angola would pay Abalone the $1.5 billion in full. Angola's state oil company Sonangol started paying money into the Abalone account via the controversial and secretive oil trader Glencore. In February 2001, after 16 of the 31 notes (or $774 million) had been paid off, the Swiss judge froze the remaining 15 notes.

19. Global Witness, *Time for Transparency,* March 2004, p. 44.

20. Over $160 million went to an account called "Treasury Ministry of Finance" in Moscow, though knowledgeable sources in Switzerland told me that despite its name, this account may have been a front, with other interests behind it.

21. *Le Monde,* April 3, 2002: "Le règlement de la dette angolaise aurait donné lieu à des détournements de fonds," quoted in Global Witness, *Time for Transparency,* March 2004. I asked Gaydamak if the money had simply disappeared into private pockets, offshore. No, he said: Instead of paying Russia in cash for the promissory notes, Abalone paid Russia in "Russian obligations"—Russian debts he bought on secondary markets via these mysterious offshore companies and then redeemed to Russia— and Abalone had legally profited on those debt trades too. It was a "huge stupidity," he said, to assume that he would pay Russia back directly, rather than via intermediary accounts.

22. Dev Kar and Devon Cartwright-Smith, "Illicit Financial Flows from Africa: Hidden Resource for Development," Global Financial Integrity, March 26, 2010. Dev Kar is a former senior IMF economist.

23. See "'Angolagate' Revisited," Global Financial Integrity, Task Force on Financial Integrity & Economic Development, April 7, 2010, http://www.financialtaskforce.org/2010/04/07/angolagate-revisited/.

24. IMF data, "Angola: Selected Issues and Statistical Annex," April 1999 and Sept. 2003, and "Angola, Recent Economic Developments," Dec. 1995, Dec. 1997, Sept. 2000; "IMF Executive Board Concludes 2004 Article IV Consultation with Angola," July 2005.

25. The Soyo-Palanca Trust and the Cabinda Trust were used as efficient mechanisms for routing Angola's oil money, enabling Angola to provide trustworthy collateral for oil-backed loans, ring-fenced from the inefficiencies of Angola's domestic financial system. The problem was, essentially, that this ring-fencing also meant it was off the Angolan state's balance sheet, and therefore outside any normal budgetary or political procedures, playing havoc with Angola's ability to run a coherent budget.

26. Some economists, many with ties to the financial services industry and to tax havens, have tried to dispute these numbers—none successfully. In fact, the numbers are quite compatible with the only comparable official estimate available—a World Bank study from 1994, which estimated total capital flight from developing countries at $155–377 billion in 1992: Simply extrapolating this figure to 2006 dollars (using the IMF conversion rate of 287.2 percent) yields a figure of $443 billion to $1.1 trillion; evidence is, however, that the growth rate has significantly exceeded the inflation rate. For counterarguments and detailed discussions, see "Time to Bury the Oxford Report," Tax Justice Network, July 16, 2009.

27. Léonce Ndikumana and James Boyce, "New Estimates of Capital Flight from Sub-Saharan African Countries: Linkages with External Borrowing and Policy Options," Political Economy Research Institute, April 8, 2008.

28. Although one might argue that the problem of climate change is a bigger threat.

29. Letter to John Snow from Phil Gramm, February 19, 2003, republished by Center for Freedom and Prosperity, http://www.freedomandprosperity.org/ltr/gramm-irs/gramm-irs.shtml.

30. James S. Henry, *The Blood Bankers: Tales from the Global Underground Economy* (Thunder's Mouth Press, 2003), p. 73.

31. "The Future of Money," *Wired News* 4, no. 10 (October 1996), http://www.wired.com/wired/archive/4.10/wriston.html?topic=&topic_set=.

32. Eric Helleiner, *States and the Reemergence of Global Finance: From Bretton Woods to the 1990s* (Ithaca, NY: Cornell University Press, 1996), p. 177.

33. Michael Hudson quotes are a mix of the author's interview with Hudson and "An Interview with Michael Hudson: An Insider Spills the Beans on Offshore Banking Centers," Counterpunch, March 25, 2004, http://www.counterpunch.org/schaefer03252004.html.

34. Luca Errico and Alberto Musalem, "Offshore Banking: An Analysis of Micro- and Macro-Prudential Issues," IMF, January 1999.

35. Todd Moss, Gunilla Pettersson, and Nicolas van de Walle, "An Aid-Institutions Paradox? A Review Essay on Aid Dependency and State Building in Sub-Saharan Africa," Center for Global Development, Working Paper 74, January 2006.

36. "Address by Trevor Manuel, MP Minister for Finance of the Republic of South Africa," 4th Meeting of the Forum on Tax Administration Cape Town, January 10, 2008.

37. Chinese ministry of commerce. Total for Hong Kong was $27.7 billion, BVI $16.6 billion; the next largest was South Korea, with $3.7 billion.

38. See, for example, "India Gets 43% FDI through Mauritius Route," Press Trust of India, April 20, 2009.

39. It was a French colony until Britain invaded during the Napoleonic Wars.

40. Author's interview with Elmer, 2009.

41. Telephone interview with Rosenbloom, December 1, 2009.

CHAPTER 8   RESISTANCE

1. "Harmful Tax Competition: An Emerging Global Issue," Organization for Economic and Cooperative Development, 1998, http://www.oecd.org/dataoecd/25/26/44430243.pdf.

2. The last major attempt at attacking the havens had been the so-called Gordon report published by the U.S. Internal Revenue Service in January 1981: "Tax Havens and Their Use by United States Taxpayers—An Overview," report to the Commissioner of Internal Revenue, the Assistant Attorney General (Tax Division) and the Assistant Secretary of the Treasury (Tax Policy), submitted by Richard A. Gordon, Special Counsel for International Taxation, January 12, 1981. This was almost entirely ignored.

3. Though the 1998 report did not list the havens, the content was clearly aimed at smaller island centers.

4. Author interview with Dan Mitchell, Washington, D.C., Jan. 16, 2009.

5. David Cay Johnston, "Behind the IRS Hearings, a GOP Plan to End Tax Code," *New York Times,* May 4, 1998, http://www.nytimes.com/1998/05/04/us/behind-irs-hearings-a-gop-plan-to-end-tax-code.html?pagewanted=1.

6. David Cay Johnston, *Perfectly Legal: The Covert Campaign to Rig Our Tax System to Benefit the Super Rich—and Cheat Everybody Else* (New York: Penguin, 2003), p. 148.

7. See "The Liberalizing Impact of Tax Havens in a Globalized Economy," presentation by Dan Mitchell, Capitol Hill, March 23, 2009, http://www.youtube.com/watch?v=ISfsY1nqoaM&feature=related.

8. Ibid.

9. Paul de Grauwe and Magdalena Polan, "Globalisation and Social Spending," Cesifo Working Paper No. 885, March 2003, https://lirias.kuleuven.be/bitstream/123456789/119409/1/cesifo_wp885.pdf.

10. "Table A. Total Tax Revenue as Percentage of GDP," OECD, http://www.oecd.org/dataoecd/48/27/41498733.pdf.

11. "A Fair Share: Has the Tide Turned for Corporate Profits?" *The Economist,* August 27, 2009, http://www.economist.com/research/articlesBySubject/displaystory.cfm?subjectid=2512631&story_id=E1_TQPNSGGV. In 2006, for example, just ahead of the economic crisis, U.S. corporate profits were higher as a share of national income, and wages and salaries were lower, than at any time since the Second World War.

12.   See David Cay Johnston, "Tax Rates for Top 400 Earners Fall as Income Soars, IRS Data," *Tax Analysts,* undated, 2010, http://www.tax.com/taxcom/features.nsf/Articles/0DEC0 EAA7E4D7A2B852576CD00714692?OpenDocument.

13.   Mitchell's own book quotes a seminal 2006 European study that baldly explains the problem: "The effect [of falling tax rates] on incorporation is significant and large. It implies that the revenue effects of lower corporate tax rates—possibly induced by tax competition—partly show up in lower personal tax revenues rather than lower corporate tax revenues. . . . There *is* reason (after all) to worry about tax competition." "Corporate Tax Policy, Entrepreneurship and Incorporation in the EU," CESifo Working Paper No. 1883, December 2006. Also see Lucas Bretschger and Frank Hettich, "Globalisation, Capital Mobility and Tax Competition: Theory and Evidence for OECD Countries," *European Journal of Political Economy* 18, no. 4 (November 2002); and S. Ganghof, *The Politics of Income Taxation: A Comparative Analysis* (European Consortium for Political Research Press, 2006).

14.   Michael Keen and Alejandro Simone, "Is Tax Competition Harming Developing Countries More Than Developed?" *Tax Notes International* 1317, June 28, 2004.

15.   Alexander Klemm and Stefan van Parys, "Empirical Evidence on the Effects of Tax Incentives," IMF Working Paper No. 09/136, July 1, 2009, http://www.imf.org/external/ pubs/cat/longres.cfm?sk=23053.0.

16.   One such incentive was the tax holiday, which the IMF economists said was "widely regarded as the most pernicious form of incentive." Britain had briefly tried this gimmick under Prime Minister Margaret Thatcher until it became clear they did not work: set up a ten-year tax holiday, and companies will pack up and leave after nine years and 11 months, or will transfer the business to another subsidiary and get another ten-year holiday. After these failures, however, Africa was still encouraged to embrace them: In 1990 only one sub-Saharan African country offered tax holidays, but a decade later they all did. Often these holidays are available in special export processing zones, which are a bit like small offshore jurisdictions lodged inside the state. When these zones pop up, wealthy locals who want to invest at home inevitably send their money overseas, dress it up in an offshore secrecy structure, then return it, slashing their tax bill in the process.

17.   Daniel J. Mitchell, *The Moral Case for Tax Havens,* video, Center for Freedom & Prosperity, October 2008.

18.   This history is explored in more detail in the UK edition of this book, in chapter 3 on Switzerland. See also Sébastien Guex, "The Origins of the Swiss Banking Secrecy Loans and Its Repercussions for Swiss Federal Policy," *Business History Review,* Summer 2000, the President and Fellows of Harvard College, pp. 237–266.

19.   "The Moral Case for Tax Havens," Center for Freedom and Prosperity Foundation video, http://www.youtube.com/watch?v=Xf14lkyH2dM; and "Tax Justice Network Sides with Europe's Tax Collectors, Ignores Critical Role of Low-Tax Jurisdiction in Protecting Human Rights and Promoting Pro-Growth Policy," Center for Freedom and Prosperity, April 7, 2005.

20.   Joel Bakan, *The Corporation* (London: Constable & Robinson Ltd., 2005), p. 154.

21.   "Why Do I Have to Deal with People Like Dan Mitchell?" J. Bradford DeLong, February 12, 2009, delong.typepad.com.

22.   When the tax writer David Cay Johnston challenged Norquist, noting that his views were at odds with those of most economists, and taxes were needed to pay for civilization, Norquist responded that "we are not the successor of, we are not a continuation of, western civilisation. We are a unique and different civilisation." From David Cay Johnston, *Perfectly Legal: The Covert Campaign to Rig our Tax System to Benefit the Super Rich—and Cheat Everybody Else* (New York: Penguin, 2003), p. 3.

23. See, for example, "Historical Top Tax Rates," Tax Policy Center, October 26, 2009, http://www.taxpolicycenter.org/taxfacts/displayafact.cfm?Docid=213.

24. Jason Sharman, *Havens in a Storm: The Struggle for Global Tax Regulation* (Ithaca, NY: Cornell University Press, 2006), p. 85.

25. "The Moral Case for Tax Havens," Center for Freedom and Prosperity Foundation video, http://www.youtube.com/watch?v=Xf14lkyH2dM.

26. David Cay Johnston, "Treasury Chief: Tax Evasion Is on the Rise," *New York Times,* July 19, 2001, http://www.nytimes.com/2001/07/19/business/treasury-chief-tax-evasion-is-on-the-rise.html?pagewanted=1.

27. "OECD Tax Haven Crackdown Is Out of Line, O'Neill Says," Center for Freedom and Prosperity news summary, May 11, 2010, http://www.freedomandprosperity.org/Articles/sum05–11–01/sum05–11–01.shtml.

28. Martin A. Sullivan, "Lessons From the Last War on Tax Havens," *Tax Notes International,* July 30, 2007.

29. David Cay Johnston, "Treasury Chief: Tax Evasion Is on the Rise," *New York Times,* July 19, 2001.

30. Sharman, *Havens in a Storm.*

31. Johnston, *Perfectly Legal,* p. 2. A new study in October 2008 based on unpublished IRS data found that the rich hide much more of their income than the poor do. Taxpayers earning true income between $500,000 and $1 million a year understated their adjusted gross incomes by 21 percent overall in 2001, compared to just 8 percent for those earning $50,000 to $100,000. For poorer people, cheating was even lower. See "Rich Cheat More on Taxes, New Study Shows," *Forbes,* October 21, 2008, http://www.forbes.com/2008/10/21/taxes-irs-wealth-biz-beltway-cz_jn_1021beltway.html.

32. Martin Wolf, *Why Globalization Works* (New Haven, CT: Yale University Press, 2005), p. 283.

33. For useful explorations of this topic, see Monique Morrissey and Dean Baker, "When Rivers Flow Upstream: International Capital Movements in the Era of Globalization," Center for Economic and Policy Research, March 22, 2003; or Dani Rodrik and Arvind Subramanian, "Why Did Financial Globalization Disappoint?" IMF staff papers, vol. 56, no. 1, 2009, pp. 112–138.

34. Ryszard Kapuscinski, *Shah of Shahs* (New York: Vintage Books, 1992).

35. *Caymanian Compass,* July 8, 1991.

36. "Framing Cayman," *The Lawyer,* March 29, 2004, http://www.thelawyer.com/framing-cayman/109308.article.

37. Anthony Travers, "An Open Letter to President Obama from the Cayman Islands Financial Services Association," OBE, May 5, 2009.

38. "Tax Havens Batten Down as the Hurricane Looms," *The Observer,* March 29, 2009.

39. The G20 declared this on April 2, 2009; the blacklist was empty by April 7. See "The Empty OECD Black List: Where Did All Tax Havens Go?" Eurodad press release, April 16, 2009; Richard Murphy, "The TIEA Programme Is Failing," Tax Research blog, November 27, 2009; and "A Progress Report on the Jurisdictions Surveyed by the OECD Global Forum in Implementing the Internationally Agreed Tax Standard," OECD, May 10, 2010, http://www.oecd.org/dataoecd/50/0/43606256.pdf.

40. Michael J. McIntyre, "How to End the Charade of Information Exchange," *Tax Notes International,* October 26, 2009.

CHAPTER 9   THE LIFE OFFSHORE

1. Now known as the Big Four, following the demise of Arthur Andersen.

2. Michael Bronner, "Telling Swiss Secrets: 222 Billionaires," *Global Post,* August 5, 2010.
3. Michael Bronner, "Telling Swiss Secrets: The Golden Goose," *Global Post,* August 5, 2010.
4. "Doom-mongers Huddle over Island under Threat," *Financial Times,* November 11, 1998.
5. Patrick Muirhead, "Jersey's Culture of Concealment," *The Times,* April 24, 2008.
6. Author's interview with Syvret, 2009.
7. Stuart Syvret's blog, "Jersey's Media and Its Role in the Culture of Concealment," July 29, 2010, http://stuartsyvret.blogspot.com/2010_07_01_archive.html.
8. Austin Mitchell, Prem Sikka, John Christensen, Philip Morris, and Steven Filling, "No Accounting for Tax Havens," *Association for Accountancy and Business Affairs* (2002).
9. "Economics and Development in the Twenty-First Century," remarks by Kenneth Galbraith on the occasion of his receipt of the Leontief Prize at Tufts University, March 27, 2000.
10. Companies can, if they prefer, set their own rates of tax, with a minimum of 2 percent, if they want to climb over the bar of a minimum rate specified in their country of origin. At the time of writing, Jersey is considering changes to its tax system.
11. Author's interview with Elmer, 2009.

CHAPTER 10   RATCHET

1. The main research for this was undertaken by myself and Ken Silverstein of *Harper's* magazine in 2009.
2. Some interviewees said May 1980, but Henry Beckler's resume says June 11, 1980, http://www.wtcde.com/HenryBeckler.pdf.
3. According to the *New York Times,* "Others who might have raised questions about the bill, including other state officials, the press and the public, were intentionally kept in the dark, according to bankers and state officials" ("New York Banks Urged Delaware to Lure Bankers," *New York Times,* March 17, 1981, http://www.nytimes.com/1981/03/17/business/19810317BANK.html?&pagewanted=1).
4. Biondi is a former president of the Delaware State Bar Association, a Democrat who served as an adviser to both Republican and Democrat governors, and an attorney for business interests, the Teamsters union, and many others. Delaware Grapevine, a local political website, called him "a tough-minded political operative capable of delivering corporate contributions or muscling up votes." Celia Cohen, "I Heard You Picket Newspapers," Delaware Grapevine, July 13, 2005, http://www.delawaregrapevine.com/7-05sheeran.asp.
5. Interview with Hayward and Hayward's comments in Larry Nagengast, *Pierre S. Du Pont IV, Governor of Delaware, 1977–1985* (Delaware: Delaware Heritage Press, April 2007), p. 109.
6. "Birth of a Banking Bonanza," *Delaware Lawyer* (Fall 1982): 38.
7. David S. Swayze and Christine P. Schiltz, "Keeping the First State First: The Alternative Bank Franchise Tax as an Economic Development Tool," *Delaware Banker* (Fall 2006), http://www.pgslegal.com/CM/FirmNews/Fall%202006%20Delaware%20Banker%20Article.pdf.
8. Adrian Kinnane, *Durable Legacy: A History of Morris, Nichols, Arsht & Tunnell* (Morris, Nichols, Arsht & Tunnell, 2005), http://www.mnat.com/assets/attachments/MNAT_Book_Web_Version.pdf.
9. "New York Banks Urged Delaware to Lure Bankers," *New York Times,* March 17, 1981, http://www.nytimes.com/1981/03/17/business/19810317BANK.html?&pagewanted=1.
10. Nagengast, *Pierre S. Du Pont IV, Governor of Delaware, 1977–1985*, p. 113.
11. In 2010 the so-called Whitehouse Interstate Lending Amendment was introduced in the U.S. Senate, cosponsored by Senators Cochran, Merkley, Durbin, Sanders, Levin, Burris,

Franken, Brown, Menendez, Leahy, Webb, Casey, Wyden, Reed, Udall, and Begich, aiming to restore to the states the ability to enforce interest rate caps against out-of-state lenders. At the time of writing, it had made no progress.

12. Nagengast, *Pierre S. Du Pont IV, Governor of Delaware, 1977–1985*, p. 114.

13. A description of the Bank Franchise Tax, Delaware Department of Finance, http://finance.delaware.gov/publications/fiscal_notebook_09/Section07/bank_franchise.pdf.

14. "New York Banks Urged Delaware to Lure Bankers," *New York Times,* March 17, 1981, http://www.nytimes.com/1981/03/17/business/19810317BANK.html?&pagewanted=1.

15. Nagengast, *Pierre S. Du Pont IV, Governor of Delaware, 1977–1985*, p. 110.

16. Author's interview with Swayze, Delaware, November 24, 2009.

17. See "Consumers Turn to Plastic as Home Loans Slow," Reuters, September 11, 2007. Credit card debt stood at $907 billion, and this would rise to $975 billion by December 2008. From "US Credit Card ABS: 2006 Outlook," Barclays Capital, January 26, 2006; and Mark Furletti, "An Overview of Credit Card Asset-Backed Securities," Philadelphia Federal Reserve, December 2002; and "Fed Report: Consumer Credit Card Balances Keep Plummeting," http://www.creditcards.com/credit-card-news/federal-reserve-g19-consumer-credit-december–09–1276.php.

18. This research was undertaken by myself and Ken Silverstein of *Harper's* magazine in Delaware in 2009. As far as I know, nobody has ever deeply explored this Delaware episode and linked it to its wider impacts, apart from the early *New York Times* article cited in this chapter. For Geoghegan quote see Thomas Geoghegan, "Infinite Debt: How Unlimited Interest Rates Destroyed the Economy," *Harper's,* April 2009.

19. Paul Tucker, "Shadow Banking, Financing Markets and Financial Stability," remarks by Mr Paul Tucker, Deputy Governor for Financial Stability at the Bank of England, at a Bernie Gerald Cantor (BGC) Partners Seminar, London, January 21, 2010, http://www.bis.org/review/r100126d.pdf.

20. From Biondi interview and David S. Swayze and Christine P. Schiltz, "Keeping the First State First: The Alternative Bank Franchise Tax as an Economic Development Tool," *Delaware Banker* (Fall 2006), http://www.pgslegal.com/CM/FirmNews/Fall%202006%20Delaware%20Banker%20Article.pdf.

21. See, for example, JP Morgan CDO Handbook, May 29, 2001, p. 31; and Scott E. Waxman, "Delaware Statutory Trusts," Potter Anderson & Corroon LLP, 2010, http://www.potteranderson.com/news-publications–0–127.html. Biondi did not say he was involved in the Delaware Statutory Trust Act.

22. Scott E. Waxman, Nicholas I. Froio, Eric N. Feldman, and Ross Antonacci, "Delaware: The Jurisdiction of Choice in Securitisation," Potter Anderson & Corroon LLP, May 19, 2004, http://library.findlaw.com/2004/May/19/133435.html.

23. David S. Swayze and Christine P. Schlitz, "The Evolution of Banking in Delaware," published by Parkowski, Guerki & Swayze, http://www.pgslegal.com/CM/FirmNews/evolution-of-banking-in-delaware.asp.

24. See John Dunn and Prem Sikka, "Keeping the Auditors in the Dark," Association for Accountancy & Business Affairs, 1999, http://visar.csustan.edu/aaba/dunn&sikka.pdf.

25. The UK Companies Act of 1948, for example, required this.

26. Author's interview with Konrad Hummler, November 4, 2009.

27. Jim Cousins, Austin Mitchell, and Prem Sikka, "Race to the Bottom: The Case of the Accountancy Firms," Association for Accountancy & Business Affairs, 2004.

28. David Cay Johnston, *Perfectly Legal: The Covert Campaign to Rig Our Tax System to Benefit the Super Rich—and Cheat Everybody Else* (New York: Penguin, 2003), p. 15.

29. From the UK Companies Act of 1989.

30. From author's interview with Southern, March 13, 2009.

31. "Voter Turnout," International Institute for Democracy and Electoral Assistance, 2010, http://www.idea.int/vt/survey/voter_turnout_pop2.cfm.

32. "Offshore Hazard: Isle of Jersey Proves Less Than a Haven to Currency Investors," *Wall St. Journal,* September 17, 1996.

33. A letter in October 1996 from Colin Powell, Jersey's Chief Adviser, to Pierre Horsfall, President of Jersey's Finance and Economics Committee, suggests the uncertain official position at the time. "Some might hold the view that there is nothing wrong with States members being directors of local companies," the letter read. "Indeed, for as long as States members are not full-time and salaried it is almost inevitable." The answer that had been put forward, Powell said, was to set up a Jersey Financial Services Commission to supervise the finance industry—though that, he conceded, may not be very different. "The Commission will include those who have a direct interest in the finance industry." The answer, Powell said, was to make sure that those in the future commission would not be involved in particular areas where they had a conflict of interest, and that the matter should be debated further. (Letter from Colin Powell, O.B.E, Chief Adviser to the States, to Senator P.F. Horsfall, President, Finance and Economics Committee, October 25, 1996.)

34. "Finance: Damage Might Be Done to Jersey's Reputation," *Jersey Evening Post,* February 15, 1996.

35. *Accountancy Age,* March 29, 2001, p. 22.

36. Prem Sikka and Hugh Willmott, "All Offshore—The Sprat, The Mackerel, Accounting Firms and the State in Globalization," Essex Business School Working Paper No. WP 09/05, February 2009.

37. Luca Errico and Alberto Musalem, "Offshore Banking: An Analysis of Micro- and Macro-Prudential Issues," IMF, January 1999. Also: "Favourable regulatory treatment in OFCs increases the operational leeway of offshore banks for balance sheet management," the IMF said: "exemptions from reserve requirements on deposits; liquidity requirements; liability and asset concentration restrictions; capital adequacy thresholds; and stringent foreign exchange position limits, allow offshore banks to more freely manage their balance sheets."

38. For example, in *When Genius Failed,* Roger Lowenstein's otherwise excellent analysis of the episode, the offshore structure is almost ignored. Roger Lowenstein, *When Genius Failed* (New York: 4th Estate, 2002).

39. See, for example, "Report on Special Purpose Entities," the Bank for International Settlements, September 2009.

40. As the BIS report puts it: "The onshore (Delaware) versus offshore (Cayman) decision will generally be driven by factors outlined in the previous section (on tax considerations of SPEs), while other (non-taxation related) considerations (such as clarity of legal regime, ease of incorporation, etc) will generally be similar to those outlined for European SPEs immediately above." Note that "clarity of legal regime" and "ease of incorporation" stem specifically from these jurisdictions' offshore status, as defined in this book.

41. See Jim Stewart, "Shadow Regulation and the Shadow Banking System: The Role of the Dublin International Financial Services Centre," *Tax Justice Focus* 4, no. 2 (July 18, 2008); and Jim Stewart, "Low Tax Financial Centres and the Subprime Crisis: The IFSC in Ireland," presentation, Tax Justice/AABA research workshop, University of Essex, July 3–4, 2008. Also, draft version of Jim Stewart, "Low Tax Financial Centres and the Financial Crisis: The Case of the IFSC in Ireland," May 15, 2010.

42. Dublin's lures for the shadow banks were not especially its low-tax regime—though that helped—but other features: Ireland's wide array of tax treaties, and the fact that it ticks certain boxes that fund regulators require in their home countries, including the fact that certain EU directives apply. Being within the Euro currency zone is also crucial.

43. See Goldman Sachs, "Abacus Prospectus and Abacus Indicative Terms," February 26, 2007, http://www.scribd.com/doc/30054003/Abacus–2007-AC1-INDICATIVE-TERMS.

44. Goldman's offshore deals deepened global financial crisis: "Goldman's Offshore Deals Deepened Global Financial Crisis," *McClatchy's*, December 30, 2009.

45. Author's interviews with Elmer, 2010.

46. "Debt Bias and Other Distortions: Crisis-Related Issues in Tax Policy," IMF Fiscal Affairs Department, June 12, 2009.

47. 2003–2007 data from the IMF and from "Private Equity Fund Raising up in 2007: Report," Reuters, January 8, 2008.

48. Julie Cresswell, "Profits for Buyout Firms as Company Debt Soared," *New York Times*, October 4, 2009.

49. Andrew G. Haldane, "Small Lessons from a Big Crisis," Bank of England, May 8, 2009. Haldane is executive director, financial stability. For some excellent examples of this, see Gretchen Morgenson, "Private Equity's Trojan Horse of Debt," *New York Times*, March 12, 2010; and Julie Cresswell, "Profits for Buyout Firms as Company Debt Soared," *New York Times*, October 4, 2009.

50. The GFI studies present a range of estimates, with net flows into deficit countries worth hundreds of billions of dollars. See chart 7 in Dev Kar and Devon Cartwright Smith, "Illicit Financial Flows from Developing Countries 2002–2006," Global Financial Integrity, Washington, D.C., 2008, http://www.gfip.org/storage/gfip/economist%20-%20final%20version%201–2–09.pdf.

51. See Rebecca Smith, "Monty's £10,000 Credit Limit," July 28, 2003, http://www.wilmslow express.co.uk/news/s/63/63903_montys_10000_credit_limit.html.

CONCLUSION

1. The IASB issues International Financial Reporting Standards, which are currently in a process of "convergence" with U.S. accounting standards under the U.S. Financial Accounting Standards Board (FASB), which has a complex, private-led ownership structure but also does not require country-by-country reporting.

2. The World Bank says it "meets the cost/benefit test"; see the World Bank submission to the IASB, June 28, 2010, http://www.ifrs.org/NR/rdonlyres/7FAC2D52-A064–41BD–8BA8–445245232E0B/0/CL55.pdf.

3. Currently the most comprehensive source of updated information available on the topic of information exchange is a section entitled "On Exchange of Information for Tax Purposes" on the website of the Tax Justice Network, http://www.taxjustice.net/cms/front _content.php?idcat=140.

4. "Double Tax Treaties and Tax Information Exchange Agreements: What Advantages for Developing Countries?" *Misereor*, February 2010.

5. "Tax for Development," *OECD Observer*, December 2009–January 2010.

6. Campaigns have been established to pursue this. See, for example, *Tax Justice Focus* 6, no. 1 (2010), which explores land value taxation.

7. This example of the street musician is borrowed from Henry Law, "A Tax That Is Not a Tax," *Tax Justice Focus* 6, no. 1 (2010), www.taxjustice.net.

8. Raymond Baker, "Transparency First," *The American Interest*, July–August 2010.

9. This last paragraph is taken from my article coauthored with Raymond Baker and John Christensen in the September–October 2008 edition of the *American Interest*, entitled "Catching Up with Corruption."

INDEX